Intellectual, Sensory, and Motor Impairments

Development and Disabilities offers the first "multidisability" developmental approach to children with mental retardation, deafness, blindness, and motor impairments. Part I describes the organismic and contextual aspects of modern-day developmental approaches, and discusses the origins of these approaches in the work of such developmental thinkers as Werner, Piaget, and Vygotsky. Part II then examines the most interesting aspects of development – and describes studies that explore the child's development, mother–child interactions, and family work in each of the four disabilities. Part III outlines theoretical and applied implications. Both similarities and differences are noted in development across disabilities, with the aim of achieving better research and intervention. This book should be of interest to a wide range of researchers and practitioners interested in the development of children with disabilities.

Robert M. Hodapp is Associate Professor in Special Education at UCLA's Graduate School of Education and Information Studies. Trained as a developmental psychologist, Hodapp served on the faculty of the Yale Child Study Center between 1982 and 1992. He is a major proponent of developmental approaches to mental retardation and other disabilities. The author of more than 50 papers, Hodapp has also coauthored Understanding Mental Retardation and coedited Issues in the Developmental Approach to Mental Retardation and the Handbook of Mental Retardation and Development.

DEVELOPMENT AND DISABILITIES

Intellectual, Sensory, and Motor Impairments

Robert M. Hodapp

CAMBRIDGE
UNIVERSITY PRESS

PUBLISHED BY THE PRESS SYNDICATE OF THE UNIVERSITY OF CAMBRIDGE
The Pitt Building, Trumpington Street, Cambridge CB2 1RP, United Kingdom

CAMBRIDGE UNIVERSITY PRESS
The Edinburgh Building, Cambridge CB2 2RU, UK   http://www.cup.cam.ac.uk
40 West 20th Street, New York, NY 10011-4211, USA   http://www.cup.org
10 Stamford Road, Oakleigh, Melbourne 3166, Australia

First published 1998

Printed in the United States of America

Typeset in Sabon 11/13 pt, in Quark XPress™ [RF]

A catalog record for this book is available from
the British Library

Library of Congress Cataloging-in-Publication Data
Hodapp, Robert M.
Development and disabilities :   intellectual, sensory, and motor
impairments / Robert M. Hodapp.
p. cm.
Includes bibliographical references and index.
ISBN 0-521-48294-1 (hb). – ISBN 0-521-48338-7 (pbk.)
    1.   Handicapped children – Development.   I. Title.
RJ137.H63   1998
155.45 – dc21   97-49940
                                                                        CIP

ISBN 0 521 48294 1 hardback
ISBN 0 521 48338 7 paperback

To Elisabeth,
with whom the best is yet to come

Contents

Preface

This book applies a theory to a population – or more precisely, it applies a set of related approaches to several disabled populations. The theory is a loosely knit group of "developmental approaches"; the application is to children with mental retardation, deafness, blindness, and motor impairments. A few words about both theory and application seem in order.

As many have pointed out, no single theory of development exists within developmental psychology. For one thing, researchers interested in children's development study a dizzying collection of topics. Moreover, they disagree vehemently about what development is, what its end point(s) are, or even who develops (e.g., the child alone, the child in context, or the contexts themselves). These researchers also employ a variety of techniques, and examine children and their environments at different ages (including adulthood), further complicating the situation.

And yet, within most research on children today, a developmental perspective stands out. This perspective has both a content and a history. The content includes those changes, usually leading to more advanced functioning, that children undergo as they proceed from the cradle to adulthood. This first more organismic sense of development continues to influence many studies of cognitive, linguistic, physical, motoric, and social development. The second, contextual sense of development involves children's relations to their many environments. Motivating studies of caregiver–child interactions, peers, schools, and families, this contextual sense of development is bidirectional: It concerns how children influence their environments and how their environments influence them.

This two-pronged developmental perspective also features a history that spans the twentieth century. From Piaget, Werner, and Vygotsky until today's focus on modularity, ecology, and transactions, a clear, identifiable tradition stands out. Different workers may emphasize, pointedly ignore, or reject different parts of that tradition, but none can claim to be unaffected by its major viewpoints and debates. As Chapter 2 demonstrates, this history strongly influences present-day work on development in children with disabilities.

In applying a developmental perspective to children with disabilities, I have chosen four disabilities: mental retardation, deafness, blindness, and motor impairments. To quote a reviewer of the proposal for this book: "Why these four disabilities? Why not autism, learning disorders, and giftedness?" My answer must be partly personal: These four disabilities most interest me. Mental retardation, in particular, has been my disciplinary home throughout my professional career; though I am a newcomer to deafness, blindness, and motor impairments, I have been struck by the similarity of developmental issues and concerns among all four disabilities.

My answer is also partly professional. To me, mental retardation, deafness, blindness, and motor impairments constitute a loosely related set of mental-motor-sensory impairments. Although some would disagree, all four are relatively easily and reliably diagnosed and have been characterized by a fairly substantial body of developmentally oriented work. This is not true of most other disorders. Learning disabilities have been the subject of only a few studies on sequences, cross-domain relations, or families; they are also among the least clear-cut of all disorders to diagnose. Autism is marginal in both respects: A small (but growing) developmental literature exists, and there is some diagnostic ambiguity. Finally, giftedness has been the focus of few developmental studies, its definition is debated, and one might even question whether it is a disability at all.

While applying a developmental perspective to these four disabilities, I have attempted to remain cognizant of criticisms that have been leveled against developmental approaches over the years.

Specifically, I have tried to keep in mind the notion that developmental findings are somehow unimportant, too theoretical, or sterile. I cannot disagree more strongly. To me, developmental studies provide exciting insights into both theoretical and practical issues. In my more enthusiastic moments, I even argue that several of today's most interesting theoretical debates – linguistic modularity and critical age come to mind – cannot be resolved *unless* one utilizes developmental data on children with disabilities. Practically as well, more extensive applications of developmental findings have begun to allow for more consistent, targeted, and effective programs of intervention.

Development and Disabilities is divided into three parts. Part I defines developmental approaches and provides a history of developmental thinkers who continue to influence work on children with disabilities. Part II examines organismic and contextual issues in each of the four disorders; due to the greater amount of theoretical and empirical work devoted to mental retardation, the discussion of this disability is subdivided into one chapter on organismic issues and one on contextual issues. Part III draws the general lessons of such findings for both theoretical and practical approaches.

A few words about what this book is not: This book is not a comprehensive review of all the developmental information on these disorders. The coverage in Part II is therefore selective, with discussion centered on only certain aspects of cognition, language, interaction, and families. My goal has been to highlight the most interesting developmental findings in each disability in order to show how developmental approaches are currently being applied. Readers should consult more specialized volumes for more comprehensive treatments of each disorder.

Finally, I would like to thank my friends, family, colleagues, and collaborators for their continued and unfailing support. Mike Faulkner, Maren Jones, Vicki Seitz, Nancy Apfel, Julia Denes, David Evans, and Connie Kasari have all been close friends and colleagues over the years. My family, including my mother, father, two sisters, and their families, has been especially supportive. I would also like to thank my collaborators on developmental work in mental retardation, Ed Zigler and Jake Burack. My thanks go also to Mary Racine, who ably copyedited this book, to Donald MacMillan and four anonymous reviewers who commented on different chapters of the manuscript, and to Julia Hough of Cambridge University Press. Julia, in particular, provided careful, critical comments on each chapter, and has always been helpful, encouraging, and professional.

But my greatest thanks go to Elisabeth Dykens, my closest friend and collaborator. On this book, as on everything I have written, Elisabeth has been my toughest, most insightful critic. Just recently, I am happy to report, she has become my wife. To the person who has always made life "funner," I dedicate this book.

Robert M. Hodapp

Part I

Introduction and History

1

What Are Developmental Approaches?

Children with disabilities can be examined from a variety of perspectives. One can study what causes a specific disability or how children with disabilities perform in school. One can examine how society treats these children, how they interact with their families and communities, how legal, economic, political, and medical issues affect them, and how different cultures conceptualize disabilities.

This book focuses on a specific perspective toward children with disabilities: the developmental perspective. As we will see, this perspective might best be characterized as comprising several related approaches, all grounded within a few basic principles. In the broadest sense, developmental approaches examine children with disabilities through the lens of normal development. Such approaches thus incorporate the theories, findings, and methods used to study typically developing children to examine children with disabilities.

Before considering these approaches to children with disabilities, we must ask what constitutes a "developmental" approach. Like many things that are commonplace, the term has become watered down over time. Nowadays, many people seem to be interested in "development" and many espouse a developmental approach. But we need to take some care to spell out clearly what is and is not a developmental approach.

The Developmental Perspective

Defining the developmental perspective is problematic in that it has two components that have only recently been joined. The first and more well known part includes what might be called classical developmental approaches, which focus almost exclusively on children themselves. The second and more recent component is referred to as "development in context," with the main context being the environments in which children develop. Researchers in this area have examined how the child interacts with others and how larger social systems – the neighborhood, school, town, or culture – influence the child's development. Let us discuss each in turn.

Classical Developmental Approaches

Best exemplified by Jean Piaget, classical developmentalists conceptualize the child as an active, living system. According to philosopher of science Steven Pepper (1942), such a view falls under the "organicist" or "organismic" worldview. As we will see, the organismic view is just one of several views concerning children's development. Six basic principles undergird the classical developmentalist's perspective.

The first is that the child is an *inherently active, constructing organism*. In the eternal debate between those who feel they are "the captain of my ship, the master of my fate" and those who feel themselves "buffeted about by the seas," the classical developmentalist is the captain par excellence. Turn at random to any of Piaget's books (e.g., Piaget, 1954) and you will read observations of children doing things. To Piaget, the child is a little scientist, a nonstop actor, experimenter, tester, creator, constructor – all with the aim of making sense of the world.

The second principle stipulates a focus on the *entire organism*. Piaget concluded that developments in different areas were closely synchronous with one another; hence, the child who was in the sensorimotor stage for one behavior was also thought to be in that stage for all other behaviors. Although they question such a high degree of horizontal organization, modern-day developmental workers remain interested in how one thing goes with another, the interrelations among developments in different areas.

The third principle is that *behavior* provides an indication of the child's thinking, a window on the mind. The goal is always to understand the child's mind as well as the processes by which the child comes to understand his or her world. Behavior plays a critical role in indicating what the child knows at any one time, but it mainly reflects the child's underlying competencies.

The fourth principle concerns the *directedness of development*. Developmentalists everywhere are struck by the orderly and sequential nature of children's development – its tendency to lead toward specific end points. Although many developmental workers currently chart idiosyncratic pathways – across individual children (see Wells, 1986) or for children in one culture versus another (J. G. Miller, 1984) – most developmental theories still adhere to a set sequence of development that ends at some highest or most adaptive point.

The fifth principle is that reaching these developmental end points requires *qualitative changes* – changes such that the child's experience is different from everything that has come before. These changes might be considered akin to Kuhn's (1970) revolutions in science. The world is never the same once one has achieved a particular development. Consider Helen Keller's thrill upon being able to speak (i.e., sign) "in winged words that need no interpretation" (Keller, 1954). For Keller (as for anyone who has acquired language), it was difficult to conceptualize what her thoughts were like before she was able to use language.

The sixth principle is the role of the *environment,* which to classical developmentalists has less significance than the other five principles. Piaget, for instance, always considered himself an interactionist, but the interaction he recorded was generally between an active, constructing child and a relatively passive environment (often an object). Although Piaget speaks of the environment as "aliment" – food – to the child's developing schemes, it plays a secondary role.

Table 1.1 highlights these six principles by contrasting classical developmental with behaviorist views. Whereas the developmen-

Table 1.1. *Classical developmental versus behaviorist models*

Classical Developmental	Behaviorist
Development is active, constructive	Development is passive, reactive
Organism is an organized whole	Organism consists of accumulated parts
Behavior reflects schemes	Behavior itself is of interest
Development is directed	Development is nondirected
There is more focus on qualitative change	There is more focus on quantitative change
There is little focus on the environment	There is much focus on the environment

talist sees the child as an active, constructing organism, the behaviorist sees the child as passive and reactive. While the developmentalist is fascinated by the way different skills work together, the behaviorist is interested in training specific behaviors. In contrast to the developmentalist's interest in children's thinking processes, the behaviorist's interest revolves around behavior . . . period. Finally, the behaviorist generally speaks of quantitative rather than qualitative change.

The most distinct difference between developmentalists and behaviorists concerns the role of the environment. As just mentioned, classical developmentalists pay relatively little attention to the environment. Although they are aware of the way the environment can foster a child's development, they generally think of the environment the way most of us think about air: We all realize that we need air to live, but most of us don't stay awake at night pondering its importance. In contrast, behaviorists are entranced by the environment. They consider it extremely powerful, serving to strengthen or weaken behavior at every moment. They strive to understand which rewards or punishments, provided in certain ways at certain times, elicit more or less of a particular behavior.

These differences between classical developmentalists and behaviorists are so fundamental that most consider them irreconcilable (Reese & Overton, 1970). But even many of those interested in developmental approaches have become disenchanted with one aspect of classical developmentalism – that concerning the environment.

Contextual or Ecological Developmental Perspectives

Many modern developmentalists dislike both the classical developmentalist and the behaviorist views of the environment. In essence, contextual developmentalists assert that the environment is more than aliment (as it is to the classical developmentalist) and more than a source of rewards and punishments (as it is to the behaviorist).

What do we mean by the environment? Although no precise definition exists (Kessen, 1968), we can describe some of its features. One involves the world of objects versus the world of people. Although Piaget and others focused on the object-world – and children's interactions with that object-world as they develop a variety of skills – many developmentalists have recently become interested in children's world of people. In addition, the two worlds are connected. Children in different cultures are surrounded by different objects and live in different physical settings (Super & Harkness, 1986). Toys, picture books, computers, even a separate crib or bed in a separate bedroom are more characteristic of middle-class Western homes than homes in many other societies throughout the world. The object-world is therefore influenced by the person-world, and both differ markedly from one society to another.

Which aspects of the person-world are most important for development? At the very least, in industrialized societies the personal environment consists of interactions between mothers and their children, between children and their peers and family members (and among family members themselves), and between children and individuals in their schools, churches, clubs, sports teams, neighborhoods, towns, and countries. Following Bronfenbrenner (1979), we are increasingly aware of the many interconnected personal environments in which children participate as they develop.

Furthermore, these environments change as the child develops. The environment of the newborn obviously differs from that of the 7-year-old, which differs again from that of the 15-year-old. Who the child interacts with and how that interaction proceeds differ in each case. This has led some modern developmentalists to examine development in context. These workers insist that we can understand development only by examining the interplay between children and their environment.

Through their interests in personal environments, contextual developmentalists have also moved beyond organismic developmentalists' sole focus on children and children's internal processes of development. Whereas Piaget and other classical developmentalists examine children themselves, contextual developmentalists have also examined mothers, fathers, siblings, peers, teachers, schools, and families. Bryant (1985) took a neighborhood walk with 7- and 10-year-olds to ask these children whom they went to for emotional reassurance in times of trouble or whom in their neighborhood they could ask for information, money, or a place to play. Such concerns would have seemed totally "out of discipline" to developmental psychologists only 20 or 30 years ago.

In a sense, then, developmental approaches join organismic and contextual perspectives. To some, this marriage has been rocky (Bronfenbrenner, Kessel, Kessen, & White, 1986; Labouvie-Vief & Chandler, 1978). For our purposes, though, let us simply assert that the developmental perspective combines two viewpoints that we will assume coexist reasonably harmoniously. On one hand, the perspective borrows heavily from organismic developmental thinkers such as Piaget, with his focus on the child's developmental processes. On the other, it employs contextual developmentalists' wider sense of the ecologies of development, the many interconnected people and institutions (e.g., family and school) that affect children as both they and their environments change over time. We are interested in an active, developing child within an active, developing environment.

Uses of Developmental Approaches

Given a working definition of developmental approaches, we now consider how these approaches relate to children with disabilities. Here we can identify three distinct elements: conceptualizing development in children with disabilities; gaining a better understanding of normal or typical developmental processes; and increasing the effectiveness of intervention efforts.

Conceptualizing Development in Children with Disabilities

At their most basic level, developmental approaches provide a benchmark, a metric against which to compare the child with disabilities. Such comparisons can involve the rate of development, the relation of one domain to another (i.e., the structure of development), or the sequences of development. Thus, one might ask whether a child who is blind is behind sighted children in language development (rate); whether a child with Down syndrome has a strength in social skills relative to language (structure); or whether a child with motor impairments is progressing in the usual order of sensorimotor cognitive developments (sequences). All are questions that can be answered only through comparison with typically developing children.

But the benchmark provided by developmental approaches also involves the environment. Are the interactive behaviors of the parents of a child who is deaf appropriate, or should they change in some way to better assist the child's development? Similarly, are families of children with a disorder similar to families of nondisabled children of the same age? Again, one needs a reasonably precise sense of what is normal among parents and families of typically developing children.

As already mentioned, the development of children with disabilities often differs from that of nondisabled children. The families of such children, as well as the family dynamics involved in their upbringing, also differ. These differences – and their ramifications – are the focus of many studies and much theorizing among those interested in developmental approaches to children with disabilities. Such concerns underlie many of the discussions in this book.

Understanding Process of Typical Development

In most developmental approaches, the goal is to examine children with disabilities through the lens of normal development. But applying developmental principles to disabled populations is akin to driving in only one direction down a two-way street. One might also turn the car around, examining children with disabilities in order to learn more about typical development.

Such an approach starts from the simple idea that developmental processes are complex, with different developments occurring quickly and simultaneously. As a result, when one is studying typical development, it is often difficult to determine which developments cause other developments to occur or which ones must be present (i.e., are prerequisites) before another is even possible. We can get some sense of these interrelations when studying typically developing children, but our knowledge remains limited.

From children with a sensory impairment we can learn something about the typical processes of development in a particular domain. To take the simplest case, by examining children who are blind we can determine the degree to which vision is needed to achieve various levels of sensorimotor development. In the same way, children who are deaf and have no productive language can help us determine whether a specific level of language is a prerequisite for the development of certain cognitive or social skills.

Children with retardation can also help us learn about normal developmental processes. The development of these children is slowed down. But because it may not be slowed down equally in all areas, children with retardation display some domains that are at higher levels than others. Such discrepancies between high- and low-level domains may occur either in certain children or in most children with a particular type of retardation (e.g., Down syndrome). In examining these children, we can begin to see which domains must be at the same level in development and which domains can be, but need not be, at the same level. Similarly, the three other disability conditions discussed in this book can tell us something about typical developmental processes.

Refining Intervention

A final use of developmental approaches is more practical. By knowing about typical developmental processes – and by examining how processes operate in children with disabilities – we get a better sense of how to intervene. The ultimate test of the success or utility of developmental approaches may well be whether they lead to improved intervention techniques.

When we know, for example, that a child who is blind is behind in language development relative to functioning in other areas, we have identified an important area of intervention. Knowing instead that a child who is blind is at age-appropriate levels in language implies that our intervention efforts might be better spent elsewhere. This issue can also be examined on a group level: In several disability conditions, most children show strengths in certain areas over others. Children who are relatively strong in language, for example, might benefit from being taught even nonlinguistic skills by means of language-based methods. Children showing relative weaknesses in language will have more difficulty benefiting from such a language-based intervention. Using these profiles of development, interventionists can design more informed, fine-grained interventions for children with various disabilities.

Similarly, we can give more help to parents, siblings, and families as we come to know what occurs in families of same-age children and how such processes are disrupted by children with disabilities. Once again, both child-centered and environment-centered interventions are possible. Both are aided by attention to developmental processes in children with specific disability conditions.

Structure of the Book

This book is divided into three parts. Part I discusses theoretical issues. In addition to this chapter's introduction to organismic and contextual developmental perspectives, Chapter 2 presents a historical perspective, highlighting how Werner, Piaget, and Vygotsky conceptualized children with disabilities.

Part II then applies developmental perspectives to children with mental retardation, deafness, blindness, and motor impairments. As the oldest, most explicitly formulated developmental approach, the developmental approach to mental retardation is described in two chapters. Chapter 3 overviews organismic issues, whereas

Chapter 4 discusses contextual issues. Chapters 5, 6, and 7 overview organismic and contextual issues in deafness, blindness, and motor impairments, respectively.

Part III takes a step back, applying theoretical and intervention issues to all four disability conditions. Chapter 8 gleans general theoretical lessons from the prior discussions, while Chapter 9 proposes more effective interventions for children with each disability. Chapter 10 considers the state of the art in developmental approaches to children with disabilities, indicating what we do and do not know about development in children with each disability.

2

Historical Precursors

Over the past several hundred years, many philosophers and scientists have been interested in children with disabilities. Philosophers have debated such questions as whether children who are blind can hear better or are more musical than sighted children or whether children with retardation are imbued with simple but enduring truths. Scientists have been intrigued by cases such as Victor, the "wild boy" discovered in a French forest in 1799, who was later the subject of Itard's "scientific teaching" (the start of the special education field; Lane, 1976). And yet along with this interest has come a fear of the differences these children represent. While few would be so harsh, many once subscribed in part to Martin Luther's feeling toward persons with retardation: "The Devil sits where their soul should be" (Scheerenberger, 1983). Although society's views have often been too negative (and occasionally too positive), people have been sporadically interested in children with disabilities for generations.

Yet not until the early 1900s did developmentalists begin to apply their findings and methods to children with retardation, deafness, blindness, and motor impairments. Much of this early work was led or inspired by three great developmental thinkers: Heinz Werner, Jean Piaget, and Lev Vygotsky. Since development in children with disabilities was not the main interest of any of the three, each could only prepare the way for later, more formal and elaborate developmental approaches. To understand these theorists' contributions and limitations, it is necessary to provide a brief biography of each thinker, then to illustrate how each man's views of development were applied to children with disabilities.

Heinz Werner

Heinz Werner lived from 1890 to 1964. Born and educated in Vienna, he pursued his career over a period that can roughly be divided into three phases. During his early career, after receiving his Ph.D. in 1914 until leaving Germany in 1933, Werner conceptualized his general theories of development and began his work on aesthetics (Witkin, 1964). Situated within a rich German intellectual climate, Werner read and consulted with many of the most important contributors to child and comparative psychology, philosophy, anthropology, art, and linguistics. During this time Werner wrote monographs on metaphor, perception, and language, as well as the first (German) edition of his classic book, *Comparative Psychology of Mental Development* (1926/1948).

In the summer of 1933, with the rise of Hitler, Werner lost his position at Hamburg. What followed was the second phase of Werner's career. This period, from 1933 until 1947, was characterized by change and uncertainty. As one among many German expatriates, Werner scrambled to secure an academic position in the United States. He was a visiting professor at the University of Michigan for three years, then spent a year at Harvard. Unable to return to the University of Michigan, Werner then took a position as research psychologist at the McGregor Laboratory of the Wayne County Training School outside Detroit. There, along with Alfred Strauss, Werner applied his theories to children with retardation. This second period ended when Werner moved to Brooklyn College, where he stayed from 1945 to 1947.

It was the final phase of his life, the years he spent at Clark University, that established Werner in American psychology. This period, from 1947 until his death in 1964, was marked by tremendous productivity and influence. Almost single-handedly, Werner revived the once-famous Psychology Department at Clark so that it again ranked among the period's most prominent institutions of developmental psychology. Led or supported by Werner, professors and students investigated symbolic development, dream states, schizophrenia, musical and artistic development, adults in "primitive" societies, microgenesis (i.e., development "in the moment"), field dependence, and comparative psychology.

And yet, as influential as Werner's theories became, today he is less widely known than many other great developmentalists. Part of the problem is that many of Werner's ideas have become thoroughly incorporated into modern developmental thought. Ideas and methodological innovations implicit in the work of Werner or his students have been expounded more explicitly by later workers. As Glick (1992) notes, "Particularly in comparison to his rough contemporaries, Vygotsky or Piaget, Werner seems to have precipitously faded from view" (p. 558; see also Franklin, 1990).

Applications to Children with Disabilities

Like his influence on developmental psychology, Werner's influence on those studying children with disabilities is today more implicit than explicit. For example, Werner was the first major Western psychologist to apply developmental perspectives to children with disabilities, notably in a series of studies with Alfred Strauss on children with retardation.

Several specific findings arose from this work. First, Werner discovered that it is important to distinguish between developmental processes – the psychological structures underlying behavior – and contents – the behaviors themselves. Indeed, Werner found that, under specific circumstances, children with retardation can perform some behaviors even better than same-age nonretarded children. Examining how children with and without retardation perform on a picture completion task, Werner and Strauss (1939) noted that children with retardation were not led astray by their sense of the completed picture; instead, they simply matched the edges of different pieces with one another. "By this 'chain-like' procedure, characteristic of a genetically lower level, they performed better than most children of the same age but of far superior intellectual ability" (p. 39). Such findings alerted Werner (1937, 1938) to a major tenet of organismic developmental thought, that development does not involve behavior, but underlying mental processes.

This focus on developmental processes led Werner to his view of developmental sequences. In his efforts to probe the development of children with retardation (Werner, 1959/1978), Werner found that the development of these children often occurred in sequences, or orderings, similar to these found in typically developing children. For example, Werner and Strauss (1939) noted that children with retardation showed "genetically lower level" functioning, that is, functioning typical of younger children. Although Werner never directly stated this, he implied that these children developed in the same order as, only slower than, nonretarded children.

In order to characterize development in children with retardation, Werner also proposed various methodological innovations. Since his goal was to determine the psychological processes underlying behavior, some studies focused on individual cases (e.g., Werner, 1941), others evaluated groups of children with specific problems. In one study, Werner and Strauss (1939) compared children with specific reading problems to those children, also with retardation, who did not demonstrate these deficits. The purpose was to determine what caused children to show strengths and weaknesses so that processes aiding or impeding developmental change could be determined.

Finally, like many workers of his day, Werner realized that all mental retardation was not the same. Whereas retardation in some children had no clear organic cause (i.e., it was "endogenous"), retardation in others appeared to have a district organic cause (i.e., it was "exogenous"). As Werner (1941) noted, "The assumption seems justified that deficiencies of this sort [exogenous] must impede the learning processes in a way peculiar to the type of mental deficiency" (p. 235).

These four findings – concerning the processes of development, sequences, methodology, and types of mental retardation – all persist in modern developmental work. A focus on underlying developmental processes is partly what differentiates developmental from behaviorist researchers, as does an interest in sequences followed by children with or without disabilities (see Chapter 1).

Modern developmentalists employ a variety of research techniques when examining children with disabilities. Single- versus multi-subject designs, control or contrast groups matched on mental age, language age, chronological age, and other variables – all continue to be debated. And, as we will see in Chapter 3, researchers disagree on whether a child's type of mental retardation differentially influences rates, regressions, strengths and weaknesses, or other aspects of development. Although Heinz Werner may be partially forgotten, his ideas continue to influence developmental work on children with disabilities.

Jean Piaget

Born in 1896, Jean Piaget enjoyed a long, productive career until his death in 1980. Following an early and continuing interest in nature, Piaget began as a teenager to read widely in philosophy. Specifically, he was interested in the way we come to know what we know (epistemology). To Piaget, such philosophical problems were never solved rationally, but instead yielded themselves to active experimentation. Piaget spent his entire life combining these two interests – natural science and epistemology.

After receiving his Ph.D. from the University of Neuchatel in 1918 for a study of mollusks, Piaget worked in the Binet Laboratory in Paris as a research assistant to Theophile Simon. Along with Binet, Simon had developed the first IQ tests. Piaget's job was to standardize the British psychologist Burt's test of logic on French schoolchildren. That is, Piaget was responsible for determining the number and types of problems correctly, answered by children of different ages, and how any particular child's number of passes compared with those of other children of the same age. For two years, however, he mostly ignored this part of his job, instead examining how children answered the questions. As Piaget (1952) notes in his autobiography, "I engaged my subjects in conversations patterned after psychiatric questioning, with the aim of discovering something about the reasoning process underlying their right, but especially their wrong answers" (p. 244). Most important to Piaget was *how* children of a particular age thought about a problem. Like Werner, he came to value the processes of development over behaviors per se.

Shortly thereafter, Piaget took a series of research, academic, and administrative jobs, most notably at the University of Geneva. Along with such co-workers as Inhelder and Szeminska, he produced detailed studies on many topics related to children's thinking. By 1952, he had published 22 books and countless articles. Prolific throughout his life, Piaget continued working until his death in 1980.

Applications to Children with Disabilities

Although Piaget's work did not become widely known in the United States until the early 1960s, several workers attempted to apply his findings to children with disabilities early on. These earliest studies – scattered throughout the late 1930s to the early 1960s – took many of Piaget's cognitive tasks and examined the performance of children with retardation. A few studies applied these tasks to children with other disabilities (e.g., Fraiberg, Siegel, & Gibson, 1966; Higgins, 1973).

Several issues arose from these early investigations. First, children with retardation and other disabilities developed along roughly the same sequences of cognitive reasoning as did nondisabled children. Given the inherently logical nature of such developmental orderings, such cognitive reasoning in the child with retardation, "while following the same rule of application, follows a much slower rhythm and remains forever unfinished" (Piaget & Inhelder, 1947, p. 403).

Indeed, early studies had already shown that one could apply Piagetian sequences to children with retardation. As early as 1939, Lane and Kinder examined children with retardation at four different levels of mental age on Piaget's egocentrism tasks (Piaget, 1928). They noted that these children's functioning on Piagetian tasks seemed much more closely related to the child's mental age than to his or her chronological age. Lane and Kinder thus concluded that, while the amount of time that a child has interacted with others may have some effect on solving Piagetian tasks (particularly familiar tasks; Granich, 1940), by far the more important factor is the child's overall level of mental functioning, or mental age.

Most important, Lane and Kinder (1939) found that children with retardation showed the same sequences of development as had already been found for typically developing children (Piaget, 1928). In looking across all groups, they noted clear orderings of difficulty. These orderings were related to the mental age of the child and were identical to the sequences or orderings earlier found in typically developing children.

But sequential development was not the only way to characterize functioning in children with retardation. Inhelder (1943/1968, 1966) noted that, while such children showed similar sequences in their development, they differed from typically developing children in other ways that are harder to characterize. For example, Inhelder (1943/1968) found that these children were much more likely to show regressions and oscillations. Thus, a child who had previously answered a particular item correctly at one session might regress, answering the same question incorrectly when examined two weeks later. Even within a single test session, children with retardation were more likely than other children to oscillate from one level to another within a single answer.

In addition to sequences and oscillations, Piaget was interested in horizontally organized stages of development. Piaget (1952) examined "structures of the whole" throughout his life; his notion of developmental stages, that aspects of development in different areas, or domains, are equivalent within a single child is probably his best-known idea. In the earliest work applying Piagetian constructs to mental retardation, however, all children did not appear to develop equally on all tasks within a stage. Prothro (1943) noted that children at a given mental age are not consistently at one or another level on certain Piagetian tasks. Similarly, in Woodward's (1961, 1962) studies of early number and spatial concepts, children with retardation did not always perform at identical levels in different tasks. In examinations of sensorimotor functioning in 7- to 9- and 14- to 16- year-olds with profound mental retardation, Woodward (1959) noted that only 43% of the children showed identical sensorimotor substages on tasks of object permanence and means–ends relations. Although the lack of horizontally organized structures might be due to the difficulties inherent in scoring certain tasks, children with mental retardation did not seem to adhere to Piaget's idea that development is "all of a piece" from one domain to another.

Despite such difficulties, Inhelder, Woodward, and others realized the importance of Piaget's sequences and structures for work with children with disabilities. Woodward (1963, 1979) noted that children with severe and profound mental retardation are often "below the floor" on commonly used IQ tests; that is, these children are unable to answer any items correctly. As such, examiners can only report that such children are "untestable" or make gross estimates of their levels of functioning. With Piagetian tasks, however, children can be assessed on concepts that are "level-appropriate" for each child's functioning. Children or adults of any age can be assessed using sensorimotor, preoperational, concrete operational, or formal operational tasks, whichever are most appropriate.

In addition, because Piagetian tasks are not psychometric instruments, more flexibility is allowed in both test administration and scoring. Since the tasks are not timed, a child with motor impairments may spend extra time completing a particular task. Moreover, a child who is blind can be assessed on items involving sound. Any item can be administered several times, and it is acceptable to administer an item using slightly different materials or with other minor variations. Since the concept, not the behavior, is of interest, improved estimates of the child's level of functioning can often be generated using Piagetian versus psychometric testing.

A further influential aspect of Piaget's theory involves interactions between the organism and the environment. Piaget always considered himself an interactionist, although the interaction he observed generally featured an active, exploring child and a passive, usually object, environment. As a result, teachers of children with disabilities provide environments in which the children can develop. In a sense, the interventionist moves from "teacher" to "facilitator" of the child's own, internally directed developmental processes.

Piaget's modern-day influence, then, relates to his sequences of development, his sense that development proceeds in parallel from one domain to another, and his colleague Inhelder's findings of variable, up-and-down patterns of development in children with retardation. For example, contemporary developmentalists debate the degree to which various cognitive abilities are "modular," or separate from one another during development. In addition, in recent studies, young children with Down syndrome showed higher rates of regressions (Dunst, 1990) and of within-session oscillations (Wishart, 1995) than found in nonretarded children. The writings of Piaget and Inhelder also have practical implications. Piagetian sequences serve as the basis of scales for testing children with many different disability conditions (e.g., Dunst, 1980) and for teaching early and later cognitive skills. Researchers, examiners, and interventionists use Piaget's and Inhelder's findings every day.

Lev Vygotsky

Lev Semenovich Vygotsky was born in 1896 near Minsk in Belorussia. Like Werner and Piaget, Vygotsky had a wide variety of interests, particularly philosophy, theater, and literature. From early childhood, he was acknowledged as brilliant.

Because Jews were limited in their occupational choices, Vygotsky's family convinced him to study medicine at Moscow University. After a month, however, he switched to law, the field in which he received his degree in 1917. In addition, Vygotsky enrolled in Shanyavskii's People's University, a semiunderground university whose faculty was composed of professors fired from other universities by the czar. There he studied history and philosophy; through his sister and friends, he also learned much about linguistics and other areas. Thus, although officially trained in law, Vygotsky was actually educated in a variety of fields.

Moscow in 1917 was a city awash in revolution, and young Vygotksy was caught up in this movement. Along with other young Soviet intellectuals, he helped form the "new Soviet society." Upon returning to his hometown after graduating from Moscow University, Vygotsky contributed to the Soviet effort by writing book and play reviews, corresponding with leading figures in the arts, performing his first psychological experiments, and founding a short-lived publishing company, all while teaching at the local teacher's college (van der Veer & Valsiner, 1991).

Vygotsky emerged from his hometown seven years later when, in early 1924, he gave a speech to the Second All-Russian Psychoneurological Conference in Leningrad. This speech propelled him into the midst of the reorganization of psychology in the Soviet Union. Recalling this speech, his soon-to-be colleague Alexandr Luria declared that "it was clear that this man from a small provincial town in western Russia was an intellectual force who would have to be listened to" (1979, pp. 38–39).

Soon thereafter, Vygotsky joined Kornilov's Institute in Moscow, the main psychological laboratory in the new USSR. With the help of Luria and Leont'iev, Vygotsky developed an entirely new Soviet psychology. For the next 10 years, from 1924 to 1934, he performed an incredible amount of work. Children's development, changes in the thinking of nonliterate peoples caused by the imposition of writing, development in children with various forms of disability – all constituted Vygotsky's research topics during this hectic time. He also performed various administrative duties, taught classes, gave public lectures, corresponded widely with colleagues in and outside the Soviet Union, edited journals, and traveled throughout the USSR to establish new outposts of psychological study.

Although such hard work would tax anyone, Vygotsky was particularly unfortunate. As early as 1920, he had been hospitalized for tuberculosis. Periodically thereafter, he had to be rehospitalized. Yet he continued working, traveling, and lecturing at a frenetic pace, committed to his cause but also perhaps realizing that his disease would soon overcome him. After several years of variable health, Vygotsky died from tuberculosis in June 1934. He was 37 years old.

Vygotsky's posthumous reception is almost as interesting as his life itself. It was an accident of fate that the years of his productive career, 1924 to 1934, coincided with a societal tolerance for fresh ideas. This period of openness was already ending during Vygotsky's last few years. By 1936, reference to Vygotsky was illegal throughout the USSR, and his later writings were not published in

Russian until after Stalin's death in 1953. Since that time, Vygotsky has influenced psychologists, anthropologists, and educators alike. In addition to his two major works, *Thought and Language* (1934/1962) and *Mind in Society* (1978), collections and translations of Vygotsky's many articles and speeches continue to appear.

Applications to Children with Disabilities

In addition to his other achievements, Lev Vygotsky is known for his role as one of the founders of the modern Soviet field of "defectology." Yet since many of the papers he wrote in this area have only recently been collected and translated (Rieber & Carton, 1993), Vygotsky's influence on the Western developmental disabilities field is only beginning to be felt.

Before we examine Vygotsky's views, the term *defectology* requires explanation. To our modern ears, the word sounds pejorative. It seems to imply that individuals with disabilities are incapable or undeserving of a full life within society. To Vygotsky and his colleagues, however, the term had a much more neutral connotation. It simply referred to children with a problematic condition. As such, the term is akin to our term *developmental disabilities,* which applies to those persons who require special education.

Vygotsky was interested in children with a wide range of disabilities. He examined, wrote about, and held a weekly discussion group (similar to our medical rounds) on children with deafness, blindness, mental retardation, and emotional disorders (van der Veer & Valsiner, 1991). Most of this work was undertaken during the period from 1924 to about 1930 – indeed, Vygotsky's interest in disabilities was more pronounced in his earlier than in his later career.

Vygotsky emphasizes three main themes: developmental analysis, mediation, and sociogenesis (Wertsch, 1985). First, Vygotsky adopts a strong *developmental perspective* toward children with disabilities. His concern throughout is how children with disabilities develop. Like both Piaget and Werner, he criticizes atheoretical measures of completed development. To Vygotsky, these measures – most prominently IQ tests – are static and do not provide the examiner with much information about the child's future development. Similarly, Vygotsky decries all static systems of classification. He notes that any atheoretical classification system "is powerless to solve questions of origin, development, and growth" (Rieber & Carton, 1993, p. 154).

Intrinsic to this developmental approach is Vygotsky's *mediation*, or the use of an object (e.g., a book), person (mother), or ability (language) to help comprehend the world. One instance of mediation involves the actions of adults, the cultural representatives who mediate children's experiences. Mothers, for example, label objects, describe how things work, comfort children, and in thousands of ways make the world comprehensible to their children. In contrast to adults who help children without disabilities, adults who help children with deafness, blindness, or mental retardation need to consciously structure their actions. He notes that all of special education involves discovering "roundabout ways" in which adults can best help these children develop.

Mediation also involves language, since language constitutes the tool that individuals use to clarify, extend, and make explicit their thoughts. Vygotsky was therefore interested in children with sensory impairments, for these children are hindered in their comprehension of visual or spoken language. In considering the development of children who are blind, for example, he disagreed with those who dislike Braille. He noted that, through Braille, a child who is blind learns to read and write, thereby sharing the legacy of the most advanced human societies. Vygotsky realized that the important thing about language is not its form, but its functions. Thus, through Braille, a medium of literacy that is different from printed words, the child becomes literate.

Also for this reason, Vygotsky held strong views concerning intervention with children who are deaf. He was a strong proponent of a certain type of oralism for such children. He attacked the methods of his day, by which these children were taught to utter one sound, then another. To Vygotsky, language develops through necessity. He therefore advocated a more natural, interactive style of intervention. Surprisingly, though, Vygotsky generally did not favor sign language training. He felt that signs do not constitute a complete language and that all children – including those who are deaf – ultimately need to live and interact within the larger society, not becoming "a special breed of people." Although some researchers claim that Vygotsky softened his views against sign language in later years (Knox & Kozulin, 1989), most of his writings champion a more interactive approach to oral training.

Both development and mediation relate to Vygotsky's third main idea, *sociogenesis*. In contrast to Werner and Piaget, Vygotsky felt that all developments first appear in collaboration with more competent adults. For example, school children are helped by their teachers, who gives hints or clues or in other ways help children to develop. Later, children can perform identical behaviors on their own. Vygotsky therefore proposes that all behaviors occur first in conjunction with helping adults, later by children themselves without assistance. This movement from the "interpsychological" to "intrapsychological" planes helps explain Vygotsky's "zone of proximal development." There is a gap, or zone, between what the child can do only with help versus what the child can do alone. Vygotsky calls this gap between levels of "potential development" (with help) and "actual development" (by oneself) the "zone of proximal development." This gap can inform both intervention and assessment efforts.

Views concerning sociogenesis take interesting twists when related to developmental disabilities. Vygotsky considered such disabilities primarily a social problem. Disabilities become troublesome only when children feel themselves inferior to or ostrasized by others. "What is important is not the deficiency, the abnormality, the defect or handicap by itself, but the ensuing reaction, that is, how the child's personality develops in response to the encountered difficulties stemming from the handicap" (Rieber & Carton, 1993, p. 125). Given such a social definition of disability conditions, compensatory processes also involve social factors. Special education and Braille, oral training done in a natural way, full participation in work and in life – all are considered social compensations for children with disabilities.

Later workers have attempted to apply Vygotskian thinking to children with disabilities. Specifically, Brown and Ferrara (1985) have applied Vygotsky's zone of proximal development to children with mental retardation and learning disabilities. Their goal has been to examine whether the zone of proximal development might, as Vygotsky predicted, serve as an assessment tool for children with disabilities. Although such work has only begun, the hypothesis is that children with larger discrepancies between potential and actual development might have better prognoses than children with smaller discrepancies (see also Budoff, 1974).

Vygotsky has also influenced intervention. If development is best enhanced by environments that are only slightly above the child's level of (actual) abilities, then interventions might capitalize on this fact. Although the idea of a "staged curriculum" that is slightly ahead of the child is common in work with typical children (e.g., Bruner, 1982; Kaye, 1982), an explicitly Vygotskian perspective has only occasionally been used in interventions with children with disabilities (e.g., Feurstein, Rand, Hoffman, Hoffman, & Miller, 1979; Jamieson, 1994).

Overview

The work of Werner, Piaget, and Vygotsky constitutes the pre-history of developmental approaches to children with disabilities. Although none of these thinkers proposed a formal developmental perspective, each contributed ideas and approaches that led to later formulations. Several points should be highlighted in comparing and contrasting the three theorists.

Role of Children with Disabilities in the Career of Each Theorist

The careers of Werner, Piaget, and Vygotsky ranged over a wide variety of topics. From childhood, each was acknowledged as exceptionally bright, with many diverse interests. Werner was concerned with children, aesthetics, linguistics, and psychopathology, all from a developmental perspective. In addition to his psychological work, Vygotsky wrote essays on *Hamlet* and other plays, was intensely interested in Hegel, Marx, and other philosophers, and regularly commented on and corresponded with several Russian poets. Even the interests of Piaget, possibly the most "child-focused" developmentalist of the three, ranged across biology, epistemology, and children.

Within each theorist's broad view of development, the emphasis on children with disabilities occurred early in their careers. Werner studied mental retardation during his transitional period after coming to the United States; after moving to Clark University, he rarely concentrated on development in these children (see Witkin, 1964). Piaget never actually studied children with disabilities, although he did write occasional articles on the topic in collaboration with Inhelder (e.g., Piaget & Inhelder, 1947). Vygotsky, among the three the most interested in disabilities, performed most of this work in the early part of his career, from 1924 to about 1930 (van der Veer & Valsiner, 1991). None exclusively devoted his productive life to children with disabilities. Indeed, the disability work of each sometimes led to later work, sometimes extended earlier formulations, and sometimes appeared to have no connection with remaining work.

Probably the issue most consistent with the remaining work of each theorist is the process–content distinction. For all three theorists, studies on children with developmental disabilities illustrated the need to examine the processes of development over behavior per se. Each theorist criticized the use of IQ and other psychometric tests of children's behavior. Werner spoke of the need to start – but not finish – an assessment with IQ tests; Piaget and Inhelder declared that IQ tests tell us little about cognitive processes; and Vygotsky railed against such tests, attacking their inability to predict a child's future development. Each thinker examined children's underlying psychological processes, not specific behaviors.

Other issues served as transitions to each theorist's later career. Consider, for example, Werner's finding that, under specific conditions for selected tasks, children with retardation performed better than did nonretarded agemates. Such results undoubtedly led to Werner's more mature view of development, his "orthogenetic principle" that development "proceeds from a state of relative globality and lack of differentiation to a state of differentiation, articulation, and hierarchic integration" (1957, p. 126). By defining development in terms of differentiation and hierarchic integration, Werner equated development with the degree of cognitive sophistication underlying a particular behavior. According to this more abstract view of cognitive behavior, children with retardation perform at more primitive levels than nonretarded agemates, even if the peculiarities of a task sometimes allow these children to answer correctly more often.

In a similar way, Vygotsky's zone of proximal development was developed partly through his sense that children with disabilities – even those of similar mental ages – differed markedly in their capacity to benefit from adult help. As a result, Vygotsky realized that zones of different sizes relate to differing prognoses for individual children with and without disabilities (van der Veer & Valsiner, 1991, p. 342). Given Vygotsky's preoccupation with rising above one's disability (and his own attempt to rise above tuberculosis), the zone of proximal development seems partially a result of his earlier work in developmental disabilities.

And yet, while some aspects of their work on developmental disabilities were either closely tied to or preparatory for later work, other aspects of each theorist's ideas were never significantly connected to development in children with disabilities. For example, while Werner may have used his earlier findings on retardation to formulate his concepts of development, the orthogenetic principle was never explicitly applied to these children. Similarly, in his preface to Inhelder's (1943/1968) book, Piaget (1943/1968) notes that "we must admit that we did not suspect that this [Piagetian] method would become central in her [Inhelder's] everyday practice" (p. 10). Children with retardation may thus have served as a population about whom Piaget generalized his theory, but these children were otherwise peripheral to his theory and interests.

Nor does Vygotsky always link his later ideas to children with disabilities. In his writings on disabilities (Rieber & Carton, 1993), he repeatedly discusses the social nature of disabilities, the idea of compensation, and the need for roundabout ways to intervene with these children, but his statements remain general. Vygotsky never explains how his zone of proximal development might make use of the child's transitional thinking to inform intervention efforts, or how children with deafness, blindness, or mental retardation might benefit from tasks that are within each child's zone. So Vygotsky's studies on children with disabilities are also sometimes preparatory, sometimes connected, sometimes unconnected to his later work.

Organicism Versus Contextualism

In addition to their similarities, Werner, Piaget, and Vygotsky display differences in their stands on the organicist–contextualist distinction. Werner and Piaget were primarily organicist in orientation, whereas Vygotky was primarily a contextualist.

Piaget and Werner. Werner and Piaget primarily studied children themselves. Though they acknowledged the importance of the environment, both theorists (and their followers) emphasized functioning in children with retardation or other disabilities. They usually ignored the interplay between children and their environments, and said only a little about the practical consequences of their theories for assessment and intervention.

The main similarity between Werner and Piaget involved sequences. Both noted that children with retardation developed in set order, through the usual sequences of development. Given his precise developmental sequences, Piaget's developmental patterns were explicit; Werner and Strauss (1939) more implicitly assumed similar sequences in children with retardation.

The two organicists also differ slightly as well. Piaget – not so much Werner – considered the "wholeness" of development in children with retardation. Thus, Piaget's colleague Inhelder (1943/1968) examined children at various stages of development, the idea being that children with retardation – like all children – showed horizontally organized stages of development. Although even early workers (e.g., Prothro, 1943) had noted that such children may not always function at the same stage in every domain, the idea of horizontally organized stages was adopted in future work with children with disabilities.

In addition, Inhelder (1943/1968) found that children with retardation more often show oscillations, regressions, and unstable functioning than do nonretarded children. While these children generally developed in accord with the usual sequences and stages, they also demonstrated certain differences. Children with disabilities might therefore simultaneously be the same as and different from normally developing children. This combination of similarities and differences has greatly influenced later developmental thinking concerning children with disabilities.

While Piaget and Inhelder presented more elaborate ideas concerning structures and performance in children with retardation, Werner and Strauss offered more precise views of the population itself. Piaget and Inhelder did not examine the effects of different types of mental retardation on children's performance. In contrast, Werner (1941) clearly distinguished between types of retardation with clear organic causes and those without obvious organicity. Werner even argued that, in certain (unspecified) ways, children whose retardation has organic causes might differ in development, showing "peculiar" aspects of development compared with children whose retardation does not show organicity. To Werner, only this endogenous group necessarily follows the usual sequences of development.

Despite these differences, Werner and Piaget approached children with disabilities from similar perspectives. On certain issues (e.g., sequences, structures, regressions), Piaget and Inhelder presented more elaborate, precise views; on others (causes of retardation), Werner and Strauss were more specific. On balance, however, the similarities of the two theorists far outweigh their differences.

Vygotsky. In contrast to Werner and Piaget, Vygotsky was primarily a contextual developmentalist: He was concerned with the interaction between a child with disabilities and that child's environment. Vygotsky also differs from the others in that he directly examined children with a wide variety of disabilities – including deafness, blindness, motor impairments, and emotional disorders.

In keeping with his focus on the environment, Vygotsky, unlike Werner and Piaget, explicitly mentions interventions in his writings on disability. He advocated instruction in Braille for children who are blind. He took on the entire sign–oral debate, usually advocating a more naturally occurring oral intervention for children who are deaf. Vygotsky declared that special educators must continually search for a roundabout means to reach children with disabilities, although he remained troubled by the societal isolation of children in special schools that offered unique educational methods. His concerns were much more practical and social than those of Werner and Piaget.

Given his interest in the relation between society and the individual, Vygotsky was particularly interested in the social effects of disability. He often spoke of the total change in personality brought about by a child's disability, and of the need for adaptation and compensation. Although Vygotsky granted that disabilities have intrinsic effects, he saw their main effects as social and cultural. Moreover, even his "child-centered" provisions related to other people (e.g., changes in personality due to the child's disability, which in turn affect the child's interactions with others). Vygotsky's zone of proximal development involved the child's functioning with and without adult help, and the size of the zone helped the adult to determine the appropriate stimulation. In all his writings, Vygotsky championed contextualist developmental concerns for children with disabilities.

Werner, Piaget, and Vygotsky were all developmentalists who, to various degrees, applied their ideas to children with disabilities. Although none of the three could be considered the founder of a formal developmental approach, all proposed ideas that have enlivened modern developmental perspectives. We now explore how these and later ideas apply to children with each of the four disability conditions.

Applications of Developmental Approaches to Children with Disabilities

3

Mental Retardation:
I. Origins and Organismic Issues

Although developmental concerns arise in all disabilities, most disabilities have not been the subject of a coherent or widely known developmental approach. Only mental retardation has received such treatment. Spearheaded by Edward Zigler and his colleagues beginning in the late 1960s, the developmental approach to mental retardation has been considered one of the field's most important theoretical perspectives (Baumeister, 1987). For this reason, we begin by discussing children with mental retardation.

Before describing this approach, we must address a few issues. Like any long-lasting scientific theory, the developmental approach to mental retardation has evolved with the passing years. New theories have expanded the definitions of development and how it operates. New developmental findings have been applied to children with retardation. And new tasks, methods, and analytical tools have been imported into the mental retardation field from the larger field of developmental psychology. All of these innovations, to be described in this chapter, have allowed mental retardation researchers to expand their work.

This chapter also continues to develop several themes from the first two chapters. By reviewing the changes in the developmental approach to mental retardation since the late 1960s, the chapter extends the historical perspective outlined in Chapter 2. Here, we discuss how both early and modified developmental approaches continue to influence modern work in mental retardation.

In addition, this chapter makes more specific the developmentalist's interest in organismic issues. Historically, the original developmental approach to mental retardation dealt exclusively with organismic concerns. Sequences, structures, and personality-motivational functioning (described later in this chapter) all pertained solely to the child. Only recently have other, more contextualist concerns been added to the picture.

To cover the history of the developmental approach and its organismic and contextualist roots, two separate chapters are devoted to work on mental retardation. This chapter discusses historical and organismic issues. Chapter 4 then examines contextualist issues, emphasizing mother–child interactions and families.

The Original Developmental Approach to Mental Retardation

Chapter 2's history provides the background for our discussion of the original developmental approach to mental retardation. In their early work, Werner, Piaget, and Vygotsky all examined children with retardation, although Vygotsky in particular also examined children with other disabilities.

Edward Zigler, who is today Sterling Professor of Psychology at Yale University, entered the field in the mid-1950s. His dissertation and early studies focused on disproving Lewin's (1936) and Kounin's (1941a, 1941b) views of rigidity, the idea that children with retardation were inherently more "rigid" than their nonretarded peers (Zigler, 1984). These studies introduced several substantive and methodological ideas. First, motivation plays a role in how children with mental retardation perform on any type of task. Second, the life histories of children with mental retardation are often different from those of nonretarded children; for example, children with retardation are more likely to have been institutionalized or to have been schooled in special classes. Third, when one is examining cognitive or linguistic abilities, it is often better to compare children with mental retardation with nonretarded children of the same mental age as opposed to chronological age. These issues continue to influence modern developmental work in mental retardation.

For our purposes, the next period of Zigler's career is of particular interest. Until the late 1950s, Zigler was a follower of Clark

Hull, who advocated a (now little-known) learning theory that was widely followed at the time. As part of his training as a clinical psychologist, Zigler interned from 1957 to 1959 at Worcester State Hospital in Worcester, Massachusetts. There he engaged in a friendly, long-running argument with the developmentalist Bernard Kaplan, a young professor at Clark University and collaborator of Heinz Werner (Werner & Kaplan, 1963). This clash between the young learning theorist and the ardent developmentalist deeply influenced Zigler's career. "Losing that argument," recalls Zigler, "is probably the best thing that ever happened to me."

In subsequent years, Zigler began applying developmental approaches to various disabled populations. With Leslie Phillips and Jacob Levine during the 1960s and 1970s, and with Marion Glick from the late 1970s until today, Zigler applied developmental perspectives to adult schizophrenia and depression (Zigler & Glick, 1986). He also began work on various aspects of development in typically developing children.

Zigler formalized what was later to be called "the developmental approach to mental retardation." From his dissertation and follow-up studies in the early 1960s, Zigler advanced the idea that persons with retardation are affected by motivational-personality factors, and that a child's motivational-personality structure is influenced by his or her history of rewards and punishments, living status, and other environmental influences. From the earlier work of Werner (1941) on mental retardation, Zigler realized that there may be several types of retardation. From Piaget and Werner, he adapted developmental ideas such as sequences and stages.

In summarizing this work, two basic issues must be addressed: application of the developmental approach and the nature of the approach itself. Since these two issues are central to later discussions, they are described in detail here.

Applying the Developmental Approach

It may seem strange to apply an approach that has not yet been defined or explained. However, Zigler (1967, 1969) first applied the developmental approach, and only later described its nature and definition. The reasons for such a backward ordering will become clearer as we explore the mental retardation field during the 1950s and 1960s.

To simplify a little, during the early 1960s different theorists postulated different primary causes of mental retardation. Zeaman and House (1963) held that the basic problem concerned attentional processes. Luria (1963) – extending Vygotsky – felt that the basic problem was related to inadequate verbal mediation of thought. Ellis (1963) contended that the problem concerned brain mechanisms relating to inappropriate stimulus traces. In short, the field was full of researchers who were searching for *the* basic problem in mental retardation.

The Two-Group Approach. In considering how to apply developmental ideas to children with mental retardation, Zigler rejected the idea that all persons with retardation are the same. Here he borrowed the idea from Pearson and Jaederholm (1914), E. O. Lewis (1933), and Werner (1941) that there are two types of mental retardation (cf., Burack, 1990). The first type consists of retardation with one or more definite organic causes. Those causes that occur prenatally include genetic defects, thalidomide exposure, rubella, and accidents in utero. Causes that occur perinatally include prematurity and anoxia at birth, and those that occur postnatally include head trauma and meningitis – among many others.

At last count, there were approximately 750 organic causes of mental retardation (Opitz, 1996), with new (primarily genetic) causes being discovered every year (Moser, 1992). Several of the most interesting organic forms of mental retardation include the genetic disorders Down syndrome (earlier called "mongolism"), fragile X syndrome, Williams syndrome, and Prader–Willi syndrome. These disorders, about which more will appear later, are summarized in Table 3.1.

Even though many different organic causes exist, most affect relatively few individuals. Altogether, organic causes affect slightly less than 50% of all persons with retardation (Zigler & Hodapp, 1986). Such individuals usually fall in the low IQ ranges, with IQs generally below 50 or 55. Most persons with moderate (IQ 40–54), severe (IQ 20–39), and profound (IQ below 20) retardation show an organic cause, with higher and higher percentages of

Table 3.1. *Genetic forms of mental retardation*

Disorder	Genetics	Prevalence	Prominent physical and behavioral features
Down syndrome	95% involves 3rd chromosome at 21st pair (trisomy 21)	1–1.5 per 1,000 live births	Moderate mental retardation; epichanthal folds around eyes; blocky build; reputedly social and outgoing demeanor; speech and language problems
Fragile X syndrome	Fragile site (thin, threadlike portion) on long arm of X-chromosome	0.73–92 per 1,000 live births	Moderate mental retardation; more males than females; males often show large ears; long, thin faces and (after puberty) large testes; hyperactivity and autistic-like behaviors (e.g., gaze aversion)
Prader–Willi syndrome	Two-thirds involve deletions on chromosome 15; one-third involve maternal disomy (both 15s from mother)	1 per 15,000 live births	Mild mental retardation; proneness to obesity (and short stature); food foraging and preoccupations; stubbornness and proneness to obsessive-compulsive disorder.
Williams syndrome	Deletion on chromosome 7	1 per 50,000 live births	Mild mental retardation; "elfin" or "pixie-like" facial appearance; friendly and hyperverbal demeanor; possible anxiety beginning in adolescence

organicity as one goes lower down the curve of IQ (Zigler & Hodapp, 1986).

The second type of mental retardation has no obvious organic cause. Individuals with this type of retardation appear to be normal in their health, appearance, and development, the only difference being their lower levels of intelligence. Demographically, these individuals are likely to be of low socioeconomic status and from minority backgrounds. They are also likely to come from families in which one or more family members are also of low intelligence (Broman, Nichols, Shaughnessy, & Kennedy, 1987).

For more than 30 years, a controversy has existed as to what percentage of the retarded population has this form of mental retardation. Although some researchers claim a figure of 75%, prevalence studies show rates of about 50% (Zigler & Hodapp, 1986). This percentage is influenced by a variety of factors. For example, the 50% figure is derived from population-based studies (usually in Scandinavian countries) of all persons whose IQs are below 70. But in studies that adopt different definitions of mental retardation, the prevalence of persons with cultural-familial mental retardation changes. Specifically, with the American Association on Mental Retardation's revised definition of mental retardation providing a cutoff score of "IQ 70 to 75," many more persons could potentially be diagnosed with mental retardation (MacMillan, Gresham, & Siperstein, 1993). Disproportionate percentages of these individuals have cultural-familial as opposed to organic forms (Gresham, MacMillan, & Siperstein, 1995). Thus, although the prevalence of persons with cultural-familial retardation is probably not as high as the 75% that is typically noted, the actual percentage will vary according to the definition of mental retardation used and the way in which the prevalence study is performed.

Many hypotheses have been advanced as to the causes of retardation primarily affecting individuals who are poor, of minority backgrounds, and from homes in which other family members have low IQs (Hodapp, 1994). These hypotheses range from the environmental to the genetic. Proposed environmental causes include under- or overstimulation during the formative years, and different cultural or subcultural "mismatches" between the dominant (i.e., White, middle-class) culture and the child's home environment. These mismatches might affect the child's cognitive abilities, test-taking skills, or motivation to succeed – all of which might depress IQ scores. Other environmental causes include the effects of poverty, racism, and poor educational opportunities.

A variety of genetic views have also been advanced for the lower intellectual abilities of persons with cultural-familial mental retardation. This form of retardation has been hypothesized to result from "polygenic" factors, or from the effects of many single genes working together (each individually accountable for only a small portion of one's total intelligence). The best example of polygenic inheritance is height: Short parents generally produce short offspring. So too might "intellectually short" parents be likely to produce children with mental retardation.

At present, no one knows which environmental or genetic factors, in which combinations, cause this type of retardation. In most studies of IQ, approximately 50% of the variance in any one individual's intellectual abilities seems inherited and 50% seems due to environmental factors (Plomin & Rende, 1991), allowing ample room for both genetic and environmental determinants. Such discrepant ideas are apparent in the many names proposed for this type of retardation (Table 3.2). Here we use the term *cultural-familial.*

Since many mental retardation professionals dispute the existence of cultural-familial mental retardation (e.g., Baumeister & MacLean, 1979), a few more words seem necessary. The two-group approach – and the concept of cultural-familial mental retardation – is an argument about the normal distribution of intelligence. Virtually all continuous human traits are distributed along a Gaussian curve, or bell curve, with most individuals falling in the middle, slightly fewer individuals falling a little away from the mean, and fewer and fewer persons falling at either high or low extreme. Such is the case with adult height and weight (by gender), resting heart rate, blood pressure, reading abilities, and almost anything else one can think of. So too with intelligence. At least for nonretarded persons and for persons with cultural-familial mental retardation, a bell curve presumably exists. Some persons fall two or more standard deviations below the mean on this bell curve (i.e., in the retarded range, with IQs below 70). Zigler therefore reasoned that, like IQ differences throughout the bell curve, nothing "unusual" caused the lower intellectual levels of individuals with cultural-familial retardation. Whatever causes a person with IQ

Table 3.2. *Names for mental retardation with no clear biomedical cause*

Cultural-familial (or sociocultural-familial) retardation. This term suggests that the child's retardation is caused by either environmental or genetic factors. Cultural factors include mismatches between the child's home environment and the surrounding culture, or under- or overstimulating environments. Familial factors may also be involved, meaning that the child's background is environmentally deprived or that the family's genetic background is substandard.

Familial retardation. Although this term can denote either sense of "familial" causes, it often emphasizes the effects of a substandard polygenetic background.

Retardation due to environmental deprivation. This term implies that this form of retardation might be prevented or reversed.

Nonspecific mental retardation. Probably the most neutral, this term denotes only that the cause of retardation remains unspecified.

Nonorganic mental retardation. This term implies that the retardation does not involve organic causes, implying a substandard environment as the primary cause.

Idiopathic mental retardation. This term implies that the retardation is peculiar, stemming from causes that are unknown and/or are unique to the child.

130 to be more intelligent than a person with IQ 100, a similar cause (or causes) makes a person with IQ 90 more intelligent than a person with cultural-familial retardation with IQ 60. We just do not know what those causes are.

Original Applications. With the two-group approach as a background, we can discuss Zigler's original applications of the developmental approach. At first, Zigler did not apply his approach to all children with mental retardation. Citing the different causes of lower intelligence in children with cultural-familial versus organic retardation, he noted that "it is far from logical to assert that the course of development is the same, or that even similar contents in their behaviors are mediated by exactly the same cognitive process" (Zigler, 1969, p. 553).

Zigler at first therefore excluded children with organic mental retardation from the developmental approach. Reasoning that children with clearly organic forms of retardation are in some sense damaged or deficient, Zigler was uncertain whether a developmental approach would apply to them. Given their organic defects, these children might not traverse Piagetian or other sequences of development in order or have similar horizontal stages. In contrast, children with cultural-familial mental retardation seemed like typically developing children. They simply developed more slowly. As a result, Zigler hypothesized that children with cultural-familial retardation developed as nonretarded children do. The usual developmental sequences and structures should apply.

Contents of the Original Developmental Approach

What, then, was the nature of this original developmental approach? Three ideas predominate: similar sequences, similar structures, and personality-motivational factors.

Similar-Sequence Hypothesis. The similar-sequence hypothesis states that children with mental retardation develop, in order, through the usual or normative stages of development. Like typically developing children, they are assumed to develop from Piaget's sensorimotor, to preoperational, to concrete, to formal operational stages. Even within a particular large stage, children with mental retardation should progress in the usual ordering. Children with and without mental retardation should progress from substages 1 to 2 to 3, and so on, in Piaget's six substages of sensorimotor development (Dunst, 1980). There should be few instances of "incorrect ordering" – of developing from sensorimotor stage 1 to 4 to 3 to 2.

Although sequential development had long been implicitly accepted in developmental circles, this idea had yet to be applied to children with retardation. Specifically, Werner and Strauss (1939) had earlier commented on the "genetically lower functioning" of children with mental retardation, and Piaget and Inhelder (1947; see also Inhelder, 1943/1968) had noted the universal ordering (with more regressions and oscillations) in such children. Zigler (1969) made these ideas explicit, proposing that children with retardation should also traverse in order both the larger and the smaller substages of development.

Similar-Structure Hypothesis. The similar-structure hypothesis states that, when matched on overall mental age (MA) with non-retarded children, children with retardation should perform similarly on a specific cognitive or linguistic task. For example, groups matched on overall mental age (i.e., MA matches) should perform similarly on linguistic, attentional, or other cognitive-linguistic tasks. In essence, there should be no outstanding strengths or weaknesses in the intellectual abilities of children with mental retardation – these children should be developing at a slower rate than nonretarded children, but their developmental profiles should be flat or even.

The similar-structure hypothesis has two sources, one explicit and one implicit. Explicitly, Zigler was arguing against the many defect theorists in mental retardation. He argued that, if in children with cultural-familial retardation there was no single defect causing the retardation, then these children should show MA-level performances on Zeaman and House's attentional, Luria's language mediational, or Ellis's stimulus trace tasks. Zigler has long been criticized for arguing that finding of no differences support the similar-structure position (Spitz, 1983); technically, when two groups do not differ statistically, one can state only that they do not differ, not that their performances are necessarily the same (see also Weisz, Yeates, & Zigler, 1982). Such studies do imply, however, that no single skill appears as a deficit below the child's overall MA. By inference, no single deficit seems to be the cause of the child's mental retardation. Such reasoning led to Zigler's advocacy of MA matches in retarded – nonretarded comparisons of intellectual or linguistic functioning.

Implicitly, Zigler was also influenced by Piaget's horizontal stages of development. If children with cultural-familial mental retardation were developing like nonretarded children, then they should show identical or nearly identical levels of functioning across various cognitive tasks, as Piaget had proposed (Kessen,

1962). Although such views of Piagetian structures have since been criticized (Fodor, 1983; Gardner, 1983), Zigler implicitly followed the idea of horizontally organized developments in his theorizing about children with cultural-familial mental retardation.

Personality-Motivational Factors. An area rarely discussed by Piaget, Werner, or Vygotsky, personality-motivational functioning is among the least classically developmental of the ideas in the original developmental approach. But it follows directly from Zigler's dissertation work and from experiments performed during the 1960s and 1970s (Zigler, 1971).

Although Zigler assumed that children with cultural-familial mental retardation develop identically to nonretarded children in terms of sequences and structures, he also acknowledged that these children have different life experiences. In the mid-1960s, such children were more likely than nonretarded children to be institutionalized. Even today, children with retardation are more likely to attend special classes and resource rooms or to receive special help within mainstream classrooms.

In addition, children with retardation were assumed to fail more often than other children on intellectual tasks. Such failure was hypothesized to change the child's style of solving problems. Instead of welcoming new, challenging intellectual tasks, children with retardation were thought to avoid such tasks, to expect to fail them, and to look to others for solutions whenever possible. Zigler (1984) has referred to children with retardation as often having "vexing, 'I can't do it'" approaches to intellectual problems. Such personality-motivational styles do not cause the child's retardation, but they do make the problem solving of these children less efficient than it might otherwise be.

The personality-motivational work of Zigler and his colleagues over 35 years has profoundly affected the field of mental retardation. Most important, Zigler and his colleagues have engendered among researchers and health care practitioners an appreciation that children with mental retardation are "whole people" who consist of more than their cognitive or linguistic limitations (Zigler, 1971). Recently, such work has tied motivational-personality functioning to emotional-psychiatric problems in retarded groups

(Zigler & Burack, 1989) and to the presentation of intellectual tasks to children with retardation (Bybee & Zigler, 1992). As we will see later, motivational styles may also influence how children with Down syndrome approach intellectual tasks (Wishart, 1993). Along with the similar-sequence and similar-structure hypotheses, Zigler's personality-motivational findings have justly been considered a lasting legacy of his developmental approach to mental retardation (Weisz, 1990).

More Recent Developmental Approaches

Applications of Developmental Approaches

Zigler limited his developmental approach to individuals with cultural-familial mental retardation. Due to their organic defects, children with pre-, peri-, or postnatal organic etiologies were excluded from his studies.

Gradually, however, various workers began applying developmental perspectives to children whose retardation had organic etiologies. Most prominent was the work of Dante Cicchetti. In a chapter examining development in children with Down syndrome, Cicchetti and Pogge-Hesse (1982) distinguished "conservative" from "liberal" developmental approaches to mental retardation. They noted that Zigler's approach was conservative in that he applied the similar-sequence and similar-structure hypotheses only to children with cultural-familial mental retardation. But to Cicchetti and Pogge-Hesse (1982), development should be viewed from a more general perspective, much as it had been by Werner, Kaplan, and other developmental theorists. Cicchetti and Pogge-Hesse thus called for a more liberal developmental perspective that would include development in children with Down syndrome and with other organic impairments.

In later work, Burack, Hodapp, and Zigler (1988) noted that the organic group needed to be better characterized. Comparing the trajectories of intelligence in Down syndrome (Cicchetti & Beeghly, 1990; Hodapp & Zigler, 1990) and fragile X syndrome (Dykens et al., 1989; Hodapp et al., 1990), Burack et al. (1988)

noted that it is simplistic to treat as identical the behavior of children with various forms of organic mental retardation. Hodapp and Dykens (1994) described differences among the genetic etiologies of mental retardation. Intellectual, adaptive, and linguistic strengths and weaknesses, the timing of slowed and accelerated periods of development, even the presence of distinct predispositions to particular emotional-psychiatric disturbances (Dykens, 1995, 1996) – all seem to vary from one etiological group to another.

Organic retardation is, therefore, not a single entity. The child with Down syndrome differs from the child with fragile X syndrome, Williams syndrome, or Prader–Willi syndrome, who may differ yet again from the child with fetal alcohol syndrome or some other, nongenetic but organic form of mental retardation. Although not every genetic (or organic) condition will be unique in every aspect of behavior (Hodapp, 1997a), etiology nevertheless influences many aspects of behavioral development.

Newly discovered organic conditions also change the prevalence rates of cultural-familial mental retardation. Cultural-familial retardation is defined by exclusion. If an individual does *not* have any other known condition, that person is considered to have cultural-familial mental retardation. As a result, each time a new genetic condition is discovered, fewer individuals remain in the cultural-familial group.

Consider the case of fragile X syndrome. Although geneticists had long suspected this condition to be a prevalent, genetically related type of mental retardation, only in the late 1960s did Lubs (1969) discover that the retardation of certain individuals was caused by a fragile, threadlike segment on the X-chromosome – hence the name "fragile X syndrome." Only later, in the mid-1970s, did genetic diagnoses of this syndrome become reliable (Sutherland, 1977). Even later, researchers realized that fragile X syndrome was the second most common genetic form of mental retardation (after Down syndrome). Given that fragile X syndrome "runs in families," these individuals had earlier been considered to have cultural-familial mental retardation (Dykens & Leckman, 1990). Although cultural-familial mental retardation will never disappear completely as a category, its prevalence will inevitably decrease below its present estimate of 50% to 75% of all persons with mental retardation. Most developmental work during the past 10 years has focused not on children with cultural-familial mental retardation, but on children with different genetic conditions.

As a by-product of this work, developmental approaches are being applied to children with organic conditions. In contrast to earlier workers, researchers now acknowledge that such children suffer from a clear organic defect, but that developmental approaches can still be tried. Hodapp and Zigler (1995) refer to such attempts as examining development "in the face of defect." Such developmental examinations go beyond Zigler's original focus on development in children with cultural-familial retardation, to investigate how development occurs in children with various types of mental retardation.

Changing Ideas of Development: Organismic Issues

In exploring how organismic issues have changed over the years, we will consider four topics. Two of these–sequences and cross-domain relations – were first discussed in the late 1960s. The other two – regressions and rates – Although sporadically discussed within developmental circles, have only recently received systematic evaluation.

Sequential Development. As the hallmark of any developmental approach, sequential development has been the concern of many developmentally oriented researchers. Many studies have therefore examined whether children with retardation traverse Piagetian or other, presumably universal sequences in the usual ordering. Such studies have both examined the similar-sequence hypothesis and contributed to the discussion of universal sequences in typical and atypical populations.

Similar-Sequence Studies. Most studies show that children with mental retardation do develop in the same sequences as do nonretarded children. Overviewing 3 longitudinal and 28 cross-sectional studies of development on a host of Piagetian tasks, Weisz, Yeates, and Zigler (1982) found that in almost all tasks, children with retardation followed the same sequences of development as nonretarded children. As for the distinction between cultural-familial and organic mental retardation, few differences emerged. Like children with cultural-familial retardation, children with organically caused retardation (usually Down syndrome) also demonstrate development along identical sequences (Cicchetti & Mans-Wagener, 1987; Cicchetti & Sroufe, 1976, 1978). Children with different organic forms of mental retardation may develop more slowly than children with cultural-familial retardation, but they too develop in order through Piagetian and other developmental sequences.

Yet a few exceptions should be noted. Children with severe abnormalities shown by EEG – causing uncontrollable seizures many times each day – often do not show sequential development (Wohlheuter & Sindberg, 1975). Their different sequences, however, may be as much a reflection of problems in testing as an indication of their development: It is difficult to know when such children are not having a seizure so that they can attend to the task at hand.

An additional complication appears in later-occurring developments. Mahaney and Stephens (1974) found that development did not proceed in the usual sequences for some questions involving moral reasoning. Specifically, adolescents with retardation were often unable to distinguish between the effects and the intent of an actor's action; that is, they did not treat a child's reactions as different based on whether a child inadvertently or deliberately broke a window by throwing a ball.

Sequentiality in Developmental Psychology. Just as exceptions to sequential development occur in children with retardation, typically developing children do not always show sequential development. For this reason, even within the field of (typical) developmental psychology, disenchantment with universal sequences has arisen among researchers over the past 15 to 20 years (Kessen, 1984).

In assessing these modifications of universal sequences, we can distinguish two types of developments, those that occur early versus later in typical development and those that are "cognitive-linguistic" versus "social-moral" in nature (Hodapp, 1990). For the most part, children's earliest developments and those that appear most closely tied to biological domains (i.e., cognition and language) seem to be most sequential. In contrast, less reliable sequences have been noted for later-occurring developments and for those domains that are more social or cultural.

Such issues arise most prominently in studies examining the development of children from different cultures. What it means to act morally, for example, varies between U.S. and Hindu children. The sequences of acquisition differ, as do the end points of development (J. G. Miller, 1984). Such differences often exist in many of the later-occurring, social and moral developments that were at one time considered to follow universal developmental sequences.

In contrast, sequences in infant cognition seem much less variable from culture to culture. Such universality in development has led Scarr-Salapatek (1975) and McCall (1982) to hypothesize that infant behavior is "channelized." That is, the human species may be biologically programmed to develop such early (and important) behaviors in a single, fixed ordering. Differences may occur across cultures in the speed of development or in the conceptualization of developments by adult caregivers (Super & Harkness, 1986), but the basic developmental sequences are identical.

To provide a few examples, children around the world develop in fixed order such early cognitive skills as object permanence and the use of two-word utterances concerning the existence of objects ("That ball"), the nonexistence of objects ("all-gone milk"), and the recurrence of objects or events ("more milk," "more tickle"). Later, however, children of different cultures develop different views of right and wrong, of why people behave the way they do, and of other, culturally based issues. Such differences between early biologically related developments and later, culturally related developments may influence which developments occur in sequential order throughout every society and which seem unique to different societies and cultures.

Such patterns of development exist among children with retardation as well. Early cognitive (and, possibly, grammatical) abilities appear to be channelized. Later and less cognitive developments are not necessarily sequential, and are more subject to cultural and neurobiological influences. Although not foolproof, these distinctions – early versus late and biological versus social – serve as useful guideposts as to whether a set sequence can be expected to occur in any child's development, whether or not that child has mental retardation.

Cross-Domain Relations. According to Zigler's similar-structure hypothesis, children with cultural-familial mental retardation, when matched on overall MA with nonretarded children, will show no obvious areas of "defect." Advanced in response to the defect theorists, the similar-structure hypothesis implicitly followed from Piaget's ideas concerning horizontal structures of development. Thus, the child at a particular developmental level in a certain area was thought to be at a similar level in all other domains. Again, we will first examine similar-structure studies, then the connection between cross-domain relations and wider issues in developmental psychology.

Similar-Structure Studies. Unlike studies of sequences, studies of the similar-structure hypothesis vary with the type of retardation under investigation. Briefly stated, the similar-structure hypothesis has held up reasonably well – with some exceptions – for children with cultural-familial mental retardation, but not as well for various organic groups.

In most studies, the performance of children with cultural-familial mental retardation was similar to that of MA-matched nonretarded children. Examining 32 studies involving 113 different comparisons, Weisz and Yeates (1981) noted that children with cultural-familial mental retardation performed at MA levels on a wide variety of Piagetian tasks. These tasks included animism, causality, classification, class inclusion, identity concepts, and classification of area, color, continuous quantity, length, mass, and number. With few exceptions, the MA-level performance of children with cultural-familial mental retardation was identical to that of nonretarded children.

When examinations center on information processing as opposed to Piagetian tasks, however, the picture changes slightly. In a later article, Weiss, Weisz, and Bromfield (1986) noted that children with mental retardation performed worse than MA-matched nonretarded children on certain aspects of information-processing tasks. Unlike Piagetian tasks, information-processing tasks require looking for long periods of time at a computer screen and responding again and again when a certain letter or symbol appears, or repeatedly deciding if two or more figures are identical or different.

No one really knows why children with cultural-familial mental retardation perform at MA levels on one type of task and show deficits (relative to MA levels) on others. One possibility involves differences between Piagetian and information-processing tasks (Weisz, 1990). Maybe, unlike nonretarded MA matches, children with cultural-familial mental retardation simply do not enjoy spending an hour or so at a computer screen, deciding again and again whether the geometric figure on the left differs from the one on the right. Alternatively, the distinction may be one of level of analysis. In this sense, Piagetian tasks might be considered global in nature, whereas most information-processing tasks are more detailed and specific. It may be that children with cultural-familial mental retardation may be deficient on the smaller, more detailed tasks, even as they perform at MA levels on the larger Piagetian tasks (Mundy & Kasari, 1990). For now, we cannot say for certain.

We do know, however, how children with organic mental retardation perform. In many studies, they perform worse than nonretarded MA-matched children (Weisz et al., 1982) on both Piagetian and information-processing tasks.

With the recent shift in emphasis from general organic retardation to retardation with particular organic etiologies, the picture has become more complex. It now appears that children with different types of mental retardation show different strengths and weaknesses. Children with different etiologies show weaknesses *and* strengths relative to MA matches.

A few examples will serve to illustrate this growing line of work. Boys with fragile X syndrome demonstrate a specific profile on the Kaufman Assessment Battery for Children, or K-ABC (Kaufman & Kaufman, 1983). Specifically, the K-ABC is divided into three parts: Sequential Processing, Simultaneous Processing, and Achievement. *Sequential Processing* involves the processing of information in serial or temporal order. For example, the child might be asked to repeat a series of three or four hand movements made by the examiner or to repeat a series of digits ("When I'm finished I want you to tell me which numbers I said. Ready? 11 . . . 5 . . . 6 . . . 14 . . . 3 . . . Go ahead"). *Simultaneous Processing* involves the understanding of the gestalt, or whole. Tasks involve identifying a drawing in which certain lines are missing or using a set of colored triangles to reproduce a larger figure. *Achievement* involves reading, general information, and math abilities. Boys with fragile X syndrome perform exceptionally poorly on those subtests involving Sequential Processing, whereas they do better on Simultaneous Processing and Achievement (Dykens, Hodapp, & Leckman, 1987). Further, this weakness in Sequential Processing is not demonstrated by children with Down syndrome (Hodapp, Dykens, Evans, & Merighi, 1992; Pueschel, Gallagher, Zartler, & Pezzullo, 1986). Table 3.3 presents an overview of the intellectual strengths and weaknesses of children with different organic etiologies of mental retardation. Some of these strengths and weaknesses occur in several groups, whereas others seem unique to a single etiological group.

Cross-Domain Relations in Developmental Psychology. Whatever the tasks or the type of retardation, the similar-structure hypothesis implies horizontal organization from one domain to another. Whether they are typically developing or retarded, children are expected to perform at the same level as children of the same MA on any cognitive or linguistic task.

While Piaget's horizontal cross-domain organization may be straightforward, it has generally not been supported by recent developmental work. Many researchers and theorists have observed that even in typically developing children levels of development are not the same from one domain to another. For instance, a child who has exceptionally good language skills may often show below-average skills on visuospatial tasks. On the basis of these findings, Gardner (1983) identified distinct "multiple intelligences": linguistic, musical, logicomathematical, spatial, bodily kinesthetic, and personal skills. Similarly, Fodor (1983) proposed that language (specifically, grammar) is a "modular" system that is separate from and does not interact with other abilities. Although these two theorists disagree on the number and nature of distinct human abilities (Gardner, 1985), both emphasize the disconnectedness of development from one domain to another.

Yet in spite of the strongest claims for disconnectedness, many abilities do appear to hold together to some degree, although rarely as consistently as described by Piaget. Skills in vocabulary and

Table 3.3. *Strengths and weaknesses in different genetic forms of mental retardation*

Disorder	Strengths	Weaknesses
Down syndrome	Social skills Protection from some forms of psychopathology	Grammar, articulation, and expressive language Mathematics
Fragile X syndrome	Simultaneous processing Most achievement tasks	Sequential processing Mathematics Proneness to hyperactivity and autistic-like behaviors
Prader–Willi syndrome	Long-term memory Receptive language Visuospatial perception	Auditory short-term memory Mathematics Social skills Fine and gross motor skills
Williams syndrome	Grammar, semantics, and vocabulary Music Social skills and interpersonal relations	Visuomotor integration (e.g., drawing) Spatial localization

pragmatics (i.e., the uses of language) seem closely related to the child's overall MA. Such links to MA occur in children with and without retardation (Rondal, 1996).

At the same time, as already mentioned, striking discontinuities also exist, and many can be seen in the functioning of children with retardation. Major support for the existence of discontinuities comes from studies of exceptional individuals (most with retardation) from the early 1970s on. The most dramatic story is that of Genie (Curtiss, 1977). "Genie" is the pseudonym for a young woman living in the Los Angeles area who was severely neglected and abused by her father until she was discovered at the age of 14 years by social service workers in the early 1970s. Having lived in a closet without any exposure to language, Genie at first displayed no language. After a great deal of intervention, however, she made remarkable linguistic progress. As the psycholinguist Susan Curtiss later noted, "Genie learned how to encode concepts through words. She used language as a tool: she could label things, ideas, emotions. It was from her we learned of her past. She told us of her feelings" (Rymer, 1993). Yet she was never able to acquire grammar. To this day, Genie uses language productively, but has never become adept at ordering words or at using the many English word endings (morphemes) that denote plural, tense, and ongoing activity ("ing").

Other children with unusual linguistic characteristics have also been discovered. Laura, a young woman with a nonverbal IQ of 44, shows remarkably intact grammatical abilities (Yamada, 1990), and Françoise, a woman with Down syndrome, has unimpaired grammar (Rondal, 1995). Table 3.4 lists examples of the grammatical abilities of Genie, Laura, and Françoise.

In addition to these individual cases, individuals with one etiology of retardation may display "language without comparable abilities in thought." Williams syndrome is a rare genetic disorder of mental retardation that affects approximately 1 in 50,000 children (Pober & Dykens, 1996). Many of these children show specific high-level abilities in language and language-like tasks compared with MA-matched children with or without retardation (Bellugi, Wang, & Jernigan, 1994). They have vocabulary levels that are several years ahead of overall MA (Bellugi, Marks, Bihrle, & Sabo, 1988). For example, a child with Williams syndrome who had an overall MA of approximately 5 years understood such words as *peninsula* and *spherical* (Bellugi et al., 1988). Similarly, some children with Williams syndrome can tell stories using high-level grammar, as well as sound effects and other storytelling devices (Reilly, Klima, & Bellugi, 1990). But clearly, not all children with Williams syndrome can perform linguistically at such a high level (Udwin & Yule, 1990), and several recent studies have questioned the degree to which linguistic grammar is "intact" (i.e., occurs at chronological age levels) in children with Williams syndrome (Karmiloff-Smith et al., 1996). Still, such discrepancies show that language – primarily grammar – may develop separately from other areas of development (Tager-Flusberg & Sullivan, 1998).

We see, then, that cross-domain relations reflect changes that have occurred over the past 25 to 30 years. On one hand, the developmental approach to mental retardation has been applied more broadly, to children with organic retardation who were not

Table 3.4. *Grammar in three exceptional cases of language acquisition*

Genie, aged 13–17 years, shows high-level vocabulary but very poor grammatical abilities, as shown by this conversation with her foster mother:
G: Genie have yellow material at school.
M: What are you using it for?
G: Paint. Paint picture. Take home. Ask teacher yellow material. Blue paint. Yellow green paint. Genie have blue material, teacher said no. Genie use material paint. I want use material at school.
M: You wanta paint it, or are you trying to tell me you *did* paint it?
G: *Did* paint. (Curtiss, 1977, p. 172)

Laura, 32 years old (IQ 44), has extremely high-level linguistic abilities, as shown by the following sentences produced during various conversations:
"He was saying that I lost my battery powered watch that I loved; I just loved that watch." (Yamada, 1990, p. 28)
"He's my third principal I've had since I've been here." (p. 29)
"Did you hear about me not going to this school in Altadena?" (p. 29)

Françoise, a young woman (32 years old; IQ 64) with Down syndrome, has relatively intact grammatical abilities:
"La secrétaire joue au tennis avec le professeur. Il vous telephonera demain." (The secretary plays tennis with the professor. He [the professor] will telephone you tomorrow; Rondal, 1995, p. 439; my translation.)
"Et ça m'étonne pas parce que les chiens ont toujours trop chaud quand ils vont à la port." (And that does not surprise me because dogs are always too warm when they go outdoors; Rondal, 1995, p. 117).

considered in the earliest formulations. On the other, developmental psychology proper has moved beyond views of horizontally organized development. Researchers no longer consider the child's levels in one domain (e.g., grammar) to necessarily be congruent with levels in another (e.g., cognition). In short, changes have occurred in the choice of populations to which developmental principles have been applied, as well as in the principles themselves (Hodapp, 1997b).

Developmental Rates. Although clinicians and interventionists may be interested in promoting faster development, speed of development per se has rarely interested developmental workers. Some of this neglect has theoretical roots: Until recently, most developmental researchers have been organismically inclined, while most researchers interested in behavior change (including the speed of development) have been behaviorists and behavior modification specialists.

But there may be a deeper explanation. Historically, most developmental researchers have been interested in understanding the basic processes of development. They have striven to ascertain why children develop, how children at a certain level of development understand the world, what sequences characterize all development, and in what ways developments in different areas are related. In short, developmental psychology has often been characterized by a basic research orientation.

Given this orientation, practical issues have been granted a relatively low status. Such issues have often been of greater concern to educational psychologists and those in other applied disciplines than to most developmental psychologists. Piaget's (possibly apocryphal) response to the issue of rate shows this disdain for practical issues. During several of his lectures in the United States, he was asked whether children's development through his various stages and substages could be accelerated. But Piaget showed little interest in this issue. He came to call this concern "la question américaine," noting that only Americans could be obsessed with faster development.

Nonetheless, developmental rate can sometimes shed light on theoretical issues. Consider McCall, Eichorn, and Hogarty's (1977) studies using the Bayley Scales of Infant Development (Bayley, 1969). Examining many children longitudinally over the first few years of life, McCall et al. noted that infants appeared to maintain their rank in relation to other infants at certain ages more than at others. An infant with a high DQ (developmental quotient, or infant IQ score) at 3 months was likely to show a high DQ at 6 months. At certain points, however, earlier performance did not predict later performance. The same infant who showed above-average DQ at 3 and 6 months might not show above-average performance at 9 months. Specifically, when testing was performed before and then after the ages of 2, 8, 13, and 21 months, earlier performance did not predict later performance. McCall et al.

(1977) noted that these break points seemed to occur at times when the very nature of infant intelligence was changing.

Changes in rate of development may also provide useful indications of developmental changes within groups with retardation. Figure 3.1 plots two children's rates of development, which are steady (though slow), until the children reach a particular chronological age (CA), when their development slows down. This type of "slowing" might be called a "CA wall"; that is, it is a slowing down of development due to the child's having reached a specific CA.

Evidence for such "slowings" based on CA can be found in several types of mental retardation. The intellectual growth of boys with fragile X syndrome slows down from approximately 8 or 10 through 15 years (Dykens et al., 1989; Hodapp et al., 1990). Certain types of development may slow down in children with Down syndrome at specific CAs, usually at approximately 6 through 11 years. During this time, "slowings" may occur in IQ scores (Gibson, 1966), adaptive skills (Dykens, Hodapp, & Evans, 1994), and possibly grammatical development (Fowler, 1988). Although the age-related slowing in Down syndrome has not been as well demonstrated as the later slowing in fragile X syndrome, CA walls may represent one major source of rate changes in several retarded populations.

A second type of slowing down of development seems related not to the child's age but to the task with which the child is struggling. As shown in Figure 3.2, two children develop at a given rate until they reach a certain level of development – each at a different CA – after which development slows down. This type of "slowing" might be called an "MA wall," in that development slows down at a certain MA. But since different MA levels require different skills (e.g., productive language beginning at age 2), the slowing down of development at a particular MA level may be related to an inability to perform one or more MA-appropriate tasks.

Again, children with Down syndrome show such MA walls during development. Examining sensorimotor development, Dunst (1988, 1990) showed that the development of such children slows down as they progress across several Piagetian sensorimotor stages, most notably from sensorimotor Stage IV to Stage V (which occurs at around 12 to 13 months for typically developing chil-

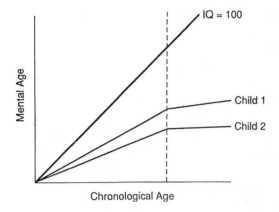

Figure 3.1. Effects of changes in neurobiological structure on rate of development.

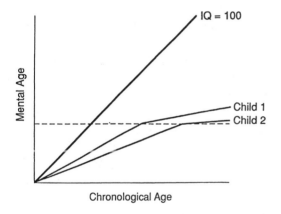

Figure 3.2. Effects of changes in type of task on rate of development.

dren). At slightly later ages, children with Down syndrome may have particular difficulty with Brown's (1973) Stage III grammar, the stage when children begin acquiring complex syntactic structures such as negatives, wh-questions, and yes–no-questions (Fowler, Gelman, & Gleitman, 1994; Rondal, Ghiotto, Bredart, & Bachelet, 1988).

Although such findings are intriguing, more research is needed on both MA and CA slowings in different etiological groups. At present, we cannot be certain whether many of these slowings occur or, if so, whether they are more closely related to the child's CA or to difficulties with specific developmental tasks. Even when such slowings are identified, we will still need to determine why they occur. Why, for instance, does the development of children with Down syndrome slow down from 6 to 11 years of age, or the development of boys with fragile X syndrome slow down from age 8 to 10 through 15 years? Similarly, we do not understand why children with Down syndrome have such difficulties with Brown's Stage III grammar or with the transition from Piagetian sensorimotor Stage IV to Stage V. Like McCall et al.'s (1977) findings on typically developing infants, future MA and CA wall studies might help us understand the nature of development or, in this case, the interplay between behavioral and neurobiological development in children with many different etiologies of retardation.

Regressions. From Piaget and the similar-sequence hypothesis, one might surmise that development is an uncomplicated affair. The child progresses from one stage (or substage) to the next, acquiring more and more skills with each passing day.

Although in general this may be the case, few children develop in such a perfect manner. Indeed, like a child first learning to walk, development is often characterized by fits and starts, a few steps forward, one back, and an occasional fall in between. While the general direction may be forward, most children experience temporary setbacks, times when what was accomplished today cannot be performed tomorrow.

Regressions are an old topic that has been revisited in new, exciting ways. Piaget's colleague Inhelder sensed that the development of children with retardation was more fragile than that of nonretarded children. Inhelder found evidence of regressions from one testing session to another, as well as of oscillating responses even within a single session.

Such regression and fragility have recently been found in children with Down syndrome. These children appear to regress much more often than do nonretarded infants. Whereas in one study typically developing children regressed an average of 7% of the time across all testing sessions and all sensorimotor domains, infants with Down syndrome regressed 17.6% of the time, or 2.5 times as often (Dunst, 1990). Certain domains seemed particularly susceptible to regression. Rates of regression over 20% occurred in tests measuring gestural imitation, vocal imitation, and symbolic uses of objects (using a cup to drink; at later ages, using words to refer to objects). These children really were performing in a "two steps forward, one backward" manner.

But the story may be even more complicated. In a series of studies examining many diverse developments, young children with Down syndrome were found to be particularly unstable in their development (Wishart, 1993; see also Morss, 1983). These children were more likely than typically developing children to regress on a single test (e.g., object permanence) from one session to the next (Wishart & Duffy, 1988). On the Bayley and other IQ tests, these children showed gains on some items and regressions on others. A child might pass Item A during one session and not during the next, and not pass Item B during Session 1, but pass this item during Session 2.

Such instability may also have a motivational component. Pitcairn and Wishart (1994) tested three groups of young children: Down syndrome, MA-matched nonretarded, and CA-matched nonretarded. All subjects were given several impossible tasks – for example, putting a round shape into a square hole. The CA-matched children quickly realized they could not perform this task, and spent little time attempting it on the second trial. The MA-matched children took longer to realize they couldn't perform the task, but then used this knowledge to refuse on the second trial. The children with Down syndrome, in contrast, spent much time attempting the task on both trials, and also engaged in much off-task behavior on both occasions. Such behaviors consisted of looking at the experimenter, establishing eye contact and vocalizing, and performing an "act" to distract the experimenter from the task at hand. As Pitcairn and Wishart (1994) note, "The DS [Down syndrome] children were not simply more social. It was rather in their response to failure that they differed. They exploited their social skills, producing a variety of distracting behaviors that focused attention (their own and that of the experimenter) away from the task in hand" (p. 489).

Children with Down syndrome thus seem both more fragile and less motivated (or differently motivated) to solve difficult tasks. So far, little of this work has been performed with children with other etiologies of mental retardation. At the very least, the findings of Dunst, Wishart, and Morss show that development in many children with mental retardation is more complicated than originally thought.

Conclusion

Since the late 1960s, several themes have characterized developmental approaches to mental retardation. These themes involve the ongoing history of developing approaches: their changing nature and the need for more knowledge about development in children with most types of mental retardation.

The Ongoing History of Developmental Approaches to
Mental Retardation

"Plus ça change, plus c'est la même chose": The more things change, the more they remain the same. So too with organismic issues in the developmental approach to mental retardation. Indeed, it seems as if many issues come up again and again, even if they reappear in a slightly different guise or with a slightly different name.

Consider regressions. As early as 1943, Inhelder realized that development in children with retardation was more fragile, with oscillations within and regressions across testing sessions, than that of nonretarded children. More recently, Dunst, Wishart, and others have found evidence of more regressions in children with Down syndrome. Although these workers have better characterized such regressions – and limited their work to one etiological group – we again see a concern with the instability of development in children with mental retardation.

In a similar way, Zigler's personality-motivational ideas have persisted, at times returning under different guises or applied to new issues or situations. In tying personality-motivation functioning to pathology and to strategies for teaching persons with retardation, Zigler and his colleagues are putting his earlier, mostly laboratory-based findings to more practical uses. An ongoing effort to establish a quick, easy-to-use teacher-report measure of personality-motivational functioning will help in this regard. Pitcairn and Wishart (1994) have also noted oddities in the problem-solving styles of children with Down syndrome. Such personality styles further hinder the child's functioning and the interventionist's efforts to foster the child's development.

Such concerns as sequences and cross-domain relations have held a steady, continuing interest for researchers and interventionists alike. Part of the appeal is practical. As we will discuss more fully in Chapter 9, the similar-sequence hypothesis is a powerful concept that can inform teaching efforts. For children with retardation – or any other disability – who are developing in a fixed order, curricula that capitalize on the children's propensity to develop along a certain course have already been developed (Hodapp, 1990). It is no wonder that various researchers have examined sequences in many domains of development over a span of almost 50 years.

Conversely, other mental retardation findings are of interest primarily because they go against the grain of long-standing developmental views. Genie, Laura, and Françoise are fascinating because they defy Piaget's horizontal stages. In theory, these individuals simply should not have grammatical systems that are so distinct from their abilities in other areas. In the same way, children with Williams syndrome should not have such high-level language in the face of their lower cognitive abilities. But in fact these individuals do have linguistic abilities that are out of line with their other abilities.

Though to a lesser extent, changing rates of development also go against views that have prevailed for many years. Although variable rates are often seen in typically developing children during infancy (Bayley, 1955), the IQ levels of most children are reasonably stable after age 3 or 4 years (Vernon, 1979). And yet, in both

Down syndrome and fragile X syndrome, changing rates of development occur at different ages or in response to different developmental tasks. Again, part of our interest stems from the discrepancies between what we know, historically, to be the case in typical development and what we are now seeing in children with various forms of mental retardation. For developmental approaches to children with retardation then, history is not irrelevant.

The Changing Nature of Developmental Approaches

As important as history is, many exciting changes have occurred in developmental approaches since the late 1960s. Such changes have broadened the field to reflect recent developmental concerns and to encompass new populations.

Whereas Zigler did not even need to detail what he meant by development – so widespread was the adherence to Piagetian views in the late 1960s – the modern developmentalist struggles to describe development. For typically developing children or children with mental retardation, the modern developmentalist asks whether, when, and for which domains sequential development exists. Are there connections across different domains of development? If not, how unconnected are developments across various domains? In the same way, when and why do regressions or changing developmental rates occur? The work undertaken to answer these questions has led to important advances in developmental theory over the past 30 years.

Such advances have brought to the fore the question of what, exactly, is the developmental approach to mental retardation. This question has bedeviled many mental retardation researchers, particularly those who are generally not developmentally oriented. In papers written only a few years apart, major workers such as Al Baumeister have asked whether the developmental approach is indeed a theory at all (Baumeister, 1984), then lauded it as one of the two major approaches in the field of mental retardation (Baumeister, 1987). Others have ignored the developmental approach. Most common, perhaps, has been the practice of mentioning, then criticizing, Zigler's similar-sequence or similar-structure hypothesis as originally described in the late 1960s, with no acknowledgment that these issues have changed dramatically over the past 30 years.

Unlike many theories that have not changed over the years, the developmental perspective is alive for children with and without retardation. Many of the most exciting findings have occurred in the past 10 years, particularly regarding modularity and rate changes. Such issues were not a part of Zigler's early developmental approach to mental retardation. Yet these questions now represent meeting places where researchers interested in typical development can compare their findings and ideas with those interested in identical issues in retarded populations. As a result, a cross-fertilization of ideas and approaches is ensured.

Research on Different Types of Mental Retardation

As already noted, Zigler applied his original developmental approach only to children with cultural-familial mental retardation. In recent years, however, developmental approaches have been applied to children whose retardation has a wider array of organic etiologies.

To date, however, we know little about the development of such children. Most studies focus on children with Down syndrome, fragile X syndrome, and, more recently, Williams and Prader–Willi syndromes. Thus, for most of the 750 etiologies of mental retardation, few developmental studies exist.

This dearth of studies stems, at least partially, from the existence of two distinct research "cultures" – one biomedically oriented, the other behavioral (Hodapp & Dykens, 1994). Biomedically oriented workers generally belong to the professions of genetics, medical genetics, pediatrics, and psychiatry. Behavioral workers are generally psychologists (of various types), special educators, and family researchers. Most of the studies of genetic disorders of mental retardation are performed by biomedical researchers who provide only the rudiments of behavioral information. Such studies generally note only that the child with, say, Lesh–Nyan syndrome has a certain IQ and shows certain characteristic behaviors (in this case, biting and other self-injurious behaviors).

On the other side, behavioral workers (including many developmentalists) generally divide subject groups not by etiology, but on the basis of the child's level of impairment: the mildly (IQ 55–69), moderately (IQ 40–54), severely (IQ 25–39), and profoundly (IQ below 20 or 25) retarded categories that are ubiquitous in behavioral research. With the exception of children with Down syndrome, children with different etiologies of mental retardation have been the subject of very few behavioral studies.

In a sense, those researchers most interested in etiology (biomedical researchers) know little about development, and those interested in development (behavioral workers) know little about etiology. It is time for these two sides to come together in order to better examine development in children with different types of mental retardation. Fortunately, some movement along this line may be occurring. As developmentally oriented workers begin to acknowledge the importance to their own work of findings such as high-level language in Williams syndrome, they increasingly realize that all children with retardation are not the same. Only with this realization will there emerge more mature, integrated developmental studies of children with various forms of mental retardation.

We have seen, then, that developmental approaches to mental retardation have advanced greatly over the past 30 years, but still have a long way to go. Not only has our thinking about sequences, structures, rates, and regressions changed, but such issues are now being examined in children with many types of retardation. In the next chapter, we will turn to some contextual aspects of development in children with mental retardation.

4

Mental Retardation: II. Contextual Issues

One can proceed in either of two directions when discussing contextual issues in mental retardation. First, one can examine the ways in which personal environments influence children with mental retardation. Such an approach characterized earlier studies of cultural-familial mental retardation; indeed, even the terms cultural-familial, sociocultural familial, and environmental deprivation imply that the environment causes or increases the likelihood of mental retardation (see Table 3.2). Many studies in the 1960s and 1970s focused on the alleviation of mental retardation, generally by attempting to raise children's IQ scores through intensive early intervention programs such as the Milwaukee, Abecedarian, and Perry Preschool programs (c.f., Zigler & Hodapp, 1986).

Second, one can examine how children with mental retardation affect their environments. How, for example, do mothers react to having a child with retardation? Do they differ from mothers of typically developing children? What effects does the child with retardation have on fathers, siblings, or the family as a whole? Mainly due to the recent flurry of work, this "child affects the environment" approach will be emphasized in this chapter.

Like issues discussed in prior chapters, contextual issues have a research history, one that reflects multidisciplinary perspectives and new views toward families of children with retardation. Researchers have ranged from developmental psychologists, to clinical psychologists and psychiatrists, to family systems therapists and researchers. Over the past 20 years, researchers have gone from viewing these families as pathological to acknowledging that they face increased stress, though they often cope reasonably well. This shift in perspective is probably the main advance that has been made in work on families. Moreover, increased interest in individual differences and in various theoretical models has accompanied these changing perspectives. Changing histories and changing perspectives should be kept in mind as we examine maternal reactions, family effects, and mother–child interactions.

Maternal Reactions and Early Family Studies

Solnit and Stark's Model of Maternal Mourning

Like many topics in psychology, work on maternal reactions begins with Sigmund Freud. In 1917, Freud wrote an article entitled "Mourning and Melancholia," in which he described what happens when one loses a loved one. He analyzed the grief process from his psychoanalytic perspective and initiated the idea of "working through" the grief reaction over time. This article remains the classic statement about how and why humans react as they do to the death of a loved one. The article indicates how everyone reacts to "all those situations of being wounded, hurt, neglected, out of favor, or disappointed" (Freud, 1917/1957, p. 132).

Almost 50 years after Freud, Solnit and Stark (1961) returned to this theme in "Mourning and the Birth of a Defective Child." In that article, Solnit and Stark used Freud's view of mourning to conceptualize the maternal reaction to having and raising a child with retardation. Using case material from their own practices, these authors described this mourning reaction. But to Solnit and Stark, the mourning was not a reaction to the child per se, but to one's ideal child. Every mother (and father) dreams of what her (or his) child will be like: Will my child be a great historical figure, an artist, an intellectual? Benedek (1959) described the hero or heroine that each parent envisions. But such dreams are destroyed when a child is born with mental retardation. Parents realize that their child will not become president or a great historical figure. They must mourn – as after a death – the loss of their idealized child.

Effects on Subsequent Research

The Solnit and Stark model has had at least four effects on subsequent research. Although several are obvious and others more subtle, each provides background to modern work on familial reactions.

1. Focus on Pathology. The clearest, most direct effect of Solnit and Stark's formulation derives from its view of maternal reactions as pathological, as akin to the negative reactions underlying depression and other emotional problems. Influenced by the mourning model, later workers studied the adverse effects of raising a child with retardation. Researchers examined mothers' stages of mourning, the degree of depression and other psychopathology in various family members, and the ways in which these families were worse off than families of typically developing children.

Still, the implications of this mourning perspective should not be exaggerated. Mourning and other strong emotional reactions are intrinsic to everyday life. Freud (1917/1957) felt that life presents each of us with various trials, of which raising a child with retardation is one among many. Maternal mourning is therefore a normal, indeed a healthy, reaction. Even though a mourning perspective may give too much emphasis to negative outcomes, it need not be as stigmatizing as is often portrayed in recent family work.

Mothers of children with disabilities do mourn the loss of the idealized child; these mothers may also be more prone to various emotional problems, as may husbands, couples, and siblings. While an exclusive emphasis on mourning, depression, and psychopathology may be too narrow, such reactions do need to be considered.

2. Stage Models. Solnit and Stark (1961) briefly noted that the mourning process involved an initial phase of numbness and disbelief, followed by a dawning awareness of disappointment and feelings of loss, then a reexperiencing of memories and expectations that helped to "reduce the hypercathexis of the wish for the idealized child" (p. 526). These ideas imply that maternal reactions following the birth of a child with retardation occur in stages.

Subsequent workers developed theories that, although differing in their details, essentially hypothesized a three-stage process (Blacher, 1984). At birth, the mother experiences shock, in much the same way one goes into shock after a car accident or other traumatic incident. As one parent reported "I couldn't believe that it was happening to me. I thought that it was unreal and that I would soon wake up" (Drotar, Baskiewicz, Irvin, Kennell, & Klaus, 1975, p. 712). The mother's knowledge is disconnected from her feelings; she knows, intellectually, that her child has mental retardation, but she cannot yet emotionally accept this fact.

During the second stage, called emotional disorganization, strong emotional reactions arise. Some mothers report extreme sadness and depression, while others experience anger – even rage – toward doctors, or God, or whomever they blame for their child's condition. In psychoanalytic terms, anger is turned inward toward oneself (depression) or outward toward others (anger).

During the final stage, called emotional reorganization, mothers accept their child as he or she is. They begin working for the child's best interests, and their own emotions become less acute. As one mother noted, the birth of her child with retardation was due to "nothing I had done" and her child was "very special" (Drotar et al., 1975, p. 713).

Figure 4.1 shows one variant of this three-stage model. Although Drotar et al.'s (1975) model features five stages, it is typical of most mourning models in other respects. Shock and disbelief come early, and as these subside depression and anger emerge, followed by adaptation and emotional reorganization. Note that the time spent traversing each stage is left undefined, with individual mothers progressing at different rates. Nonetheless, an orderly, sequential process is implied.

Although most mental retardation workers originally accepted the maternal mourning model, a few have always questioned it. Writing around the same time as Solnit and Stark, Olshansky (1962, 1966) noted that the term maternal mourning may not adequately convey the experiences of most mothers of children with retardation. He noted that such mothers do not simply work through their grief over having a child with retardation. Instead, most "suffer chronic sorrow throughout their lives," with the intensity varying "from time to time for the same person, from situation

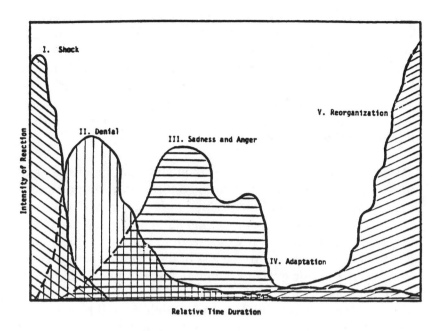

Figure 4.1. Hypothetical model of a normal sequence of parental reactions to the birth of a malformed infant. From Drotar et al., 1975 (p. 715)

to situation, and from one family to the next" (Olshansky, 1962, pp. 190–191). Olshansky, then proposed what might be called a recurrent mourning model of maternal emotional reactions.

3. Emphasis on Mothers. Since even today mothers are usually the main caretakers of children (especially those with mental retardation), the mother-centered focus of early studies is not surprising. This emphasis also conforms with historical trends in developmental psychology, where until the mid-1970s fathers and families as a whole were only rarely studied (e.g., Hodapp & Mueller, 1982).

However, focusing solely on mothers skewed the examination of the effects of children with retardation on family functioning. As we now know, maternal behaviors and emotions are affected by fathers, siblings, family dynamics, and the mother's support system. To focus exclusively on mothers is to examine only part of the picture. This changes the problem of parental or familial reactions into the mother's problem. Although less derogatory than the claim that the mother caused the child's retardation (as occurred in autism), this mother-centered perspective still ignores important people and conceptualizations of familial reactions. Partly due to the influence of the maternal mourning model, paternal reactions to children with retardation have only begun to be studied (Krauss, 1993), and almost no studies exist on interactions between fathers and their children with retardation.

4. Usual or Normative Reactions. Solnit and Stark implied that all mothers of children with disabilities go through the same mourning process. The timing of the reaction may vary from one mother to another, and some mothers are angry and others depressed during the stage of emotional disorganization. But for the most part, all mothers react similarly to the loss of the expected perfect child.

An additional side effect of Solnit and Stark's maternal mourning model was the idea that the emotional reactions of mothers were similar even when children had disabilities of different types or severity. In their original article, Solnit and Stark (1961) noted that such reactions might even occur in response to the unexpected birth of twins or of premature infants. Subsequent research examined maternal reactions to children with various disabilities in single-subject groups. In the Drotar et al. (1975) study, the subjects included mothers of infants with Down syndrome, congenital malformations, cleft palate, and cleft lip. Blacher's (1984) review of maternal mourning included studies of children with mental retardation, autism, physical handicaps, and severe heart conditions.

Early Family Studies

In addition to its effects on studies of mothers, the Solnit and Stark formulation influenced how researchers examined couples, fathers, siblings, and the family as a whole. These researchers generally searched for ways in which children with retardation might adversely affect family functioning.

Couples. Several studies examined the prevalence of divorce and dissatisfaction with marriage in families of such children. Many of these studies found that parents of children with disabilities were more likely to be divorced than parents of same-age, typically developing children. For example, Gath (1977) found that in 6 of 26 families of children with Down syndrome the parents were either divorced or showed high levels of tension and dissatisfaction, compared with none of the 26 families of same-age, typically developing children.

Even in these early studies, however, suggestions emerged that the birth of a child with retardation can also strengthen a marriage. In Gath (1977), no differences emerged between the groups on overall measures; even though 6 marriages in the Down syndrome group were rated "poor," 14 (as opposed to 16 in the control group) were considered good, with much warmth and many positive comments expressed between the couple.

In summary, some indications have emerged that relationships can become either weaker or stronger due to the presence of a child with retardation.

Mothers and Fathers. Some studies examined depression in mothers. Comparing mothers of 4- to 13-year-old children with mental retardation, chronic illnesses, behavior disorders, or no disabilities, Cummings, Bayley, and Rie (1966) found that mothers of children with retardation were more depressed, more preoccupied with their children, and had greater difficulty handling their anger than mothers of typically developing children (see also Erikson, 1969; Friedrich & Friedrich, 1981). Cummings (1976) found that fathers of children with disabilities showed increased levels of depression and lower levels of dominance, self-esteem, and enjoyment of the child with disabilities, a pattern that Cummings called "neurotic-like constriction."

Again, however, not all parents showed these reactions. Mothers in two-parent families coped more effectively than those in one-parent families (Beckman, 1983), as did women in good as opposed to conflicted marriages (Beckman, 1983; Friedrich, 1979). Similarly, the mother's reactions were related to the family's socioeconomic status (SES): Mothers in higher-SES households coped more effectively (Farber, 1970). Although the effects of a good marriage and higher family income seem obvious, these studies indicated that not all mothers suffered negative reactions to an equal extent and that certain factors eased the strain of parenting the child with retardation.

Siblings. The earliest studies of siblings also centered on emotional problems. These studies found that nondisabled siblings of children with mental retardation were only sometimes more prone than siblings of typically developing children to depression and other emotional problems (e.g., Gath, 1973; Tew & Laurence, 1973). Taken as a group, siblings appeared as likely to suffer from emotional disorders as did siblings of typically developing children (Lobato, 1983).

Grossman (1972) found that older siblings generally adapted better than younger ones; the younger children suffered more than the older siblings from being deprived of their parents' attention. But older sisters seemed most prone to a variety of emotional problems (Breslau, Weitzman, & Messenger, 1981; Gath, 1974; Grossman, 1972), perhaps because they were forced to perform adult tasks at too young an age.

Growing up with a sibling with retardation may sometimes have beneficial effects. In her study of college students who were siblings of children with retardation, Grossman (1972) found that their reactions were either positive or negative. On one side were those siblings – approximately 45% – who felt strongly negative, accusing their parents of never having provided enough love and attention due to their preoccupation with the sibling with a disability. On the other were about 45% of siblings who felt that the experience of growing up with a child with retardation had been extremely positive. These siblings reported that their brother or sister with retardation had helped them become more empathic and caring, more tolerant of differences among people. As with the findings on couples, fathers, and mothers, then, there were differences among individuals.

Family as a Whole. In addition to studies of individual family members, early work focused on families as a whole. In a series of studies carried out during the late 1950s and early 1960s, Farber (1959) found that families of children with mental retardation differed in several ways from families of same-age, typically developing children. He noted that families of children with retardation – especially those in which the child is severely impaired – become "stuck" in their development: The parents are never allowed to "grow up" with their children and experience these children leaving home.

Farber (1959) also noted the role tensions often found in typically developing siblings of children with retardation, as an older sister took on more housekeeping duties, for example, or a younger brother helped an older child with retardation with a hobby. Farber (1970) further noted that many families of children with disabilities suffered from what he called "economic immobility." Unlike families of same-age, typically developing children, families of children with retardation often appeared to stagnate economically, possibly due to parental preoccupation with the child with disabilities (and possibly due to the cost of caring for the child).

Modern Family Research

Modern work on families of children with disabilities began about 1980 or 1985. From then on, researchers used new theoretical models to conceptualize their findings.

Child as Stressor

Surveying studies performed until the early 1980s, Crnic, Friedrich, and Greenberg (1983) noted that the reigning model of pathology had proved inadequate. Although many studies had shown more divorce, depression, or other negative outcomes in families of children with retardation than in those without such children, the effects of a child with retardation on family functioning were not uniformly negative. In every study, certain families and family members adapted well.

Crnic et al. (1983) proposed that these effects could better be explained by a model of stress, coping, and family ecology. Like a family member's poor health or a parent's loss of his or her job, the child with retardation could best be conceptualized as a stressor on the family system. Any family's capacity to cope depends on external resources such as money, as well as internal resources such as the parents' confidence in their ability to teach the child, their problem-solving skills, their attitude toward life, and their religious beliefs. Finally, support is also important from individuals outside the family. When friends, relatives, teachers, schools, and social service agencies are helpful and supportive, families are better able to adapt.

This model of stress, coping, and ecology is foreshadowed in the studies cited in the preceding section. That the child with retardation is indeed a stressor is attested to by the many negative consequences of having such a child in a family: the possibly higher divorce rates, the greater prevalence of depression among parents, and the larger proportion of siblings who are resentful of not receiving enough love and attention from their parents. But at the same time, many parents of children with retardation do remain close, and many young adult siblings feel enriched by having grown up with a sibling with retardation. An adequate income, two-parent families, and social supports help families raise children with retardation.

Theoretical Models

Such understanding of stress and coping has given way to several models of family adaptation. The most important of these is called the "Double ABCX" model (Minnes, 1988). According to this model, the "crisis" (the "X" in the name) of raising a child with retardation is a function of the child's personal characteristic (A), the family's internal and external resources (B), and the family's perceptions of the child (C). In addition, A, B, and C all change along with changes in the child's and in the family's circumstances – hence the "Double" in the model's name.

Although the Double ABCX model is very general, it has led to much important research. Let us look at each aspect of the model in turn.

The Child's Characteristics. Children with retardation vary considerably one from another. For one thing, the etiologies of their mental retardation vary. As shown in Chapter 3, different etiologies show different severities of retardation; different intellectual, adaptive, and linguistic strengths and weaknesses; and different associated maladaptive behaviors and psychopathology.

Some of these differences relate to familial adaptation. In most studies, families of children with Down syndrome cope better than families of children with other types of mental retardation (Hodapp, 1996). The earliest studies made comparisons between families of children with Down syndrome and those of children with autism (e.g., Holroyd & MacArthur, 1976). More recently, studies have compared families of children with Down syndrome with those of children whose retardation is of either mixed or unknown etiology. In categorizing families of children with retardation, Mink, Nihira, and Meyers (1983) identified one family type that they called "cohesive and harmonious." Almost two-thirds of these close, happy families were families of children with Down syndrome. Similar findings favoring Down syndrome have been noted in families of preschool children (Erikson & Upshur, 1989), in adolescents (Thomas & Olson, 1993), and aging parents of middle-aged adults with retardation (Seltzer, Krauss, & Tsunematsu, 1993). Thomas and Olson (1993) noted that the characteristics of families of adolescents with Down syndrome were almost identical to those of families of nondisabled children. In all cases, caring for an offspring with Down syndrome has been associated with less stress, less depression, and more social support than caring for offspring with other types of mental retardation or developmental disabilities (Table 4.1).

At present, we cannot say why Down syndrome is associated with better parental and familial adaptation. Because it is the most well known disorder of mental retardation, information and parent-group supports are readily available; these parents may thus receive more help than parents of children with other types of retardation (Erikson & Upshur, 1989). One study suggests that differences in the parents' age or in the family's SES may account for differences in coping between families of children with Down syndrome and other families (Cahill & Glidden, 1996).

Table 4.1. *Studies of families of offspring with down syndrome*

Study	Groups Examined	Offspring Ages (years)	Findings
Erikson and Upshur (1989)	DS, motor-impaired, and developmentally delayed	<2	DS mothers: greater satisfaction with support from friends and community groups
Kasari and Sigman (1997)	DS, autism, MR, and controls – all MA-matched	3–5	DS = controls; less parental stress than autistic or MR
Holroyd and MacArthur (1976)	DS, autism, and outpatient psychiatric	3–12	Less parental stress in DS than in others
Mink, Nihira, and Meyers (1983)	Severe to profound MR	12	Two-thirds of families in DS group "cohesive-harmonious"
Thomas and Olson (1993)	Two emotionally disturbed groups, DS, controls	13–18	DS identical to controls on family coherence, adaptability, and communication (better than two emotionally disturbed groups)
Seltzer, Krauss, and Tsunematsu (1993)	MR	35	Mothers of DS (vs. other MR): less caregiving stress and burden, less family conflict, more satisfying social networks

Abbreviations: DS, Down syndrome; MR, mental retardation; MA, mental age.
Source: Hodapp (1996).

Another possibility concerns the children themselves. Children with Down syndrome may be friendlier and happier than children with other types of mental retardation. Mothers (Wishart & Johnston, 1990) and fathers (Hornby, 1995) speak of the friendly, upbeat personalities of their children with Down syndrome. In addition, young children with this disorder may be especially interested in people (Pitcairn & Wishart, 1994). Although it remains debatable whether a "Prince Charming" personality should be attributed to most individuals with Down syndrome (Gibson, 1978), the presence or perceived presence of such a personality cannot be discounted.

A further possibility concerns maladaptive behaviors and psychopathology. Children with Down syndrome show low rates of many types of psychopathology; the prevalence of thought disorders and of autism among these children is especially low (Bregman, 1991; Dykens, 1995). Even within the Down syndrome group, maternal stress levels seem partially related to child behavior problems (Sloper, Knussen, Turner, & Cunningham, 1991). This connection may be even stronger in other etiological groups. Hodapp, Dykens, and Masino (1997) found that, in the child with Prader–Willi syndrome, maladaptive behaviors (see Table 9.1) – as opposed to the child's age, degree of obesity, or IQ – were most predictive of parental stress. The more maladaptive behaviors the child showed, the higher was the degree of parental stress. Certain personal characteristics of the child, then, influence parental-familial stress and coping.

Family's Internal and External Resources. Various external and internal resources effect the degree of stress involved in raising a child with retardation. One obvious resource is money: Families with higher incomes experience less stress than those with lower incomes. Recent work has shown that, especially when they are raising children with severe levels of retardation, families must pay for many services by themselves. In a survey of 326 families of children with severe and profound levels of mental retardation, Birenbaum and Cohen (1993) found that families paid an average of $2,000 per year (or 7% of total family income) for health care (12 physician visits annually), prosthetic devices, wheelchairs, and house or yard renovation to ensure the child's safety. Few of these mothers worked outside the home, and getting a babysitter was often problematic, particularly when children took medicine, had shunts to relieve fluids pressuring the brain, or were destructive to themselves or others.

An additional external resource involves the family's social support system. In contrast to earlier views of such families as isolated, we now know that most families raising children with various disabilities do have strong groups of supporters. Such supporters provide emotional, informational, tangible, and service support for parents, and allow them a respite from caring for their children.

On average, however, support networks are smaller for parents of children with disabilities than for those of children without disabilities (Kazak, 1987). In addition, these networks are generally more dense; that is, individuals within them are generally well known to one another (Kazak & Marvin, 1984). A support network might consist of the mother's own mother, her two sisters, and a close personal friend. Acquaintances, neighbors, and colleagues are not part of the network. Although a dense network is better than no support group at all, a less dense network seems more beneficial (Hirsch, 1979). As Byrne and Cunningham (1985) note, small, intimate social networks can become suffocating.

Besides a family's external resources, internal resources also influence their coping. Here we refer to the family's outlook on life, style of problem solving, and the very meaning the child with retardation has for the family. Utilizing Folkman, Schaefer, and Lazarus's (1979) scheme of five types of coping resources, Crnic et al. (1983) described the influence of parental appraisal on the amount of stress produced. Quite simply, what stresses one person may challenge or even bore another.

Recent studies of coping similarly show that how one thinks about an event – including parenting a child with retardation – strongly influences how one feels about that event (for a review see Turnbull et al., 1993). Generally, the main distinction here relates to "problem-focused" versus "emotion-focused" coping. In one study of parents of adults with mental retardation, Seltzer, Greenberg, and Krauss (1995) found that mothers were less often depressed when they made plans to address everyday problems, worked hard to alleviate those problems, and felt that they learned from their experiences. In contrast, mothers who got upset or denied problems were often depressed. As a result, though two children may objectively be similar, their parents might vary widely in their ability to cope effectively. In virtually every study, mothers who were focused on actively solving problems seemed better off than those focused primarily on their own emotional reactions.

Family's Perceptions of the Child. Related to active, practical coping is the issue of how the child with retardation is perceived by the family. To many families, such a child is a burden imposed by God; indeed, families often feel that they have been chosen to raise the child because of their special strengths and gifts (Weisner, Beizer, & Stolze, 1991; Zuk, 1959). In addition, different families conceptualize the child's and family's needs differently. As Gallimore, Weisner, Kaufman, and Bernheimer (1989) note, families engineer their everyday existence, or family ecosystem, in line with their concept of the child's and the family's goals. Gallimore et al. (1989) reported that one family felt strongly that their child with retardation should receive as much high-quality intervention as possible; this family fired a babysitter that they considered lax, and the father quit his job to ensure round-the-clock intervention. Another family felt that the needs of other family members were paramount. The parents made special efforts to ensure that the other children's needs were met; the child with retardation received intervention, but the family's environment was set up differently from the environment of the other, intervention-intensive family.

The Double ABCX model acknowledges that stress factors change over time. Like children, families themselves develop. As shown in Table 4.2, at least six different stages exist in a family's life cycle, beginning with single adults leaving home and progressing until families with grown-up children reach the parents' retirement years. Within this scheme, the meaning of the term family changes from the single-generation, nuclear family to the three- or four-generational family. Generations face different, complementary tasks at the same time: "While one generation is moving toward older age, the next is contending with the empty nest, the third with young adulthood, forming careers and intimate peer

Table 4.2. *Stages of the family life cycle*

Stage	Emotional Process of Transition: Key Principles	Second-Order Changes in Family Status Required to Proceed Developmentally
1. Leaving home: single young adults	Accepting emotional and financial responsibility for self	a. Differentiation of self in relation to family of origin b. Development of intimate peer relationships c. Establishment of self with regard to work and financial independence
2. The joining of families through marriage: the new couple	Commitment of new system	a. Formation of marital system b. Realignment of relationships with extended families and friends to include spouse
3. Families with young children	Accepting new members into the system	a. Adjusting marital system to make space for child(ren) b. Joining in child-rearing, financial, and household tasks c. Realignment of relationships with extended family to include parenting and grandparenting roles
4. Families with adolescents	Increasing flexibility of family boundaries to include children's independence and grandparents' frailties	a. Shifting of parent – child relationships to permit adolescent to move in and out of system b. Refocus on midlife marital and career issues c. Beginning shift toward joint caring for older generation
5. Launching children and moving on	Accepting a multitude of exits from the entries into the family system	a. Renegotiation of marital system as a dyad b. Development of adult-to-adult relationships between grown children and their parents c. Realignment of relationships to include in-laws and grandchildren d. Dealing with disabilities and death of parents (grandparents)

(continued)

Table 4.2. *(cont.)*

Stage	Emotional Process of Transition: Key Principles	Second-Order Changes in Family Status Required to Proceed Developmentally
6. Families in later life	Accepting the shifting of generational roles	a. Maintaining own and/or couple functioning and interests in face of physiological decline; exploration of new familial and social role options b. Support for a more central role of middle generation c. Making room in the system for the wisdom and experience of the elderly, supporting the older generation without overfunctioning for them d. Dealing with loss of spouse, siblings, and other peers and preparation for own death; life review and integration

Source: Carter and McGoldrick (1988), p. 15. Reprinted by permission of Allyn & Bacon.

adult relationships and having children, and the fourth with being inducted into the system" (Carter & McGoldrick, 1988, p. 7).

Families of children with retardation may experience different stages of family development. Families of children with severe or multiple impairments may become stuck in their development (Farber, 1959). These families may never experience Carter and McGoldrick's (1988) Stage 5 – the launching of young adult children. Or, as Seltzer and Ryff (1994) note, such launching may occur later, when the adult with retardation leaves the family home to reside in a group home. Conversely, Kazak's (1987) studies show that dovetailing across generations – the interconnectedness of grandparents, parents, and children – may occur more intensely in families of children with retardation, as grandparents, aunts and uncles, and nondisabled siblings all join in raising the child.

Regardless of how the family life cycle operates in each family, many researchers feel that differences exist between families of younger and those of older children. Many studies fail to find differences in levels of parental and familial stress between families of infants and toddlers with and without disabilities (e.g., Beckman, 1983). Indeed, the problems of parenting any young child may produce a large amount of parental stress. Later, however, differences generally do emerge between families of children with and without disabilities (Minnes, 1988).

Two partially competing ideas have been proposed to explain such findings. The first is that certain critical periods may exist during development that cause parental and familial stress. Wikler (1986) found that parents of children entering puberty (11–15) and those entering adulthood (20–21) reported the highest levels of stress. But other studies have not documented this relationship between specific age periods and stress levels (Flynt & Wood, 1989).

The second idea is that parents experience a pileup of stressors as the child with retardation gets older (Minnes, 1988). Called the "wear and tear hypothesis" (Seltzer & Ryff, 1994), this idea is simply that parents become progressively worn down by the incessant job of parenting a difficult child. Yet this hypothesis may not always hold true: In their studies of aging parents of middle-aged offspring with retardation, Seltzer and Krauss (1989) found that parents and their adult offspring mutually adapted to each other over the years. Any negative effects of increasing offspring age, then, may not pertain during the adult years.

Another age-related difference consists in the way parents use supports as the child gets older. In a study comparing parents of younger versus older children with retardation, Suelzle and Keenan (1981) found that mothers used fewer formal and informal social supports as their children got older. Many parents "burn out" on intervention programs, support groups, or parent groups as the child gets older; in addition, fewer such groups may exist for older children. Moreover, social service professionals rate the need for supportive services as higher in the early than in the later years, even as parents report a continuing need for support services as the child approaches adulthood (Wikler, Wasow, & Hatfield, 1981).

Overview of New Family Research

Modern research has greatly changed the focus in examining families of children with retardation, from a negative emphasis on pathology to an emphasis on stress and coping as influenced by the child's personal characteristics, the family's resources, and the family's perceptions. This changing perspective acknowledges that, although these families have problems, they often cope reasonably well.

Despite the fact that more has been learned in family work over the past 15 years than in all the years up to that time, much more work is needed. We continue to know little about many aspects of the Double ABCX model: about the effects of many of the child's characteristics (e.g., age or associated maladaptive behaviors); about important aspects of parental personality that influence adaptation; and about how, why, and under which circumstances internal or external supports help families cope.

An additional issue concerns individual differences. The Double ABCX and other stress-coping models highlight individual differences, yet work on different family types has only begun. Although some researchers have examined Hispanic families of children with retardation (Heller, Markwardt, Rowitz, & Farber, 1994), we know little about functioning in families of most ethnicities or languages. To a large extent, family work in mental retardation remains a White, middle-class enterprise, even as the U.S. population changes and family policy initiatives begin to address concerns of ethnically diverse families (Hodapp, Young, & Zigler, in press).

Finally, functioning in families of children with retardation needs to be joined to issues in family systems theory and therapy. At present, research on families of children with disabilities is too often isolated from family therapy. This may, however, be an area of progress. For example, in their study comparing families of typical adolescents, adolescents with Down syndrome, and two groups of adolescents with emotional disturbances, Thomas and Olson (1993) examined family cohesion, adaptability, and communication – dimensions that are commonly assessed in family therapy research but that are often ignored in research on families of children with retardation.

In essence, we have discovered the tip of the large iceberg that is the functioning of families of children with retardation, but 90% of that iceberg's mass remains under water.

Mother–Child Interactions

The study of interactions between mothers and their children with retardation has a history similar to that of family relations. At the same time, however, such research has also been influenced by movements within developmental psychology proper. The following section provides a brief history of studies on interactions between mothers and children with retardation, then discusses modern findings and thinking on this topic.

Historical Issues

Two strands characterize the early studies of interactions between mothers and children with retardation. The first parallels the larger family field. Across many studies of the 1970s, parents of children with retardation were implicitly conceptualized as incorrectly or inadequately interacting with their children. Findings of differences reinforced this view: If parents of children with disabilities behaved differently than parents of nondisabled children, then disability group parents were considered less adequate, less effective. After all, wasn't the performance of these children inferior and didn't the parents themselves have emotional problems that hampered effective interactions?

The second strand relates to developmental psychology's changing views of the nature of mother–child relations, an area that can be divided into three historical periods (Hodapp, 1988). In the years before the late 1960s, the socialization model prevailed. Socialization is the idea that parents influence children – they teach, model, discipline, and in countless other ways gradually guide their children into adult culture. In this model, the influence was unidirectional: Parents influenced children.

With Bell's influential article in 1968, however, the field shifted from a socialization to an interactional view. Bell (1968; see also Bell & Harper, 1977) declared that children affect parents too. From birth, a fussy baby elicits soothing behaviors from his or her mother, whereas a lethargic baby elicits exciting, playful interchanges. As children get older, they play a greater role in all interactions, and their behavioral level, style, and tempo influence the behaviors of their mothers and other adults. Many studies during the 1970s and 1980s documented how mothers altered their behaviors in response to various child characteristics and behaviors. Such work involved a major reorientation: Parents and children were now seen as mutually influencing one another.

The final period takes us from the early 1980s until today. Though more difficult to characterize, this period combines socialization and interactional views, while adding the dimensions of time and of parental perceptions and goals. Researchers now understand that both socialization and interaction operate in every interaction, but that each interaction also has a history. Today's parent–child interchange continues a long-running series of interactions, or transactions, that began from the moment of the child's birth (Sameroff & Chandler, 1975). In addition, interactions consist of more than back-and-forth behaviors, with the caretaker saying or doing one thing, the child responding, and the caretaker reacting yet again. Instead, each interactor brings his or her own feelings, opinions, goals, and expectations to the interactive encounter. Only by understanding such "transactions with meaning" can we understand today's interactions.

Work on mother–child interactions began in the late 1960s and early 1970s. The earliest studies examined interactions using the newly available tools of social interaction. In language studies, various researchers used Brown's (1973) mean length of utterance (MLU) to determine the complexity of maternal utterances directed to young children learning language. Marshall, Hegrenes, and Goldstein (1973) and Buium, Rynders, and Turnure (1974) discovered that mothers of children with Down syndrome produced utterances that were simpler, more redundant, and less complex than did mothers of same-age nonretarded children. Although they never explicitly stated as much, these researchers implied that the behavior of mothers of children with Down syndrome might not be quite appropriate, that their interactions might be less complex, less informative, and less helpful than they should be.

In response to this perception, Rondal (1977) studied mothers of children with Down syndrome, but his comparison group included mothers of children of the same levels of language (MLU's). Once compared in this way, the language used by the two sets of mothers was identical. Rondal (1977) concluded that "the maternal linguistic environment of Down Syndrome children between MLU 1 and 3 is an appropriate one" (p. 242).

Yet in other ways, mothers of children with Down syndrome (and other types of retardation) differed from mothers of nonretarded children, even when the children were matched on MLU or other level-of-language measure. These differences were most evident in the styles of maternal language. In various studies, mothers of children with retardation showed a more active, intrusive style. These mothers more often taught than played with their children (Jones, 1980), took interactive turns that were longer and more frequent (Tannock, 1988), more often clashed with – or spoke at the same time as – their children (Vietze, Abernathy, Ashe, & Faulstich, 1978), and did not allow their children to initiate interactions (Jones, 1980). These findings repeatedly arose when interactions were examined between mothers and young children with many different types of mental retardation and developmental disabilities.

Recent Studies

Like the research on families, studies of mother–child interactions have changed over the past 20 years. The field now acknowledges that mothers of children with retardation behave the same as but differently than mothers of typically developing children at the same levels of functioning. Mothers are identical on MLU, amount of information provided per utterance (called the type–token ratio), and other, more structural aspects of language. But at the same time, mothers in the two groups differ greatly in their interactive styles.

Recent questions concern why maternal stylistic differences occur and what effects these differences produce. Why is it that, as a group, mothers of children with disabilities are more didactic and pushy than mothers of same-level nonretarded children? Are all mothers of children with disabilities similar in this regard? Do such behaviors hinder or help the development of their children? Although we can presently answer only some of these questions, several themes emerge.

Role of Perceptions and Emotions. Partially following from studies of maternal mourning and depression, one explanation for the differences in maternal styles relates to differences in maternal expectations and emotions. These mothers may conceptualize their children differently and have a strong need to teach and instruct them. They hope that, by actively teaching their children, they can lessen the children's cognitive and linguistic delays.

This possibility receives both research and anecdotal support. Anecdotally, many parents show a strong interest in intervening to help their children with retardation. Recall the family described by Gallimore et al. (1989) in which the father quit his job to care for his child full time. Jones (1980) noted the statement of one mother of a child with Down syndrome: "It's sit him on your knee and talk to him, that's the main object. Play with him, speak to the child, teach him something" (p. 221). Other workers also documented the desire of parents to intervene with their children, even in situations where mothers of nonretarded children simply played with or became emotionally close to their offspring (Cardoso-Martins & Mervis, 1984).

In addition, mothers of children with various disabilities may worry about different things. Mothers of 1- to 6-year-old children with Down syndrome reported being extremely worried about communication milestones, such as whether the child would learn the alphabet or learn to read, whereas mothers of children with motor impairments were relatively unconcerned about communication issues (Hodapp, Dykens, Evans, & Merighi, 1992). In both informal and formal observations, the concerns of mothers cannot be discounted as a potential explanation for stylistic differences between mothers of children with and without mental retardation.

Differences between Directiveness and Sensitivity. In most early work, higher levels of maternal directiveness were thought to signify inappropriate, insensitive interactions. It now appears that the two aspects of interaction may be partially separable. In a study by Crawley and Spiker (1983), mothers interacted with their children with Down syndrome and then were rated by the experimenters on various aspects of the mothers' interactive style. Maternal sensitivity and maternal directiveness were found to be partially orthogonal – that is, many mothers showed each of four patterns: highly sensitive, highly directive; highly sensitive, less directive; less sensitive, highly directive; and less sensitive, less directive. Crawley and Spiker (1983) concluded that the best of these combinations entailed a mother who was highly sensitive to and highly directive of the behaviors of her child.

Similarly Mahoney, Fors, and Wood (1990) noted that all mothers of children with Down syndrome are not the same. Dividing mothers into "turn-balanced" versus "turn-imbalanced" interactors, they found that half of the mothers were balanced, such that the mother acted an average of 52% of the time, while the child acted the remaining 48%; these figures contrasted with those for turn-imbalanced mothers, who acted 60% of the time compared with their child's 40%. Not all mothers of children with retardation are directive in their interactive styles, and even if mothers are directive, we cannot conclude that their interactions are necessarily less appropriate, sensitive, or effective (Marfo, 1990, 1992).

Child Influences. Just as the child's personal characteristics form an important part of familial reactions, they may also affect maternal interactive behaviors. Specifically, children with retardation may sometimes require more active, intrusive interactions. If so, then researchers are incorrect in asserting that differences between mothers of children with and without retardation indicate inadequate interactions on the part of mothers of children with retardation. Instead, such differences may be necessary for sensitive mother–child interactions.

So far, few interaction studies have related maternal behaviors to specific child characteristics, although several indications exist that children require individualized interactive behaviors from their caregivers. To take an obvious example, young children with Down syndrome are often more hypotonic – that is, they have lower muscle tone – than nonretarded children or even children with retardation of the same MA and CA (Cicchetti & Sroufe, 1976). These children may also take longer to respond to their mother's requests (Maurer & Sherrod, 1987) and, before developing language, may emit fewer, more ambiguous, and more unreadable cues for the mother to interpret (Hyche, Bakeman, & Adamson, 1992). Again though, differences may not mean that the interactive behaviors of mothers with children with retardation are inadequate or inappropriate.

Effects on Development. Ultimately, we want to know how different interactive styles influence the child's development. Until recently, mothers were judged to be less adequate if they interacted in a more intrusive way than, or were not considered similar enough to, mothers of typically developing children at the same level of functioning. Recently, however, research has identified what constitutes the most effective maternal interactions, at which points during development. In a study of 28 preschool children with Down syndrome, Harris, Kasari, and Sigman (1996) found that specific maternal behaviors at a first interactive session were associated with increased levels of receptive language at a second session 13 months later. The children of mothers who allowed the children's attention to remain fixed on one toy had higher receptive language ages than did the children of mothers who more often redirected the children's attention from one toy to another.

This study calls attention to how maternal behaviors relate to outcomes in children with retardation. Like maternal behaviors in typically developing children, specific maternal behaviors at specific times seem to foster development in children with different types of mental retardation. In a larger sense, such investigations flesh out maternal scaffolding, zone of proximal development, and other ideas that have pervaded developmental psychology since Vygotsky. We need to know much more about which behaviors help children with retardation to develop, but a start has been made.

Lessons from Family and Interactional Work

Changing Perspectives

The shift from pathology to stress-coping perspectives has been the most important advance in the family field. In contrast to their depiction in the early mourning studies, mothers are now conceptualized in terms of which internal or external supports help them cope. Unlike studies of paternal depression and "neurotic-like constriction," recent studies examine how fathers and mothers differ in their adaptation and what factors affect each. From an original focus on role tensions and psychopathology, sibling studies pinpoint which nondisabled siblings are at greatest risk and focus on the positive as well as the negative consequences of growing up with a sibling with retardation.

In all these areas, the perspective has changed from depression, psychopathology, and negative outcomes to a mixture of outcomes, some good and some bad. More important, the field has shifted its focus to the factors that affect stress and coping, with the ultimate goal of describing interventions that might help every family, whatever may be their internal or external resources, family goals, dynamics, or perceptions. Within this shifting perspective, the research has become more intricate, more detailed. The factors that protect against stress have begun to be identified, and how such factors work will receive increasing attention.

Throughout this work, a combination of general and specific factors seems important. In some ways, all parents, siblings, and families need the same things: tangible and intangible support and information and an optimistic yet realistic assessment of the child's needs. Partly as a result, many things that alleviate parental stress seem obvious: a higher family income, a two-parent family, a good marriage. In addition, many things other than the child with retardation him- or herself exacerbate stresses in all families. Consider life stresses that arise in every family (Holmes & Rahe, 1967). Such "life events" include widowhood, death of a family member or close friend, divorce, moving, or loss of a job. In some studies of families of young children and of older adults with retardation, more than 50% of mothers reported having experienced one or more major life event within the past year (Krauss & Seltzer, 1998).

Other factors seem more specific to the child with mental retardation. Why, for instance, do most studies find that families of children with Down syndrome experience less stress than families of children with other disabilities? Although Down syndrome is well known and although active parent groups exist, the answer to this question may also have to do with the characteristics of the children themselves. Indeed, pleasant, sociable children with fewer and less severe maladaptive behaviors may have a positive influence on their families (Hodapp, 1996). Stoneman (1997) argues that relations with unaffected siblings may depend on the child with retardation's temperament, personality, competence, secondary disabilities, and health problems.

Just as most of these issues remain unexplored in family research, many aspects of maternal–child interactions remain unclear. The latest studies imply that specific maternal behaviors facilitate the child's development, but it is uncertain how, in what domains, or at which points during development. Again, some important factors seem to be general to all children. For example, sensitive maternal interactions are necessary for all children, with or without mental retardation. Other types of interaction may be specific to children with one or another type of mental retardation. If children with Down syndrome require a more intensive style of interaction, or if children with Prader–Willi syndrome are prone to various overeating and obsessive-compulsive behaviors, then interactions may need to be tailored to these differences.

Changing Models

A changing perspective necessitates changing models. The field has therefore moved from Solnit and Stark's maternal mourning model to models that involve stress and coping. As the most prominent model in the family field, the Double ABCX model incorporates many variables now deemed important by family researchers: the child's personal characteristics, internal and external family resources, and parent and family perceptions of the child. As researchers have realized the importance of each of these components, theories have evolved.

With these theories have come inevitable problems. For example, family researchers in mental retardation are currently debating the very meaning of the term stress. Glidden (1993) notes, for instance, that the internal and external meanings of a potentially stressful situation are not identical. She calls for a distinction between demands, stresses, and strains. Demands involve the actual, objective characteristics of a situation. A one-hour-per-day therapy session might be one demand on a family or a child with disabilities. In contrast, stresses are the difficulties that demands pose. A two-parent family with several supporters might find the demands of the child's daily therapy session less stressful than a single parent with few supporters. Finally, strains involve the way parents perceive demands and stresses. One parent might resent the daily therapy session, whereas another may welcome it. Glidden argues that in much work on the family, the concepts of demands, stresses, and strains are entangled, leading to ambiguous findings. Although the degree to which these three concepts should be differentiated remains unknown, stress and coping perspectives will become more sophisticated in future research.

Such differentiation may also lead to a closer joining of family research to family therapy and family systems theory, in which case new conceptual models will be needed. These models might include many of the components of the Double ABCX. In addition ideas such as family adaptability will become increasingly important, as families are described as falling on a continuum from rigid, to flexible but organized, to chaotic. Similarly, communication among family members will be examined, as will family coherence. For many of these variables, the middle points will indicate better family dynamics; for example, coherence will mean that family members are neither enmeshed with nor disengaged from one another, but instead enjoy a balance whereby they simultaneously feel close to but independent from one another.

Changing Research Orientations and Methods

As the focus and models shift from pathology to stress and coping, the studies change as well. One important change involves group- versus individual-differences approaches. In studies of group dif- ferences, groups of parents of children with, say, Down syndrome are compared with those of nonretarded children or children with some other condition. The goal is to determine whether, on aver- age, families of children with Down syndrome are more or less stressed or receive different amounts of social support. Within such designs, within-group variance is "error" or "noise" to be ignored; indeed, the more that one parent of a child with Down syndrome differs from another, the less likely it is that statistically significant group differences will emerge between the Down syndrome and contrast groups.

Conversely, individual-differences work highlights the differ- ences within a specific group. When examining what factors pro- tect parents of children with retardation from stress, individual- differences studies need to include parents with varying levels of stress and varying levels of protective factors. If parents vary little in their levels of stress or protective factors, low correlations emerge between the two, and it becomes difficult for the researcher to identify protective factors.

Clearly, studies focusing on both group differences and individ- ual differences are needed in family research in mental retardation. We need to know not only whether families of children with Down syndrome are less stressed than are families of children with other forms of mental retardation, but which factors can help us predict parental stress within each group. This combined approach should provide a picture of family functioning that is more complete, more accurate, and more clinically useful.

A pertinent methodological issue here is matching. In group- differences work that is concerned with the children themselves, matching on MA or other level-of-functioning measure seems best. As shown in Chapter 3, one can determine the relative strengths or weaknesses in, say, the linguistic grammar of children with a specific type of mental retardation. Level-of-functioning matching also seems appropriate when considering mother–child interactions. As Rondal (1977) notes, a mother of a 4-year-old child with Down syndrome should not speak at the 4-year level of language if her child performs at the 2-year level – appropriate linguistic input from the mother relates to the child's levels of language.

For other issues, however, CA matching may be best. Families too develop, and the family of a 2-year-old child is different from the family of a 15-year-old, regardless of the child's functioning levels. For this reason, it would seem appropriate to perform group-differences work on families by using CA matches. Parents of 10-year-old children with Down syndrome should be compared with parents of 10-year-old typically developing children (Stoneman, 1989). Only in this way can accurate assessments be made of the stress and supports available to both sets of families.

Changing Perspectives on the Nature of Development

As described in Chapter 3, the original developmental approach to mental retardation focused exclusively on the child. Issues of similar sequences and structures predominated, and these organismic concerns were joined in later years by considerations of rates and regressions. Throughout, the early developmental approaches were organismic in orientation.

Following from changes in developmental and clinical psychology, however, researchers of children with and without mental retardation now study both organismic and contextualist concerns. Today, most developmentalists would consider as limited an interest solely in sequences, rates, regressions, and cross-domain relations. But how the two can be integrated remains a mystery. Equally important is the issue of how organismic and contextual issues can be examined together, and which areas of development are more or less intertwined with changes in the child's ecology.

Although we cannot answer these questions, we acknowledge the obvious: While this book examines separately organismic and contextual issues in the development of children with retardation, the two operate together. Neither should be considered more important than or separate from the other. Both are intrinsic to all development.

5

Deafness

Research on deafness might be thought to feature less developmental work than mental retardation. Fewer studies have been undertaken on sequences, structures, rates, and regressions in children who are deaf, and most studies focus on language or the interplay between language and thought. Mother–child interaction research dates mainly to the past 15 years, and family work is only beginning. In this sense, developmental work on deafness seems less advanced than similar, longer-term work on mental retardation.

This conclusion, though, is unfair in that deafness is the only sensory impairment that is so closely related to a single domain of functioning like early language. It is therefore not surprising that most studies examine one or another aspect of language in children who are deaf, or the relations between their language and thought. Other issues, for instance the nature of mother–child interactions, are of interest by virtue of their relation to the unique linguistic development of children who are deaf. Developmental studies of deafness, then, are different from work on mental retardation or on any other condition rather than less comprehensive.

This chapter tackles only a small portion of the many developmental issues involved in studying children who are deaf and hearing impaired. Focusing only on those areas that have most intrigued developmentally oriented researchers, the chapter is generally limited to the development of children who are prelingually deaf. These are children who are unable, even with hearing aids, to hear speech (usually considered a hearing loss of 70 decibels [dB] or more). The chapter also focuses on children whose deafness occurs before language begins, usually due to genetic factors or to prenatal diseases like rubella or congenital cytomegalovirus (the major contemporary cause of deafness in the United States; Schildroth, 1994). These children stand in contrast to those who have lesser degrees of hearing loss or to children with later-occurring deafness due to meningitis or other childhood diseases. As the "more than 70 dB loss" definition suggests, however, many children who are deaf have some residual hearing.

In discussing organismic issues such as sequences and rates, this chapter is also limited to children who are in the process of acquiring American Sign Language (ASL). Although ASL is the main naturally occurring sign language in the United States, children who are deaf in this country are also taught a variety of other signed and oral systems (as discussed later). When considering contextual issues, however, we expand the discussion. In line with the majority of studies, when discussing family adaptations we focus primarily on children who are deaf but have hearing parents; when examining mother–child interactions we compare children who are deaf and have parents who are deaf versus children who are deaf and have hearing parents.

Issues Specific to Deafness

Before discussing developmental issues, it is important to review several important topics in the field of deafness. The first concerns the language that children who are deaf are acquiring; the second, "Deaf culture." Although these issues may seem to take us far afield – and one cannot hope to do justice to either in one short chapter – they are inescapable in any discussion of development in children who are deaf. Both provide a background to the organismic and contextual issues to be discussed later in this chapter.

Language Issues

In contrast to children with most other disabilities, children who are deaf are taught one of several languages. Some children are taught (or acquire naturally) American Sign Language, the main native sign language used in the United States. ASL has its own vocabulary and grammar and, from both linguistic (e.g., Klima & Bellugi, 1979; Stokoe, 1994) and clinical (Poizner, Klima, & Bellugi, 1987) evidence, it appears to be a full-fledged human language. ASL differs from British Sign Language, Langue Sign Quebec, Spanish Sign Language, and the many other sign languages used around the world.

Other sign systems are also used in the United States. These include signed English and signed exact English, both of which conform more closely to English grammar, and cued speech, which combines speech and lipreading with gestures to accentuate the production and comprehension of speech. In addition, some children who are deaf are taught by the oral method, such that they use their sight and any residual hearing to orally produce and comprehend spoken English. Although this is not an exhaustive list of the manual and oral systems used in the United States (for reviews see Nover, 1993; Paul & Quigley, 1994), it is representative of the systems used with U.S. children who are deaf.

Which language deaf individuals should use has long been debated within the Deaf community. Is it better for persons who are deaf to communicate orally and to lip-read others' speech, or is communication best achieved through "total communication," the use of ASL along with any residual hearing or speaking? This debate originated at least as early as the late nineteenth century, when Alexander Graham Bell, the inventor of the telephone and the main proponent of oralism, battled Edward Miner Gallaudet, the president of (later-named) Gallaudet University, the main proponent of total communication (Winefield, 1987). To this day, the field of deafness has two competing professional organizations, with two main research journals that differ dramatically in their orientation.

Another complication is that, no matter which method of language a U.S. person who is deaf uses, he or she must learn to read and write in English. Yet the grammar of written English is much more closely allied to the grammar of spoken English than to ASL, whose grammar is loosely associated with the French from which it arose. Similarly, although the correspondence between English speech sounds and writing is not perfect (compare the words "through" and "tough"), written phonology also generally conforms to the sound system of spoken English. Even fluent, native ASL signers, then, must learn to read and write in an English that is very different from ASL.

Cultural Issues

The issue of "Deaf culture" is a complicated matter, one on which people who are deaf hold divergent points of view. In general, however, those who belong to Deaf culture display three major characteristics. First, they are deaf, with hearing losses that, even with hearing aids, preclude the understanding of speech by hearing alone. Second, they use ASL as their primary means of communication. Third, and most important, they identify themselves as belonging to Deaf culture (Padden & Humphries, 1988). In addition to ASL (A. Neisser, 1990; Perlmutter, 1991), Deaf culture features a distinct history (Lane, 1984), theater (the National Theater of the Deaf; Bangs, 1994), social clubs, sports traditions, and universities (Gallaudet University in Washington, D.C.; National Technical Institute for the Deaf in Rochester, New York).

In some ways, one could consider the cultural issue an "either–or" question: Does one belong to Deaf or to hearing culture? But the issue may not be so simple. Indeed, most individuals who are deaf – even those most involved in Deaf culture – are essentially "bicultural." As Padden (1996) notes, "There are no towns or even blocks or areas of a city entirely occupied by Deaf residents anywhere in North America" (p. 82). Most individuals who are deaf therefore live within the larger hearing society, hold many attitudes and beliefs that are similar to those of hearing Americans, and have become reasonably efficient in dealing with hearing individuals (Humphries, 1993). Furthermore, knowledge of one culture helps one to make contacts and utilize services from the other. ASL translators and services are more readily available to those who know and are part of the Deaf community and whose skills in English writing and reading are more advanced.

Moreover, consider cultural transmission. In most cultures, parents and other adults pass on their language and culture to their offspring. But, while most persons who are deaf marry persons who are also deaf, less than 10% of the children of these marriages are themselves deaf (usually with hereditary forms of genetic deafness; Arnos & Downs, 1994; Boughman & Shaver, 1982). The remaining 90% of children who are deaf have hearing parents.

Historically, with the exception of these 10% "deaf of deaf" individuals, adults have not generally been as dominant in the transmission of culture to children who are deaf as have hearing parents to hearing children. The large majority of hearing parents have had little experience with ASL or any signed language, nor do most elementary schoolteachers of children who are deaf use ASL as the preferred form of classroom communication (although many use some type of signing plus speech; Woodward, Allen, & Schildroth, 1988). Indeed, certifications for teachers of the deaf require only a few courses in ASL, and none in Deaf culture, history, or teaching English reading and writing as a second language. Instead, the main certifying organizations have generally held a primarily oralist and speech pathology orientation for children with any degree of hearing loss (Nover, 1993). Given that few parents or teachers are fluent in ASL, children who are deaf have historically learned ASL and various aspects of Deaf culture from other children who are deaf, usually through their attendance at deaf residential schools.

In recent years, however, changes in schooling have profoundly affected Deaf culture. With moves toward mainstreaming and normalization within the larger hearing society, deaf residential schools have become smaller: Whereas the percentage of deaf children attending such schools dropped 22.5% between the 1978–1979 and 1984–1985 school years, the number of students attending local schools increased 16% over approximately the same time span (Schildroth, 1988). Further, in contrast to the full-time boarding status of most students who are deaf in past years, nowadays many more students attend such schools during the day only, and most go home to families during weekends. The child-to-child transmission of Deaf culture has thus been diluted.

In work, too, profound changes have occurred for many individuals who are deaf. Until the 1960s, most adults who were deaf worked in one of two kinds of jobs, either in solitary occupations as mechanics, shoemakers, or carpenters, or as teachers or house parents at the residential schools (Moores, 1996). Over the past few decades, however, improved vocational and academic programs have led to a growing middle-class deaf population. Partly as a result, some historic institutions – for example, the deaf social clubs in many major cities – have withered away. In addition, a class split has occurred, with working-class individuals becoming increasingly separated from middle-class individuals (Padden, 1990). These middle-class individuals, in turn, have demanded jobs involving more responsibilities and power. In this context, the 1989 Deaf President Now movement is a watershed historical event, featuring a student strike leading to the appointment of Gallaudet University's first Deaf president, I. King Jordan (for a review see Gannon, 1988).

Deaf culture is, then, in a state of flux. Various authors question what exactly is meant by Deaf culture, how various schooling, work, and other societal changes affect that culture, in what ways – and with what effects – individuals who are deaf are multicultural, a part of Deaf culture but simultaneously a part of the larger American culture and of the ethnic and other subcultures that make up the United States (e.g., Parasnis, 1996).

All of these issues affect families of children who are deaf, both children who are "deaf of deaf" and the 90% of children who are deaf and were born of hearing parents. Whether one is discussing organismic issues, such as language development, or contextual issues, such as mother–child interactions and familial reactions, both linguistic and cultural issues form the background.

Organismic Issues

Mindful of the linguistic and cultural issues just described – and limiting the discussion to children who are prelingually deaf and are learning ASL – we can now examine organismic developmental issues. Like research on mental retardation, studies of children who are deaf examine sequences and structures. But several other issues also arise, particularly those dealing with the innateness of language and the critical age for language acquisition.

Sequences and Structures

Although Vygotsky studied children who were deaf in the 1920s, modern developmental work on such children really began in the early 1960s. At that time, Hans Furth studied children who were deaf to examine an important question in Piagetian thought: whether it is possible to think in the absence of language. This question is one of cross-domain relations, although it was not called so at the time.

Simply put, Piaget and Inhelder (1969) proposed that cognition develops relatively independent of language. Theoretically, a child could attain the logical operations involved in any of Piaget's stages simply by interacting with the world. Although everyone agreed that language plays little role in sensorimotor thought, Piaget argued that older children could develop ideas of one-to-one correspondence, conservation, or even logical operations through their interactions with the world. Granted, language helps to consolidate such operations in most children, but to Piaget language was definitely not a prerequisite to thought. Piaget's subordination of language was directly opposed to Vygotsky's view of the centrality of language as a mediator of all higher-level thought.

To help disentangle the thought–language issue, Furth (1964, 1966) examined children who were deaf and could not speak, and who had not formally been taught ASL or some other sign system. Although we today would not consider these children "nonlinguistic," Furth considered them sufficiently deficient in any language – spoken or signed – to provide a test of Piaget's views. Specifically, how would these apparently "nonlinguistic" children perform on Piagetian tasks? Furth's studies showed that these children could perform tasks at sensorimotor (i.e., infancy) and preoperational (preschool) levels. However, they had increasing difficulty performing concrete operational tasks, especially those involving conservation of number, length, weight, volume, and area (for a review see Paul & Quigley, 1994). And they were almost always unable to perform tasks of formal operations – logical tasks involving hypothetical or abstract reasoning.

Why Furth's deaf children showed inadequate cognitive performance continues to be debated. Furth (1964) felt that any differences in development (e.g., difficulties with formal operational thought) were due to the children's lack of real-world experience or to task conditions that were heavily biased toward language. To Furth, these studies supported Piaget's views that thought need not rely on language. Greenberg and Kushe (1989) disagreed, noting that language does indeed affect thought, particularly when higher-level concrete and formal operations are involved (see also Parasnis, 1983). They noted that children who are deaf and whose parents are deaf (who acquire ASL as a native language) reach higher levels of formal education, and have higher reading levels and larger English vocabularies, than do children who are deaf and have hearing parents, a group of children who often have less facility in any language, spoken or sign (see Wilbur, 1979). These findings would seem to argue for some effect of language on some cognitive attainments. For our purposes, Furth's studies imply a lack of connection between these children's linguistic and cognitive levels.

Two factors complicate studies of the relation between cognition and language. The first is the difficulty of examining the intelligence of children who are deaf. As might be expected, such children perform poorly on verbal (i.e., English-language) portions of most IQ tests, even as they often show average or near-average levels on the performance (i.e., nonlinguistic) subtests. Further, Furth's "natural experiment" must be examined critically. Some children who are deaf, for example, not only are deficient in either signed or spoken language, but also differ from same-age hearing children in many other ways. For example, some children who are deaf have less extensive experiences in the world and less sophisticated interactions with others. Some studies reveal that deaf and hearing children differ in SES and in ethnicity. Age and degree of hearing loss, the type of schooling a child receives, and whether the child's parents are hearing or deaf all complicate IQ findings. Finally, surveys show that from 23% to 32% of individuals who are deaf have additional handicaps, often involving visual, orthopedic, or cognitive-behavioral disabilities. See J.P. Braden (1994) for a review of the entire IQ issue in children who are deaf.

The second complicating factor involves the association between ASL and English. As noted earlier, fluent signers generally read and write in English. To ascertain what contributes to better reading and writing, Moores and Sweet (1990) examined one group of adolescents (16 to 18 years old) who were deaf and whose parents were deaf and another group of adolescents who were deaf and were being taught by the "total communication" method (ASL plus simultaneous use of speech by teachers). Although slightly different predictors were found for a student's reading and writing skills in each group, several variables seemed consistent. Adolescents who had higher vocabulary scores and (English) grammar scores performed better on several reading and writing tasks. In the first group, the degree of residual hearing influenced both reading and writing levels. In all cases, knowledge of vocabulary and of English grammar – which seems unrelated to knowledge of ASL grammar (Moores, 1996) – was connected to skills in reading and writing English.

A host of other interesting studies have been performed on the early development of children acquiring ASL. Indeed, some of this work examines children even before they begin to sign. One common finding is that infants who are deaf produce their first stable signs at 8 to 10 months of age, a few months before hearing children utter their first words (Schlesinger & Meadow, 1972). As Bonvillian, Orlansky, and Novack (1983) showed, sign production is only loosely associated with Piagetian sensorimotor development. And, as in the mental retardation studies examined in Chapter 3, vocabulary development is unrelated to grammatical development, even when children are producing two-word (or two-sign) sentences.

Studies of sequences in the development of children who are deaf show that early sensorimotor developments occur in the usual order – and to the same degree in everything except vocal imitation – in hearing-impaired and CA-matched hearing children (Best & Roberts, 1976). When examined on nonverbal tasks, children who are deaf also develop in order through Piagetian sequences during the preoperational period (Bond, 1987); during this period these children function at levels approximating their hearing agemates. Although some children have difficulties with concrete and formal operational tasks, few researchers report evidence of incorrect orderings of development.

Yet mainly due to the nature of sign language, sequences in language development become more complex. As already noted, ASL, like any human language, has its own grammar. More than thirty-five years ago, Stokoe (1960) described the "phonology" of signs; he stated that all signs must be evaluated in terms of the shape of the hand, the location of the hand with reference to the body, and the movement of the hand. Moreover, some signs are iconic, or similar in form to the things they signify. This makes it difficult to determine the age at which an infant first signs, for many of the deaf infant's first signs are iconic.

Nonetheless, children who are deaf develop sign language in sequences that are roughly similar to those traversed by hearing children acquiring spoken English. For example, these infants' first signs include MOMMY, DADDY, and MILK (Newport & Meier, 1985; Schlesinger & Meadow, 1972), words that are also among the first 50 utterances of hearing children (Nelson, 1973). Later two-sign utterances include semantic relations for existence (THAT BALL), action (EAT SANDWICH), and state (CHAIR BROKEN); these are the same meanings encoded by the two-word utterances of hearing children (Bloom, 1970). These relations appear in approximately the same sequential ordering in children who are deaf and are acquiring sign as in young children acquiring spoken language (Newport & Ashbrook, 1977).

Other developments also occur in the expected order, although many are complicated by the sign system. Consider the deictic terms you and I. (Deictic terms are terms that change in reference to the speaker – e.g., you–I, here–there, and this–that.) In sign, each involves a pointing gesture: a finger pointing toward the listener signifies you, a finger pointing toward the speaker signifies I or me. In examining two genetically deaf children of deaf parents, Petitto (1987) found that the symbolic meaning of pointing emerged only gradually over the 1- to 2½-year period. As Figure 5.1 shows, before 12 to 14 months, these two children – Kate and Carla – pointed to desired objects and to people, although when they pointed to someone they did not always look at that person. Then, between 12–14 and 18 months, all pointing to people (self or other) ceased. Of more than 400 signed utterances during this period, not one consisted of a point signifying you or me. Only later did these children correctly point, but at first some pronoun reversals occurred. On one occasion when she wanted to eat, Kate

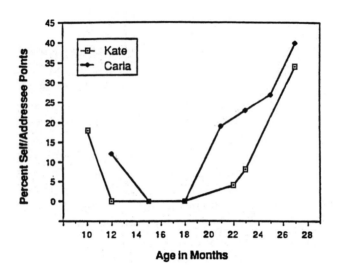

Figure 5.1. Percent of Kate and Carla's total number of pointing forms directed to see and addressee. From Petitto, 1987 (p. 19)

signed EAT YOU WANT EAT to her mother, then became upset when the mother indicated that she (the mother) had already eaten. Only when the mother understood that Kate herself wanted to eat was the child appeased. These young children thus did not make use of sign properties that to hearing adults seem iconic (see also Pizzuto, 1990). Instead, they showed the same developmental patterns – including mix-ups in the meaning of you and me before the acquisition of more stable and correct usages – as have been identified in the spoken languages of young hearing children.

Thus, the similar-sequence hypothesis (see Chapter 3) appears to hold for deaf children acquiring ASL, whereas cross-domain relations may show some areas of strengths and weaknesses.

We now turn to two organismic issues that are particular to the deaf population.

Innateness and Critical Age

Besides Furth, other researchers examined deaf children to learn about typical development. The first to do so was Eric Lenneberg

(1967), a neuropsychologist interested in language development. Influenced by Chomsky's (1968) views of the "language acquisition device," Lenneberg examined babbling in young infants exposed primarily to sign language. Lenneberg's prediction was that, if language was innately switched on at a certain point during infancy, then even infants deprived of oral input should babble vocally. Lenneberg, Rebelsky, and Nichols (1965) did indeed find that children of deaf parents showed the early stages of babbling. One of these children was himself deaf, a deaf-of-deaf infant. This infant as well showed the earliest stages of babbling; only the later, more linguistic-like babbling never occurred in this infant. Although the importance of Lenneberg et al.'s (1965) finding has since been criticized (for a review see Proctor, 1988), the presence of early babbling in infants of deaf parents lent support to the view that human language is innate, present in some rudimentary form even in children for whom aural stimulation from adults may be minimally useful.

Petitto and Marentette (1991) have provided an interesting twist to Lenneberg's early studies. These researchers examined infants who were deaf, aged 10 to 14 months, who were the offspring of deaf, signing parents and acquiring sign as their native language. These infants babbled in sign. Although both hearing and deaf infants made gestures such as holding out their arms to be picked up, infants who were deaf more often produced complex hand movements found in signed letters or numbers, and repeated these signlike gestures again and again. Further, such manual babbling became increasingly complex with age, leading to what in hearing infants is called "jargon babbling," or meaningless babbling sequences that are similar to sentences (which Lenneberg et al.'s deaf child was unable to do with speech). Petitto and Marentette (1991) concluded that infants possess an innate predisposition to babble. Be it vocal or manual, such babbling provides "the mechanism by which infants discover the map between the structure of language and the means for producing this structure" (p. 251).

Lenneberg (1967) was also concerned with the critical age for language acquisition. He felt that language development occurred during a specific "critical period," or time after which it would be difficult, if not impossible, for language to develop. Reviewing the effects of brain damage in children of various ages, Lenneberg (1967) concluded that language cannot be acquired "naturally" after the pubertal years. Obviously, adults learn new languages, but they never become as fluent as those who learn a language at younger ages. Genie, described in Chapter 3, acquired language only in the right hemisphere (whereas language usually resides in the left). In essence, the development of language, or at least grammar, may show a sensitive period that lasts until the early teen years, after which it seems less efficient, less lateralized, and less complete.

Since many adults who are deaf acquire sign language later in life, these individuals are excellent candidates for testing the critical-age hypothesis. In this context, basic word order and morphology have recently been examined. Word order refers to our understanding that in the sentence "The dog bites the cat," the actor is the dog, the recipient of the action is the cat. Morphology has to do with plural, tense, and number designations; for example, the word endings -s (e.g., cars) and -es (churches) tell us that there is more than one object, or an -ed ending tells us that an event happened in the past. In ASL, many morphological markings are denoted by subtle movements that accompany a particular sign. For example, in describing verbs of motion, hand movements signify morphemes for the category of moving object, for the path of motion traversed (e.g., straight line or circle), and for the manner of motion traversed (bouncing or rolling). Each of these actions is performed simultaneously; in comparison with spoken English, morphology in sign language often occurs simultaneously rather than sequentially.

In examining adults exposed to sign language at different points during childhood, Newport (1990) found that some linguistic abilities declined with increasing CA. All individuals – regardless of when they acquired sign language – understood the basic word order rules of ASL. But morphological knowledge appeared to be linked to the age at which the person was first exposed to sign language. Native learners exposed to sign from birth performed much better on subtle morphological tasks than early learners, who were exposed to sign beginning at 4 to 6 years. These early learners, in turn, were better still than late learners, those first exposed to sign after the age of 12 years. There thus appears to be a critical or sensitive period for grammatical acquisition. But in contrast to Lenneberg's (1967) view, this sensitive period may not suddenly switch off at puberty, but may come to a more gradual close over the childhood years.

In examining organismic issues in children who are deaf, we see many similarities with children with retardation and nonretarded children. Children who are deaf traverse similar cognitive and linguistic sequences, make similar mistakes at similar points in their linguistic development (e.g., confuse deictic terms such as you and me), and also show strengths and weaknesses (e.g., some cognitive abilities even in the absence of language). Other developments seem analogous to developments in hearing children, varying only slightly because of differences in sign versus oral input or production. Finally, the innateness and critical-age results parallel findings from language development in hearing populations.

Contextual Issues

In examining contextual issues in children who are deaf, we focus on mother–child interactions and families. For mother–child interactions, we focus mainly on the youngest years.

Mother–Child Interactions

Before we proceed, a caveat is in order. While much of the literature compares mothers who are deaf with hearing mothers of children who are deaf or hearing-impaired, the basic mother–child relationship may be similar in the two groups. Lederberg and Mobley (1990), for example, found that attachment relations are virtually identical between hearing and deaf mothers and their infants who are deaf. Although hearing mothers may more often initiate interactions – possibly by trying to get the child's attention – similar percentages of infants of mothers who are deaf and hearing mothers showed "good" (i.e., Ainsworth's B category) versus conflicted (A, C, and D) attachments. Although at later ages mother–child interactions may become more troublesome due to impaired mother–child communication (Lederberg, Willis, & Frankel, 1991), most mothers – be they hearing or deaf – have reasonably good relationships with their young children who are deaf. This basic conclusion should be kept in mind as we review studies comparing the interactive styles of hearing mothers and mothers who are deaf.

Signing Deaf Mothers of Infants Who Are Deaf. Even given the possibility of Lenneberg's "switched on" critical or sensitive period for language development – which Lenneberg thought occurred with only minimal linguistic input – all children, including infants who are deaf, seem to benefit from a simplified language input. Signing mothers who are deaf provide such input, acting analogously to mothers of hearing infants. These mothers sign at a slow rate, make sentences that involve few signs, repeat signs again and again, and talk about things on which the infant is focused. In other words, mothers who are deaf use the "motherese" that seems common to all mothers of hearing children.

Two obvious considerations influence the interactions of deaf, signing mothers and their infants who are prelinguistically deaf. First, because the baby cannot hear, instead of vocalizing to get the child's attention and to communicate, signing deaf mothers maintain almost constant physical and visual contact. Touch, in particular, allows the mother to orient the baby to see objects and signs; in addition, by touching and moving the baby, the mother can maintain the baby's attention. Typically, the mother makes tactile and visual contact while she maintains a playful, joyous affect. Mothers who are deaf smile and express more emotion than hearing mothers, and even mouth words and vocalize with their infants (Maestas y Moores, 1980). All of these behaviors – touching, visual contact, and positive affect – are more common in deaf mothers of infants who are deaf than in hearing mothers of hearing infants (Erting, Prezioso, & O'Grady Hynes, 1990; Maestas y Moores, 1980). Mothers who are deaf prepare the child for entrance into a world in which the use of vision will be critical for gathering information and for communicating to others; for their part, infants employ a very wide visual field (approximately 180 degrees) to gather information.

The second consideration concerns the language itself. Due to the visual nature of ASL, mothers who are deaf produce for their infants who are deaf more single-sign utterances, more elongated signs, and more labeling than do hearing mothers of hearing children. In one study, more than 80% of all maternal utterances to 7- to 20-month-old children who were deaf were one-sign utterances, and each mother produced one-sign utterances in more than 70% of sentences (Harris, Clibbens, Chasin, & Tibbitts, 1989). Similarly, Masataka (1992) found that Japanese mothers who were deaf held signs for a longer duration when conversing with their 8- to 11-month-old infants who were deaf than when conversing with an adult deaf friend. Signs are also repeated again and again: In one study, mothers repeated certain signs as many as 12 times (Launer, 1982; see also Masataka, 1992).

Signing deaf mothers sometimes change their signs to make them easier for the infant to see. Consider Erting et al.'s (1990) study of the signs provided by signing deaf mothers to their 3½- to 6-month-old children who were deaf. One sign, MOTHER, involves a five-finger, open handshape in which the signer's thumb touches the chin and the pinky faces the listener. But as shown in Figure 5.2, the handshape is partially obscured to the recipient of the sign. Therefore, when addressing their infants (but not when addressing adults), Erting et al.'s (1990) mothers changed the sign to make it easier to see by orienting their hand so that a full palm or a full back of the hand was visible to the infant. The infant could then determine the five-finger nature of the handshape. These mothers also continued to make the sign for almost twice as long as they signed MOTHER in their conversations with adults.

Signing mothers also sometimes modify the placement of their signs. As described by Stokoe (1960), signs are generally placed in one of several "prime" locations in front of the body. In mother–child interactions, however, mothers often sign at the very place where the infant is looking. Mothers might reach out and sign CAR above a toy car at which a child is looking. In Harris et al.'s (1989) study, mothers of infants followed from 7 to 20 months of age produced high percentages of their signs within the child's

Figure 5.2. Citation forms for the two most frequently used variants of the American Sign Language sign MOTHER. From Erting, Prezioso, & Hynes, 1990 (p. 103)

visual field: by 20 months of age, 70% of all maternal signs were produced in this way, such that the child could simultaneously attend to both the sign and the object to which it referred. Labels naming common objects are also very common, ranging from 25% to 38% of all maternal signed input in one study (Kyle & Ackerman, 1987).

Finally, mothers may shape their infant's hands to produce an appropriate sign. It is easier to shape the baby's hand when signing than it is to shape the baby's mouth and vocal chords when speaking. In Maestas y Moores's (1980) study of deaf mothers of young infants, the mothers shaped their infant's hands into signs for BATH, LOVE, DOG, MAMA, and FATHER, all before the children were 6 months of age. In this way, mothers were able to demonstrate adult signing.

Signing deaf mothers of infants who are deaf, then, are both similar to and different from hearing mothers of hearing children. They are similar in that they shorten their utterances, repeat key words, and slow the tempo of their signing. They differ mainly in aspects of linguistic input that are specific to a visual language. These similarities and differences illustrate how, within the constraints imposed by their respective languages, hearing and deaf

Table 5.1. *Similarities and differences in input language between hearing mother–hearing infant dyads and deaf mother–deaf infant dyads*

Similarities
Repetition of words
Shortening of sentences
Slowing of tempo

Differences specific to signing mothers who are deaf
Increased touching and touching as predominant attention-getting device
Constant visual contact
Increased maternal positive affect
Exaggerated signs (as opposed to spoken words)
Modified placement and orientation of signs
Signing away from body, at place of infant's gaze
Increased shaping of infant's hands
More "sequential" than "simultaneous" pattern of signing

mothers provide helpful input to their language-learning infants (Table 5.1).

Mothers Who Are Deaf Versus Hearing Mothers. Additional issues arise when one considers interactions between hearing mothers and infants who are deaf. Studies comparing mothers who are deaf and hearing mothers have proliferated in recent years, with interesting, at times counterintuitive findings.

One issue concerns control. Like mothers of children with mental retardation, hearing mothers of babies who are deaf more often use commands and other controlling language (or signs) with their infants than do hearing mothers of hearing infants. Wood, Wood, Griffiths, and Howarth (1986) describe "spirals of increasing control" in interactions of hearing mothers and their infants who are deaf, as these mothers attempt to minimize misunderstandings by providing directives and imperatives.

Recent studies have further explored the nature of maternal control. Spencer and Gutfreund (1990) distinguish several types of maternal control: response control, when mothers use imperatives and questions to elicit a response from the child; turn-taking control, when mothers provide many utterances and long turns; and topic control, when mothers initiate interactive topics that differ from the child's activities or focus of attention. Like researchers in mental retardation, Spencer and Gutfreund (1990) note that topic control seems most detrimental to the child's early communicative development.

Unfortunately, topic control commonly occurs in dyads of hearing mothers and infants who are deaf. Consider, for example, Spencer, Bodner-Johnson, and Gutfreund's (1992) study comparing dyads of hearing mothers and hearing infants (HH); hearing mothers and deaf infants (HD); and deaf infants and deaf mothers (DD). Mothers in the HD group were much more likely than mothers in the HH and DD groups to redirect their infants' focus of attention. As a result, infants in the HD group were forced to refocus their attention and to understand the mother's utterances, both at the same time.

In addition, hearing mothers may not understand how to repair interactions when the child who is deaf cannot comprehend. Hearing mothers often respond to the child's misunderstanding by simply repeating the message (Jamieson, 1993). This strategy is common in spoken language, but to infants who are deaf, such a style of linguistic repair may be counterproductive. Indeed, by using more as opposed to different language, "these [hearing] mothers responded as though their children were hearing, and in need of repetition, rather than as deaf children in need of an altered, visual approach" (Jamieson, 1993, p. 168).

Although mothers who are deaf often sign at the place where the child is looking, they most often employ a sequential interactive style. They allow the child to attend to an object, get the child's attention, and only then comment on what the child has seen. Deaf mothers of infants who are deaf realize that they must have the child's visual attention before signing. Based on their own experiences, these mothers can identify situations in which the child can see – in peripheral vision – the mother's simultaneously provided signs (Prendergast & McCollum, 1996). These mothers are thus optimally responsive to their young children, but in ways that differ from the behaviors of hearing mothers and hearing children due to the visual nature of sign language.

The studies by Spencer and her colleagues show the workings of such a sequential interactive style. In Spencer et al. (1992), only 20% of the deaf mothers' responses occurred during the child's object gaze; a full 80% of maternal signs occurred after the child had returned his or her attention to the mother. This 20:80 pattern contrasted sharply with both the HH and HD groups. In both groups with hearing mothers, almost 90% of maternal responses occurred during the child's object gaze, not after. (See Table 5.2 for examples of DD and HD interaction patterns.)

Differences between mothers who are deaf and hearing mothers lead to an appreciation of the "intuitive parenting" that parents who are deaf provide their children who are also deaf. Such parents intuitively make communicative adjustments for their children. Many of these strategies – including the use of touch, signs near the object to which the child is attending, and the sequential interactional style – involve behaviors that seem counterintuitive to most hearing parents (Koester, 1992). A greater integration of parents who are deaf as well as teachers who are deaf into intervention programs seems necessary, as does more research documenting the ways that parents who are deaf optimally – and naturally – aid their children's language development.

The intuitive parenting of parents who are deaf should not, however, be cause for discouragement among the 90% of hearing parents of children who are deaf. Indeed, particularly during the first few years of the baby's life, hearing parents can effectively communicate with their child. Adopting a sequential versus simultaneous style, recognizing the centrality of vision to every parent–child interaction, fostering physical contact, repeating signs, and performing "motherese" in sign as opposed to spoken language – all can be achieved with practice by hearing parents of young children. Other aspects of development, including social and emotional aspects, can be enhanced through various interventions during the school years (e.g., the PATHS [Promoting Alternative Thinking Strategies] curriculum of Greenberg & Kushe, 1993).

Table 5.2. *Topic change and sequential versus simultaneous communication styles in different dyads*

Hearing mother–deaf infant

Baby looks down at the seat belt fastened around his legs. While he looks down, Mom reaches out and touches his eye with her index finger, saying "Eye – Where's Eddie's eye?" After her touch, baby looks up at Mom's face, then back down toward the seat belt. While he looks down, Mom touches her own eye, saying "Mommy's eye." (Spencer et al., 1992, p. 73).

Deaf mother–deaf infant

Mother leans toward child and signs "Look, look at me." The child, who had been attempting to assemble two blocks, puts the blocks down and looks to the mother. Mother then signs "OK, you . . . look at me." Child and mother establish mutual regard, at which point mother informs the child, "You need the big ones first." Mother lowers her gaze to the blocks, and child again tries to assemble blocks. Mother pats the child's hand as a signal to look at her again. She then signs, "OK? You understand?" (Adapted from Jamieson, 1993, pp. 162–163).

Deaf mother–deaf infant

Baby looks at light on ceiling to right. Mom looks at baby during this time. Then baby looks at mom and turns her whole body to look at the light and point at it, then turns back around to face baby and signs "light" near her face several times. Mom turns again to look at and point toward the light. Baby smiles and alters his gaze to look at the light with her. Baby continues to look up toward the light and raises his arm to reach toward it. Mom begins to sign "light" near her face again but, looking toward the baby, sees that he is not looking at her. She pauses, then touches baby's uplifted arm lightly. At her touch, baby looks back at Mom and she signs "light" twice near her face. (Spencer et al., 1992, p. 74).

Families

Although much less family research exists in the area of deafness than in mental retardation, similar models have been used. Historically as well, families of deaf children were originally conceptualized as problem families. This view has now been questioned, and recent studies have focused equally on the problems these families face and on those supports and resources that might improve family adaptation.

Most work on deaf families has centered on families in which the parents are hearing and the child is deaf. The perception has generally been that, for deaf parents, a deaf child does not constitute a crisis. More than 20 years ago, Schlesinger and Meadow (1972) observed that "deaf parents of deaf children cope with the crisis of diagnosis easily and quickly, while their hearing counterparts prolong and intensify it. Once the initial diagnosis is made, deaf parents are less likely to seek confirmatory diagnosis or a miraculous cure" (p. 11). The following review thus focuses mainly on families of hearing parents and children who are deaf or hearing-impaired; only at the end does the emphasis shift to work on the dynamics of families with some of the other configurations of hearing and deaf members.

Families of Hearing Parents and a Child Who Is Deaf. Until recent years, most knowledge of families of children who are deaf came from clinical or anecdotal reports. These reports emphasized the mourning model of parental reactions (see Chapter 4). Such terms as shock, anger, depression, and constructive action (i.e., acceptance) were common (for a review see Kampfe, 1989). Reactions specific to parents of a child who was deaf were at times considered, as in discussions of the importance of age of diagnosis or the degree of hearing loss (e.g., Luterman, 1987). Generally, however, parental reactions to such a child were considered similar to parental reactions to children with other disabilities.

Yet when actual studies – as opposed to anecdotal reports – are considered, the picture is not as clear. Most studies do not show that mothers, fathers, or families of children who are deaf are worse off than families of hearing children. In comparing families of 5- to 15-year-old hearing children and children who are deaf, Freeman, Malkin, and Hastings (1975) found that the frequency of divorce and marital conflict was equal in the two groups of families. This finding is surprising in that the children who were deaf were themselves different in many ways from their hearing age-mates. Almost a quarter (23.8%) of the children who were deaf had one or more associated physical or medical handicaps, 22.6% of these children were judged to have a psychiatric disorder of moderate or severe degree, and on average these children were more often hospitalized than hearing children during the first two years of life. Nevertheless, the parents and families generally adapted well. Similarly, in examining parents of 12-year-old hearing-impaired versus hearing children, Henggeler, Watson, Whelan, and Malone (1990) noted that mothers and fathers of the children who were hearing-impaired reported that they suffered from fewer psychiatric symptoms than the parents of the hearing children.

One study, however, found differences between parents of deaf and parents of hearing children. According to Prior, Glazner, Sanson, and Debelle (1988), the mothers of preschoolers who were hearing-impaired were more anxious and depressed than were mothers of same-age hearing children; the mothers of children who were hearing-impaired were also higher overall on a scale of psychiatric symptoms. Such differences may be related to more difficult temperaments of children who are deaf and to the associated cognitive difficulties many of these children face.

In line with the movement toward stress-coping perspectives, several studies have demonstrated that various internal and external resources, as well as the child's personal characteristics, are related to parental and familial stress. For example, the child's degree of hearing loss may affect the mother's sense of marital satisfaction (Henggeler et al., 1990), and when the child wears a hearing aid the mother may experience less stress in her efforts to communicate with the child (Meadow-Orlans, 1990). In addition, mothers of children whose deafness was caused by rubella may show more overall stress, more stress related to communication, and less satisfaction with their relationships with professionals (Meadow-Orlans, 1990). Such relations appear to grow worse as the child gets older.

Other studies have related parental coping and outcomes for the child. Calderon, Greenberg, and Kushe (1991), for example, noted that a mother's problem-solving abilities were related to the child's own cognitive and interpersonal problem-solving abilities. Higher-SES and better-educated children also showed higher reading scores.

These results are both similar to and different from findings on families of children with mental retardation. Parents' decreased confidence in professionals as the child gets older, for example, seems analogous to the declining support and smaller social networks among families of older children with retardation. The benefits of good maternal problem-solving skills also are similar to those described in the mental retardation literature.

Certain diagnostic and etiological issues, though, are specific to deafness. While parents generally suspect that their child has a hearing impairment within the first year or so of life, official diagnoses are often not obtained until many months later. Indeed, when the child's hearing loss is not severe, two or more years often lapse between the time the parents first suspect the child's impairment and the final diagnosis (Freeman et al., 1975). Such periods of uncertainty undoubtedly stress parents. In the same way, different etiologies of hearing impairments – and their associated problems – may affect parents in different ways. More than 70% of babies affected by maternal rubella show some degree of hearing loss (Bradley & Miller, 1990). These children also often have mental retardation, visual impairments, and other physical or medical conditions. Compared with parenting a child who is "only deaf," parenting a deaf child with rubella may be particularly stressful.

Families with Hearing Children and Parents Who Are Deaf. Although most research focuses on hearing parents and children who deaf, research on the reverse situation is also common. Indeed, 95% of adults who are deaf marry someone who is also deaf, while 90% of the offspring of these marriages are hearing, not deaf, children. Therefore, one or more hearing children often have parents who are deaf. In general, the hearing children become fluent in both sign and oral languages; they also often serve as interpreters for their parents.

Intuitively, a child's becoming the parent's hearing contact with the outside world could prove either beneficial or harmful. Early family studies noted increased problems in these families. Many such reports were written by psychiatrists who had treated hearing offspring of deaf parents in their clinical practices. They focused on the burden children felt in translating for their parents, as well as the shame many felt about having parents who were different from the parents of their hearing peers.

More recently, however, several studies have presented a more balanced, albeit more complicated, picture. To date, most of these studies have focused on the oldest hearing child, the offspring who appears to be the designated interpreter for the parents. In 14 of the 16 families in one study (Buchino, 1993), only the oldest child translated; other hearing children were never called upon to interpret for the parents. Many of the translating children considered translating fun and helpful; younger children especially seemed to value their role as interpreter in the family.

This valued role shows itself in another way as well. Whereas hearing parents of hearing children only sometimes accepted their children's suggestions, deaf parents of hearing children often listened to their children (Rienzi, 1990). These children seem to have been accorded a privileged status in their homes, a status partially dependent on the their important role. As a result, families of deaf parents and hearing children behaved in more egalitarian and flexible ways than families of same-age hearing children and parents.

But even these more recent studies reveal that the child's role as family interpreter is not always positive. Adolescents especially resent this role, because it interferes with their social lives. Some younger children have difficulties as well. One child noted, "I'm a kid but my mom treats me like I know stuff like an adult when I have to talk to people for her" (Buchino, 1993, p. 43). These children become frustrated when they are unable to understand what their parents want or what they are trying to convey.

These problems are related, at heart, to the cultural aspects of deafness. Like U.S. immigrant children who interpret for their non-English-speaking parents, hearing children whose parents are deaf are respected by their families, while at the same time they feel shame, burdened and concerned for their parents because the usual parent–child role is reversed. These children often feel caught between two worlds, disagreeing with their parents even on the meaning of an ordinary experience like school. To their deaf parents, who in most cases attended residential schools for the deaf, school is "a place away from home where teachers and kids were like family" (Buchino, 1993); to these hearing children, school is much less personal or family-like.

In other ways, the experiences of these children recall those of nondisabled siblings of children with retardation. Hearing children whose parents are deaf face increased responsibilities. Some of these children do well, relishing the respect they receive, enjoying their experiences, and appreciating differences in ways that enrich their lives. Others feel angry, frustrated, and imposed upon. Both pluses and minuses accrue to being a "bicultural" individual, simultaneously a member of a larger hearing society and of a household with signing, deaf parents.

General Lessons

We end this chapter by discussing two issues: the need to distinguish between organismic and contextual issues and the implications of developmental similarities and differences between children who are deaf and hearing children.

Organismic Versus Contextual Issues

By considering first organismic and then contextual issues, one can discuss a range of modern developmental topics, from sequences to families, in a reasonably straightforward way. For the most part, the organismic development of deaf children learning ASL is identical to that of hearing children. For example, with some exceptions based on a visual as opposed to an oral language, sequences are identical in both cognitive and language development. Cognitive developments in the absence of a language system are similar to cross-domain findings for retarded and typically developing children. Even the findings on hand babbling and the critical age for language – while specific to ASL – parallel findings from hearing children.

In terms of contextual issues, however, the differences between the deaf and hearing worlds are striking. Therefore, it is critical that studies of interactions between children who are deaf and their mothers note whether the mother is hearing or deaf, signing or speaking. Family studies must be sensitive to the family structure: Is the child a deaf child of parents who are deaf, a deaf child of hearing parents, or a hearing child of parents who are deaf?

Organismic and contextual issues also influence one another. To take an extreme example, Furth (1964) considered his children who were prelingually deaf to be "nonlinguistic" only because oral instruction had already proved unsuccessful for them. Greenberg and Kushe (1989) found a strong relationship between early sign training and the child's academic achievement and reading levels. In addition, the PATHS curriculum has been shown to increase social-emotional development in school-age children who are deaf (Greenberg & Kushe, 1993). As elsewhere, then, a strong relationship exists between the organismic and the cultural, between the child and his or her society.

Implications of Similarities and Differences

So far, this chapter has only hinted at the implications of the many similarities and differences between the development of hearing children and children who are deaf. Partly because we have limited our discussion to children who are deaf but not hearing-impaired and to ASL (not to oral language or other sign systems), we have ignored the oral–sign controversy and the question of whether children who are deaf are better educated in public schools, in mainstream classes within those schools, or in residential schools for the deaf. Each of these issues is actively debated in the Deaf and hearing communities.

We now turn to a few of the practical ramifications of the developmental similarities between hearing children and children who are deaf. To simplify somewhat, in principle, organismic issues are identical, as are many contextual issues. Thus, while this chapter has focused on how mother–child interactions differ in deaf–deaf versus hearing–hearing dyads, the principles remain the same. Mothers simplify their input, make certain that the child is paying attention and receiving the input, and in other ways help the child to develop language. In adapting to the presence of a child who is deaf, hearing families experience stress, some of which is due to the child's personal characteristics, but they also appear to function reasonably well.

These all might be referred to as "similarities in principle, not in details." To consider some examples, it now appears that children's early language development is enhanced when the adult comments on the child's object of attention. This has been noted in studies of hearing children (Cross, 1978) as well as children with Down syndrome (Harris, Kasari, & Sigman, 1996). Studies of mothers who are deaf versus hearing mothers and their infants similarly highlight the need for mothers to comment on the child's focus of attention rather than to change the child's focus with her comments (Jamieson, 1993; Spencer et al., 1992). Yet the ways in which mothers comment on the child's focus vary depending on the child. Mothers of children with Down syndrome and of hearing nonretarded children talk about the object the child is looking at while the child is looking at it. In contrast, mothers of children who are deaf must either sign over the object or wait until the child stops looking at the object and turns to look at her (Swisher, 1992). In both cases, the principle is the same, even if the behavior differs.

In the same way, findings concerning the stresses and supports of hearing families of children who are deaf are similar in principle to those of families of children with other disabilities. While parents who are deaf conceptualize the child's deafness as normal, hearing parents generally see it as a disability. When they see it in this way, hearing parents experience stress due to delays in diagnosis or to the child's associated cognitive, physical, or medical disabilities (as in deafness caused by rubella). Social support appears to help parental and familial adaptation. The principle is the same: the child's personal characteristics, familial support, and the meaning of the child's disability to the family – the A, B, and C terms of the Double ABCX model (see Chapter 4) – affect familial adaptation. The specifics vary due to the unique aspects of deafness.

The notion of similarities and differences also encompasses the cultural aspects of deafness. As noted earlier, individuals who are deaf form a unique subculture within society. Cultural factors are more salient among such individuals than among persons with mental retardation, blindness, or motor impairments. They pervade discussions of many topics, from the acquisition of ASL, to mother–child interactions, to family adaptation, to appropriate schooling.

6

Blindness and Visual Impairments

Since most people learn about the world primarily through sight, the presence or absence of vision has long been considered an important factor in development. John Locke considered congenitally blind children a test of his "tabula rasa," the idea that an infant enters life as a blank slate and develops by accumulating sensory input. In contrast, Noam Chomsky cited blind children's normal development of language (even of concepts they cannot see) to argue that language is "switched on" in human infants, requiring only minimal environmental input (Piattelli-Palmarini, 1980). Though this debate may never be resolved, theorists have long focused on children who are blind as supposedly perfect subjects for testing the nature–nurture debate.

Although it has been of interest for several centuries, blindness remains difficult to study for a number of reasons. The most important is that blindness is not a common condition. Persons who are considered legally blind – that is, who have 20/200 vision in their better eye after correction or a visual field of 20 degrees or less – constitute less than 1% of the U.S. population. In most studies, the percentages are 0.1% or 0.2%; in others, the prevalence approaches 1%. This discrepancy exists in part because some 50% to 90% of visually impaired children are also deaf, mentally retarded, or motor-impaired (Jan, Freeman, & Scott, 1977), and the question arises as to which disability is primary for these children.

Partly due to the rarity of the condition, behavioral studies of children who are blind or visually impaired have, until recently, been less common than behavioral studies of children with men retardation or deafness. While a few large-scale studies were pe formed before the 1960s (e.g., Norris, Spaulding, & Brodie, 1957) most extensive studies have appeared in the past 20 years. Even today, research on blindness is rare and many studies examine only a few children. Indeed, Fraiberg's Insights from the Blind – a comprehensive examination of 10 children published in 1977 – continues to be the field's landmark study.

Nonetheless, the development of children who are blind or visually impaired is important to study. As noted by Vygotsky (1927/1993), blind children must compensate for their lack of vision. They receive information about the world predominantly through the modalities of hearing and touch and through the medium of language.

Blind children's compensations inevitably lead to interest in those aspects of development that are affected by a lack of sight. How, for example, does the child come to understand deictic terms such as here and there, or visual terms such as see and look? Does development proceed along the same sequences, are separate domains differentially affected by the lack of sight, and can these domains be compensated for by the child's other modalities or by behaviors that elicit information about what the child cannot see?

In social interactions as well, both the mother and child compensate. How does the mother ensure that she and the child are focused on the same topics? How can infants convey to their mothers what they are thinking and feeling? To what extent does language or touch allow the child to circumvent the loss of sight? All these issues have been addressed in recent years.

Organismic Issues

Sequences and Underlying Processes of Development

Like most other children, children who are blind or visually impaired progress in order through various developmental stages. In her early studies, Fraiberg (1977) noted that these children progress sequentially through the Piagetian stages, as well as later stages of cognitive development (Warren, 1984, 1994). Work on preoperational, concrete, and formal operational developments also show a general similarity between blind and sighted children. Children who are blind may develop more slowly – particularly in Piagetian tasks involving classification and conservation – but they generally progress along the presumably universal orderings in development.

The development of blind children, however, is not identical to that of sighted nondisabled children. It has been reported that the first words of children who are blind occur slightly later than the first words of sighted children (Moore & McConachie, 1994; Mulford, 1988), though this finding has not been substantiated by some studies. More important, blind children's first words consist of fewer personal-social words such as no and thank you, and more words that describe or accompany the child's actions (up, go) than do those of sighted children (Bigelow, 1987). In addition, the earliest vocabularies of children who are blind include more specific nominals, or words involving either proper names (Mommy) or object words that have been undergeneralized to a single object (doggie referring only to the child's dog, and not to dogs in general) than do those of sighted children. Children who are blind produce fewer overgeneralizations, such as using the word dog to refer to all four-legged animals (for a review see A. E. Mills, 1988).

Although most researchers agree about these differences in early language development, why they occur has been widely debated. Anderson, Dunlea, and Kekelis (1984, 1993) partially attribute language differences to the less developed conceptual systems of children who are blind. They emphasize that these children show more undergeneralizations and fewer overgeneralizations, more chunked, formulaic utterances and routines (Mulford, 1983), and difficulties in categorization. They conclude that "early lexical development in blind children may be constrained by delays in sensori-motor cognition" (Anderson et al., 1993, p. 27).

Other workers disagree, claiming that language deficits are due to the child's having had fewer and less widespread experiences. For example, children who are blind have less exposure to different examples of a class of objects (Bigelow, 1987; McCune, 1991) – the bird that the sighted child sees on the tree outside, in a picture book, or on television. Further curtailing their experiences are blind children's marked delays in locomotion: Using very liberal criteria, Adelson and Fraiberg (1974) reported that the blind infants in their studies reached for objects at 10 months (compared with a 5-month average for sighted children), crawled at 13 months (compared with 7 months average), and walked at 19 months (compared with 12 months). Using more stringent criteria, Norris et al. (1957) found that only half of their blind children walked independently by 24 months. Due to experiential deficits that are direct (i.e., lack of sight) and indirect (fewer movements to manipulate objects), then, children who are blind are also handicapped in their experiential bases for language.

Furthermore, such children may have different meanings for specific words. In a series of studies, Landau (1983; Landau & Gleitman, 1985) examined Kelli, a preschool girl who was totally blind. In contrast to earlier workers who felt that blind children have either no meanings or bizarre meanings for such visual terms as see and look, Landau and Gleitman noted that Kelli had consistent, logical meanings for these words. Look meant to reach out and touch an object. When the researchers asked Kelli to "look up," she generally kept her head still, but lifted her hands and arms upward as if to touch an object (Figure 6.1). Sighted children – even when blindfolded – lifted their heads upward (Figure 6.2). Thus, Kelli's meanings for selected words differed from those of sighted children, but these meanings were clear and consistent, and made perfect sense for a child developing word meanings in the absence of sight.

Young children who are blind may also differ from sighted children in their uses of language. Consider the simple problem of getting the listener's attention, then beginning and maintaining a conversation. A sighted child establishes eye contact with an adult interactor, and the two jointly attend to a single object. During the earliest years, such nonverbal cues predominate in adult–child interactions. But lacking these cues, blind children must use other means. They often touch the listener and talk about their own actions rather than the actions of others (McGinnis, 1981; Mulford, 1988). At later ages, although children who are blind eventually use language as well as nonverbal means to get and maintain

Figure 6.1. Kelli's response to "look up!" In Experiment 1, the blind child moved her hands, not her eyes and head, in the direction indicated by the command in six out of six trials. From Landau and Gleitman (1985) with the permission of Robert Thatcher and Associates, Hamilton Square, NJ.

Figure 6.2. A blindfolded sighted child's response to "look up!" in Experiment 1, each child moved her eyes and head, not her hands, in the direction indicated by the command in six out of six trials. From Landau and Gleitman (1985) with the permission of Robert Thatcher and Associates, Hamilton Square, NJ.

the listener's attention, they experience difficulties in learning how to use such skills appropriately. To gain the listener's attention, kindergartners who are blind have been reported to interrupt an adult conversation repeatedly or to pinch another child (Mulford, 1983).

These children also appear to have great difficulties with deictic terms. Consider, for example, the interactions between two young blind children (Anderson et al., 1993, p. 29):

Teddy (picking up dish): "What's this?"
Lisa   (holding brush): "This a brush.". . ."Is this a brush?"
        (holding and feeling brush)
Teddy: No it's not."

Although one might partly attribute this problem to young children's egocentrism, their lack of vision obviously hampers these two children in their development of the deictic terms this and that.

Table 6.1 lists some differences between the language development of children who are blind and sighted children.

In addition to examining sequences and processes of development, researchers have studied some aspects of cross-domain relations in children who are blind. Bigelow (1990) examined the first words of two blind toddlers and one visually impaired toddler, comparing the age of these first words with the children's object permanence skills. She found that, while the ages of first words were roughly comparable to those of sighted children, object permanence skills were not. No close relation existed between the children's object permanence skills and early vocabulary. In another set of studies, Bigelow (1995) confirmed Fraiberg's (1977) idea that crawling is related to a particular level of object permanence (Stage IV), while walking is related to the next highest level (Stage V).

One's concept of a permanent object is highly dependent on vision; hence, children who are blind acquire the object concept at later ages than sighted children. In reviewing these studies, Warren (1994) points to impairments in sensorimotor Stage VI object permanence, which requires the child to systematically search in vari-

Table 6.1. *Aspects of development in children who are blind that are delayed or different from those in sighted children*

Delayed aspects	Different aspects
Object permanence (Stage VI)	Fewer overgeneralizations of word meanings (*dog* for all animals)
Spatial abilities	More undergeneralizations (*dog* for one dog only)
Classification	Different meaning for some vision words (*look* = "explore tactually")
Conservation	More formulaic utterances
Deictic terms	More vocal attention getting
Grammar (possibly)	Greater percentage of personal-social words
First words (possibly)	More action references (to child's own actions)
Motor skills	More touching and other visual attention getting
	More passivity
	Less facial emotional expression (more with hands)
	More regressions (among children totally blind from central nervous system causes)
	Fewer back-and-forth vocalizations with adults (to avoid cluttering up vocal environment?)

ous locations for hidden objects. In contrast to earlier levels, Stage VI object permanence may require an ability to understand that one's surrounding space exists "out there" – not only in reference to one's own physical movements.

The young child's concept of self also seems impaired by lack of sight. Infants blind from birth cannot see themselves or others act, are often more passive than same-age sighted children, and may have more difficulties in differentiating themselves from others. In addition, walking and certain cognitive-linguistic skills are delayed. What might the effects of such developmental patterns be on one's sense of self?

For many years, psychoanalysts such as Sandler (1963) and

Fraiberg and Freedman (1964) have commented on ego development in children who are blind. Both total blindness and lack of stimulation from surrounding adults seem implicated in passivity, self-stimulation, and delayed development at very early periods. Still, many blind children do not have deviant self-images, and the entire area remains unclear.

Recently, however, Bigelow (1995) has distinguished between the "interpersonal" and "ecological" self during infancy (from U. Neisser, 1991). In the case of the interpersonal self, the child knows that he or she is connected to but separate from other people, whereas in the case of the ecological self, the child knows that he or she is connected to but separate from the physical environment. Bigelow notes that, while delays in attachment to the mother, you–I confusion, and a preponderance of comments about the child's own actions all point to difficulties in acquiring an interpersonal self, delays in self-concept may be even more pronounced relative to the object world. She notes the importance of crawling and walking in order to explore one's environment, and the connection of crawling and walking to object permanence skills. While children who are blind come to understand the more contingent interpersonal world (in which the mother responds when the infant cries), they may initially find it difficult to understand their own abilities to act on the object-world. These children may have trouble realizing that they themselves can bounce balls, topple cups, and squeeze toys that make a sound. Although much more work is needed in this area, it may be helpful to consider separately the effects of blindness on the different senses of "self" during the early years.

When considering cross-domain relations in young children who are blind, we are confronted with both strengths and weaknesses. Although these children more often refer to their own actions, use more proper names and "specific nominals" (as opposed to general labels for objects) when they speak, and use language differently (e.g., to get and maintain the listener's attention), their overall language development is often only slightly behind that of sighted children. However, other developments – particularly of spatial skills, locomotion, and object permanence (especially Stage IV) – seem much more delayed. Further, these strengths and weaknesses seem unique to the blind population.

Rates and Regressions

To date, few studies have directly examined blind children's rates of development. This is due in part to the difficulties such studies entail. It is often very difficult to determine any child's degree of vision, particularly a young child's. Yet even very limited vision helps young children enormously, at least with some developments (Bigelow, 1990; McConachie & Moore, 1994).

In addition, how does one test levels of development in children who are blind? Granted, several measures – most notably, the Reynell–Zinkin test (Reynell & Zinkin, 1975) and the Maxfield–Buckholz Social Maturity Scale for Blind Preschool Children (Maxfield & Buckholz, 1957) – have been designed for these blind children, but these tests are only partially comparable to more widely used psychometric tests (for a review see Sattler, 1992). Some researchers use modifications of Piagetian or other tasks. In her studies of object permanence, for example, Bigelow (1990) examined children by using noise-making objects which were moved from one location to another. In this way, she achieved a rough analogue to Piaget's object permanence task. It remains unclear, however, just how analogous such tests are to the psychometric tests administered to sighted children.

Despite these complications, it has been possible to characterize blind children's rates of development in several areas. Fraiberg (1977) noted a delay in object permanence in all of her blind infants, and more recent studies have demonstrated that object permanence in children who are blind is delayed approximately 12 months (especially at Stage VI; Rodgers & Puchalski, 1988). At later ages, classification and conservation delays become apparent.

But in other ways the development of children who are blind may not be delayed. Several studies have shown that these children speak their 1st, 10th, or 50th word (depending on the study) more or less within the normal time frame. At worst, some blind children appear slightly behind in their early vocabulary. While several studies have shown these children's grammatical development to be equal to that of same-age peers (McGinnis, 1981; Perez-Pereira & Castro, 1992), others have revealed some delay. Landau and

Gleitman (1985) noted problems in blind children's development of auxiliary verbs. Overall, though, the language of these children seems reasonably equivalent to that of their sighted peers.

To date, only a few studies have examined rates of development using a standardized intelligence test. Reynell (1978) examined three groups of children – blind, visually impaired, and sighted – with the Reynell–Zinkin test over the first five years of life. The children who were blind differed from those who were visually impaired, and both groups differed from sighted children on many domains of functioning. However, all of these differences changed with the child's age. On certain domains, blind, visually impaired, and sighted children performed nearly identically during the first year of life. Over the next 2 to 3 years, however, the sighted children outperformed the children who were visually impaired as well as those who were blind, after which the two visually impaired groups again approached the functioning levels of the sighted children. (See also Hatton, Bailey, Burchinal, & Ferrell, 1997).

In considering these findings, Reynell (1978) hypothesizes that blind and visually impaired children's conceptual abilities compensate for their experiential deficits. In contrast to those who ascribe linguistic problems to the blind child's supposed deficits in classification and cognition (e.g., Anderson et al., 1984, 1993), Reynell (1978) sees cognitive skills as a compensatory factor for these children. "When visually handicapped children are able to use intellectual means to transcend the perceptual learning, they can, to some extent, find ways around the visual difficulties, but by this time they are already 1 to 2 years behind their sighted peers in most aspects of learning" (Reynell, 1978, p. 302).

Developmental regressions further complicate the rate issue. Cass, Sonksen, and McConachie (1994) examined the Reynell–Zinkin test records of three groups of children: those who were totally blind, those whose vision improved as they developed, and those who maintained some small amount of useful vision throughout the period of study. Many more of the children who were totally blind showed regressions in development than did the partially sighted groups over the 1- to 6-year period. Thirty-one percent (10 of 32) of the totally blind group showed such regressions. All regressions involved a significant loss of language production, comprehension, or sensorimotor abilities, which began at 16 to 27 months; less than half of these children experienced partial recovery over the next few years.

In addition, both organic and environmental factors appeared to influence these regressions. The blindness of all the children who regressed had been caused by a central nervous system defect or injury, as opposed to cataracts or other peripheral factors. Moreover, for 60% of children who suffered developmental setback (as opposed to 23% of children whose development continued), the environment was characterized by marital discord, separation, or divorce, maternal depression, parental drug addiction, and/or major financial or housing problems.

Contextual Issues

Mother–Child Interactions

Parents of a child who is blind must also compensate in order for the child to develop optimally. How do most parents behave, and what behaviors seem most appropriate?

Let us first consider the child who is blind from the mother's perspective. In mothers' interactions with nondisabled infants, vision plays an essential role. Mothers and infants play "face games" as early as 2 to 4 months (Brazelton, Koslowski, & Main, 1974); these games include mutual gazing, turn taking, vocalizing, and performing physical actions. Infants smile, laugh, frown, and give other cues that enable mothers to "read" their young babies (Goldberg, 1977).

Mothers of infants who are blind are hampered by both the infant's lack of sight and several behaviors associated with the infant's blindness. Obviously, the infant's lack of vision makes back-and-forth facial–visual interactions impossible. Mothers must rely on sound and physical stimulation to elicit reactions from their babies. For the most part, mothers discover ways to interact with these infants. Als, Tronick, and Brazelton (1980a, 1980b) observed that mothers used modulations of sound and touch to develop synchronous cycles of mother–blind infant behavior like those found in mother–sighted infant pairs. During the baby's first year, mothers find that different behaviors and routines are successful with their infants (Urwin, 1978); they then repeat, expand, and elaborate such behaviors and routines as the child develops.

Employing sequential analysis to examine interactions between mothers and infants who are blind, Rowland (1983) found that, while other infant behaviors did not always elicit maternal behaviors, mothers almost always responded to the infant's smiles by vocalizing or touching the infant. But blind babies do not always smile – Rowland's infants smiled from 8% to 30% of the time – and facial expressions may not always be a reliable indication of the infant's feelings. Fraiberg (1977) realized that the baby's hands were often more expressive of the baby's intentions than was the face. At times, the baby's hand movements (e.g., opening and closing) helped adults to determine the degree to which the infant was interested in a particular object.

Blind babies tend to be more passive. Rowland (1983) noted that infant vocalizations occurred approximately 20% of the time during interactions. The infants did not consistently respond to maternal vocalizing. This nonresponsiveness may be related in part to the importance of hearing to infants who are blind. Unlike sighted infants, who can engage in back-and-forth visual games with their mothers, blind infants rely on hearing for information. They therefore risk cluttering their auditory environment if they themselves vocalize. Instead, they listen quietly to their mothers, at times moving silently or smiling.

In response to such passivity, mothers of visually impaired infants may be more directive than other mothers. They more often give commands, usually for the child to do something with a specific object (Kekelis & Anderson, 1984). They utter fewer declarative sentences and, when they do give information to their children, they more often provide labels for objects than do mothers of sighted children (Anderson et al., 1984; Moore & McConachie, 1994). These mothers do not discuss the attributes of objects as often as other mothers, thereby denying children who are blind the chance to learn more about objects and events.

The issue of which maternal behaviors most aid infants who are blind in their development has only recently received attention. It appears that when mothers are less directive and follow the child's lead, the child develops more quickly. Dote-Kwan (1995) found that when mothers complied with the child's request for help, repeated or rephrased the child's communicative behaviors, and modulated their rates of speaking and pausing to correspond to the child's level of language, the child was more advanced on both the Reynell–Zinkin and Maxfield-Buckholz scales. Granted, this study was cross-sectional, thus making it difficult to determine whether the mothers facilitated or simply reacted to more advanced levels of their children's development. Still, parental behavior that is responsive to children's utterances and focus of awareness may be most beneficial for later development.

Families

Owing to the rarity of blindness and visual impairments, few large-scale studies have been performed on families with blind children. Most researchers have instead interviewed a small number of families, usually about such topics as maternal reactions, family needs and supports, and the specific needs and supports of either minority families or families of subgroups of blind children (e.g., children who are both deaf and blind).

One recent large-scale study suggested that families of school-age children with visual impairments may be at particular risk for divorce or separation and may have lower incomes than families of nondisabled children. Hodapp and Krasner (1995) examined families of four groups of children: those with visual impairments, deafness, hearing impairments, and motor impairments. The study used data from the National Educational Longitudinal Study of 1988, which obtained questionnaire responses from the parents of 25,000 U.S. eighth-grade schoolchildren. While families in all of the disability groups had lower incomes and a higher prevalence of separation or divorce than families of nondisabled children, the families of visually impaired eighth graders seemed most seriously affected. Specifically, the 89 families in the visually impaired group showed a divorce or separation rate of more than 25%, in contrast to a rate of 15.3% in the nondisabled sample. Similarly, more than 35% of families in the visually impaired group earned $15,000 or less, compared with less than 20% of the nondisabled group.

Although no information was obtained about the extent of their impairment, the children in the visually impaired group most likely had some vision, since the study required each child to fill out a questionnaire with minimal help. In addition, these children were performing reasonably well in their neighborhood public schools; they thus constituted a higher-functioning group than the blind and visually impaired population as a whole. Moreover, although the reasons remain unknown, the visually impaired group was composed of a high percentage of African American and Hispanic families. This overrepresentation of minority families in the visually impaired group held with regard to both the sample as a whole and to the other disability groups. Once this overrepresentation was controlled, it was found that divorce and separation were more prevalent among White families, while lower family income was more common among the minority families.

Although based on smaller samples, other studies have begun to pinpoint the problems faced by families of children who are blind or visually impaired. During interviews conducted by Hancock, Wilgosh, and McDonald (1990), a small group of parents recalled their shock, depression, and anger upon receiving the child's diagnosis, much like parents of children with other disabilities. These feelings were often compounded by the scarcity of professionals trained in blindness. Many local professionals seemed of little help, because they had little experience with this condition. As one mother noted, "You soon learn that not all suggestions apply to your child, and that you may have to do your own thing" (Hancock et al., 1990, p. 412). Schools were often reluctant to provide the equipment and training that the children required. For these parents, having to spend a large amount of time interacting with their children – for example, helping them learn Braille – was stressful.

Like parents of children with other disabilities, however, these parents generally coped well, particularly if they maintained a positive attitude. As one mother noted, "If you have a positive outlook, so will the child," and as another said, "I just don't dwell on the down times" (Hancock et al., 1990, p. 412). The positive attitudes and accomplishments of children who are blind or visually impaired are also helpful, as is the support of the rest of the family.

Other studies have given greater attention to special groups, issues, and disability configurations within the visually impaired population. Several articles have highlighted those groups that may be more likely than others to have visually impaired children. Correa (1987) notes, for example, that approximately 27% of all children with visual impairments in the state of Texas are Hispanic. She emphasizes the strong family tradition within the Hispanic culture, as well as the support provided by members of the extended family and the dominant roles of the father as provider and the mother as caregiver. Intervention may thus be aided by the inclusion of extended family members and by an approach that is sensitive to the mother's need to be the primary caregiver.

Another at-risk population may be Native Americans. Orlansky and Trap (1987) provide guidelines for dealing with these families that take into account the high prevalence of diabetes, glaucoma, and other health problems in Native American groups. They suggest using cooperative rather than competitive teaching strategies and respecting the Native American family's tradition of allowing older children to care for younger children, even those with visual impairments.

Parent groups have also received attention. Although Nixon (1988) found that some parents participated in these groups, no single model of parent support seemed helpful for all families, at every age of the child. Many parents mentioned that, given the rarity of blindness, it was unlikely that they would find another local parent whose child had the same degree of visual impairment, was the same age, and had the same types of associated disabilities. A full half of these families did not join parent groups, often because the child's impairments were less severe and the parents preferred to focus on their child's normal characteristics.

Some recent work has involved children who are both deaf and blind. Among the high percentage of blind and visually impaired children with multiple impairments, many have the combination of deafness and blindness, which is often caused by rubella. Particularly during outbreaks in 1963 to 1965, many children were born with both visual and hearing problems (nowadays, the most common etiology of combined deafness and blindness in children is extreme prematurity). In recent years, this deaf–blind population has begun to receive attention. In the Deaf community, the possibility of a deaf–blind culture has been suggested (Erting, Johnston,

Smith, & Snider, 1994). In addition a special issue of the Journal of Visual Impairment and Blindness (1995) has been devoted to the deaf–blind population.

Recent years have also seen studies of families of these children. Vadasy and Fewell (1986) studied families of deaf–blind adolescents and young adults. The majority of these children had rubella, and many had associated disabilities such as mental retardation, cardiac problems, and emotional disorders. Their mothers noted a variety of difficulties, especially in garnering services for their children as they became adults. Like the parents of children with retardation, these parents feared what would happen to their children as they reached adulthood and became too old for educational services. They also expressed concern about their children's future jobs and vocational placement, as well as about their residences, particularly once the parents became older and less capable of caring for their adult deaf–blind offspring.

In overviewing the work on families of blind and visually impaired children, we see that the issues vary somewhat from those of families of children with other disabilities. Similarities include maternal reactions and the stresses that raising a child who is blind or visually impaired place on mothers, fathers, couples, and families. The problems that are unique to these families are associated with raising a child with a low-incidence condition: the lack of social service professionals with experience in blindness or visual impairments and the scarcity of parents whose child's problem is the same as that of one's own child.

We know little about these families' particular stresses and supports. A systems orientation – which has greatly influenced family work in other disabilities – is also generally lacking in most work on families of blind and visually impaired children.

Conclusion

Is Sight a Necessary Condition for Any Aspect of Development?

With the exception of obvious aspects of development such as the reading of print, sight does not appear to be a necessary condition for development. Although some of their achievements – for example, locomotion, spatial knowledge, and sensorimotor Stage VI object permanence – are especially delayed, children who are blind develop in all areas. Several areas, particularly certain aspects of language, seem less delayed than visually related aspects of cognition (e.g., spatial relations). Moreover, children who are blind develop meanings for visual terms such as look and see (Landau & Gleitman, 1985). These words meanings may differ from those of sighted children, but they are reasonable given the child's experiences. Indeed, children who are blind illustrate again how all children actively interact with and attempt to make sense of the world around them.

Is the Development of Children Who Are Blind the Same as or Different from That of Sighted Children or Children with Other Disabilities?

Children who are blind exhibit different, not necessarily deficient, development. They appear to develop in order through Piagetian and other sequences, even as they differ somewhat in what they talk about, how they use language, and in what meanings they give to particular words. Developments most closely aligned with vision are more delayed than others, such as vocabulary and perhaps grammar. The delays are worse early on, before the developing cognitive abilities of these children can partially overcome their visual deficiencies.

Underlying these findings is a sense of what might be called the fragile development of blind children. "Fragile" development refers to the overabundance of developmental regressions in children who are totally blind, as opposed even to children who have some small degree of vision or whose sight improves over the years. Fragility also seems related to the child's environment. Like children who are deaf, children who are totally blind (not so much partially sighted children) appear to be highly sensitive to their environments.

What Is the Role of the Environment?

Children who are blind may derive more benefit from good environments than do children with any other disability. One might argue, for example, that the environment has a more limited influence on children with Down syndrome or even on deaf children who have been introduced to sign language. Although these children of course benefit from an environment that is contingent and follows the child's focus of interest, a positive environment seems essential for the development of the blind child.

Like environments for children with deafness and retardation, the best interpersonal environments provide contingent responses that follow the child's focus. Mothers of children who are blind also need to expand the child's utterances and to describe the environment to them. Environments that are less didactic and in which mothers and their children are on a more equal footing also seem necessary, as do interventions that provide touch, sound, and activities so that the children can actively explore their environment. Through these techniques, blind children should become more active learners as well.

All of this work is leading to a better sense of what we mean by compensation. Just as children who are blind use touch, hearing, and language to compensate for their lack of vision, so do parents work to reach their blind children in Vygotsky's "roundabout" ways. Even though blindness and visual impairments are low-incidence disorders, they continue to tell us much about development.

7

Motor Impairments

Over the past decade, an increasing number of studies have examined children with motor impairments. These studies, which partially address a previously neglected topic, have touched on various aspects of the children themselves, mother–child interactions, and families. Although still less frequently examined than children with many other disabilities, children with motor impairments are increasingly becoming the subject of developmental approaches.

To this day, however, it remains difficult to study these children. While mental retardation, deafness, and blindness are reasonably easy to diagnose, evaluate, and study, motor impairments present a host of problems only partially encountered in other disabilities.

Research Issues Specific to Motor Impairments

One such problem concerns associated disabilities, the major disability associated with motor impairments being mental retardation. Approximately 60% of children with cerebral palsy (one type of motor impairment) have IQs below 70, placing them in the mentally retarded range of intellectual functioning (Capute & Accardo, 1991). In addition, strabismus is found in 50% of these children, seizures in 30% to 40%, and emotional, hearing, and visual problems in many others. The presence of these disabilities makes the study of children with motor impairments more difficult.

A second problem concerns how one divides the population of

children with motor impairments. One way to do so is to classify the children by their type and degree of motor involvement, as follows (from Bobath & Bobath, 1975):

Quadriplegia occurs when the motor involvement involves all four limbs.
Diplegia occurs when the legs are more seriously impaired than the arms.
Hemiplegia occurs when one side of the body is more severely affected than the other.

Another way is to classify the children by their motor difficulties: For example:

Cerebral palsy comprises a group of conditions resulting from damage to the brain early in development (Kasari, Larson, & Veltman, 1987), including a lack of oxygen at birth, prematurity, hemorrhaging, infection, trauma, or hereditary malformations at birth (G. Miller, 1992). It can be of several types, but it always involves the legs, arms, or one side of the body.
Spina bifida is a hereditary disorder in which the spinal column does not close properly. It may include weak or absent muscle functioning of the trunk and lower limbs, dislocation of the hip, clubfoot, and curvature of the spine. Tactile, bowel, or bladder problems are also sometimes found.
Hydrocephalus and myelomeningocele are two conditions often associated with spina bifida. Hydrocephalus involves a buildup of fluid surrounding (and pressuring) the brain. Myelomeningocele occurs when the spinal cord protrudes in its membrane sac from the newborn's back and must be surgically closed. This condition, which is often associated with diminished feeling and control of bladder, bowel, and lower limbs, occurs in some 70% of spina bifida cases (Wills, 1993).

This list of conditions only hints at the heterogeneity within the population of children with motor impairments. Type, severity, and cause of motor impairments can all differ from one child to another. To complicate matters, we do not generally know what the connection is between the child's motor impairments and different aspects of development. For example, motor impairments may or may not be related to the child's degree of intellectual impairment, strengths and weaknesses, or regressions.

A third problem, which, as we have seen, occurs throughout the disabilities field, concerns the adaptation of IQ and other psychometric tests. Here the major issue has to do with motor responses on common psychometric tests. Many tests require the child to provide motor responses. The WISC Object Assembly subtest, the K-ABC Hand Movements subtest (see Chapter 3), and the Stanford–Binet Copying (of line drawings) subtest all require the child to demonstrate some degree of motor behavior in order to be credited with a "correct" answer (Sattler, 1992). Some subtests are also timed, placing children with impaired motor skills at an even greater disadvantage. In all of these tests, the child may understand the concept, yet be unable to perform the behavior that demonstrates his or her knowledge.

Although these issues remain unresolved, some progress is being made. First, researchers are providing more information about the associated disabilities of the children in their samples. Studies of children with cerebral palsy often include both children who do and do not have mental retardation, or both children who were born prematurely and children born at term. With additional information, however, readers can at least determine the characteristics of the study population. They can then draw implications for their own research or clinical practice.

Second, more studies are now examining children with a single type of motor impairment. One such study, which will be described later, has focused on language in children with spina bifida. Again, such attention to different types of motor impairments will not provide a total solution to the problem of heterogeneity among children with motor impairments. Some even argue that many etiologies are vague or wastebasket categories: What does it mean, for example, to say that a child has cerebral palsy? We now know that cerebral palsy has a variety of pre-, peri-, and postnatal causes (Stanley, 1994), and such factors as maternal mental retardation, low birth weight, fetal malformation, and asphyxia at birth are among the best predictors of newborn cerebral palsy (Nelson &

Ellenberg, 1986). Though imperfect, even this amount of precision in defining samples is preferable to simply examining children with a variety of motor impairments.

Third, advances have been made in testing. Whereas new IQ tests have been devised for children who are deaf or blind, researchers in motor impairments have generally adapted existing tests to the child's capabilities (Rosenberg & Robinson, 1990). Most existing psychometric tests focus on the child's response. Tests must be given in a certain, standardized way and, while the examiner may note the child's motor difficulties, standardization requires that children receive credit for an item only when they answer in the standard way. For example, a child with motor impairments gets no credit for "sloppy" imitations of the examiner's series of hand gestures in the K-ABC Hand Movements subtest. Other subtests also tap motor or visuomotor skills to various degrees.

Given this focus on behavior alone, developmentally oriented tests have proved helpful. These tests admittedly sacrifice standardized scores and norms; one cannot determine the child's IQ or rank relative to that of his or her agemates. But developmentally oriented tests do offer good estimates of what the child knows, and provide flexible administration procedures that may be helpful in testing children with motor impairments.

The Ordinal Scales of Infant Development developed by Uzgiris and Hunt (1975) are a good example of such developmental tests. Unlike most standardized, normed instruments (i.e., all IQ, adaptive behavior, or other psychometric tests), the Uzgiris–Hunt scales allow the examiner to test the child a second or even a third time on any particular item. No test items are timed and, though many involve motor responses, the examiner is given leeway in determining whether the child truly understands the concept behind the task. If the infant shows – by gaze, head turn, or undifferentiated reach – that he or she knows that an object continues to exist even though hidden behind a cloth, the examiner gives the child credit for understanding that particular level of object permanence. Similar modifications can be made in other domains (Robinson & Rosenberg, 1987). With Dunst's (1980) modifications of the Uzgiris–Hunt scales, a greater number of items have been added to the original measure. Many of these items are less motoric; the overriding principle is that each item, whether from the original Uzgiris–Hunt scales or added later, assesses the child's understanding of a single, important developmental concept. In this way, the examiner focuses on what the child knows as opposed to what the child does motorically.

Organismic Issues

As in Furth's studies of deafness and the relations of language to cognition, developmentally oriented research in motor impairments began by studying the effects of motor impairments on cognitive development. The question was whether children could develop cognitive skills – especially during the early years – in the absence of the ability to manipulate objects motorically. Piaget and Inhelder (1969) had emphasized the importance of interactions between the infant and the environment for sensorimotor development; children with motor impairments therefore provided the perfect test of whether such motor manipulation was a necessary condition for early cognitive development (for a review see V. Lewis, 1987).

Decarie (1969) examined children whose mothers had been given thalidomide, a drug that alleviates morning sickness but that was later found to cause severe birth defects. Many of these children had missing arms or legs, others had "flippers," in which the hands or feet were directly attached to the torso (see Box 7.1 for a history of thalidomide). Decarie (1969) determined the degree to which 22 young children who had been exposed to thalidomide in utero were able to perform intellectual tasks. Her study, the first to determine whether motor manipulation was necessary for development, showed that these children did not require motor abilities to develop basic intellectual abilities. Although their average IQ was 85 (and lower IQs were found in institutionalized than in home-reared children), these children generally developed well. They had more difficulties in language than in others areas, but clearly did not require complex motor interactions to achieve basic cognitive skills.

Box 7.1. *Thalidomide: from wonder drug to teratogen*

Originally developed in 1954 as a sleeping pill, thalidomide was later found helpful in alleviating morning sickness in pregnant women. In the late 1950s, with little advance testing of harmful side effects, a German pharmaceutical company began a worldwide campaign to promote thalidomide's use as a safe, nonprescription sedative. Companies in Britain, Australia, Canada, and the United States also began to consider selling the drug.

Early on, several doctors became concerned because some patients taking thalidomide developed inflammation in the nerves of the hands and feet (neuralgia). Dr. William McBride (1961, 1977), an obstetrician in Sydney, Australia, also noted four cases of a rare, severe birth malformation in his hospital. These newborns suffered from phocomelia (from the Greek words meaning "seal limb"), in which the hands, feet, fingers, or toes were attached directly to the torso, with no arms or legs. Dr. McBride subsequently discovered that in each case the mother had taken thalidomide during the first few weeks of pregnancy. A few months later, Dr. Widakund Lenz (1961; prodded by a father of a thalidomide child, Karl Schulte-Hillen) found that many cases of the rarely occurring phocomelia had occurred throughout Germany (Taussig, 1962). Both physicians tried to get companies in their respective countries to withdraw the drug from the market, but their attempts were initially unsuccessful.

Owing to the good sense and integrity of Dr. Frances Kelsey of the Federal Drug Administration, few thalidomide births occurred in the United States. As the officer charged with approving the general sale of the drug in this country, Dr. Kelsey delayed approval until its safety could be more thoroughly evaluated. Her concern was that the U.S. distributor had not been forthright in its claims to have adequately tested the drug. During the application process, she also read preliminary British reports that the drug caused neuralgia in some recipients. Despite many months of intense pressure from the company's physicians, she continued to withhold her agency's approval (Fine, 1972).

Thalidomide's manufacturers, who originally discounted reports of its devastating effects, were eventually forced to withdraw the drug from the market in late 1961. Worldwide, more than 8,000 thalidomide children had been born – the largest number of cases of poisoning in utero ever recorded (Insight Team of the Sunday *Times* of London, 1979).

Later studies of children exposed to thalidomide also showed that motor skills – while helpful – are not necessary for development. In a study of 5- to 9-year-old children exposed to thalidomide, Pringle and Fiddes (1970) found that, on average, children with more severe motor impairments showed lower IQ scores and lower levels of academic achievement. Of equal or even greater importance, however, was the environment in which the child developed. Children whose environments were labeled "most favorable" performed much better both intellectually and academically than children in less favorable environments.

Another study examined a single child who was born with no arms or legs and who thus had none of the motor experience thought important by Piaget and others. When this child was introduced at 2½ years to prosthetic devices that allowed him to manipulate the environment, Kopp and Shaperman (1973) examined the child with IQ tests and Uzgiris–Hunt subtests. Like Decarie's (1969) children, Kopp and Shaperman's child was able to perform a variety of sensorimotor tasks and his language development was normal. From studies of children exposed to thalidomide and from Kopp and Shaperman's report, it appears that motor experiences are not necessary for the development of sensorimotor skills.

Sequences and Rates

As in other disabilities, recent studies have examined whether children with motor impairments traverse the same sequences of development as nondisabled children. In a study of 89 infants with cerebral palsy, Cione, Paolicelli, Sordi, and Vinter (1993) examined sensorimotor functioning on six domains using Dunst's (1980) adaptation of the Uzgiris–Hunt Ordinal Scales of Infant Development (Uzgiris & Hunt, 1975).

Using this measure, Cione et al. (1993) discovered several interesting aspects of early development in these children. First, while most of the children exhibited an overall delay in development, some areas seemed more delayed than others. As might be expected given the children's general lack of experience in manipulating objects, object permanence abilities were the most seriously delayed, as were the children's abilities to imitate vocally and gesturally and to use objects symbolically (e.g., to use a toy cup to "drink"). Less impaired was the children's understanding that other people cause events to occur. Though these children were delayed – and children with greater delays in one area tended to be more delayed in all areas – such delays were not uniform.

In addition, Cione et al. (1993) found that children with different degrees of motor impairment differed in their cognitive abilities. Like many children with cerebral palsy, more than 60% (54 of 89) were also born prematurely (by an average of 8 weeks). Within the sample, however, diplegic children (i.e., whose legs were more impaired than their arms) performed at higher levels than did children with quadriplegia (involving all four limbs). Although not surprising, this finding may indicate that manipulating objects speeds development during infancy.

In every area, development occurred sequentially. The degree of sequentiality was noted in two ways. First, older children performed more higher-level tasks than did younger children. Second, if a child performed a higher-level task at a particular session, that child also showed evidence of having achieved most lower-level tasks (Cione et al., 1993). While these two methods provide imperfect estimates of sequential development (Weisz et al., 1982), they do suggest that children with cerebral palsy develop along the normal sequences found in nondisabled children.

Although rarely examined, older children with cerebral palsy (and other motor impairments) also seem to develop along the usual sequences. Lister, Leach, and Udberg (1991) found that children with cerebral palsy demonstrated the same order of development in their conservation of quantity, a classic Piagetian task.

A related issue involves the rates of development for these children. For young children without disabilities, infant tests given before 12 months bear only weak relations to IQ scores when the child is 4 or 5 years old (correlations from about .20 to .35); correlations from infancy to later childhood or adulthood are essentially 0 (Vernon, 1979). In contrast, children with motor impairments develop at relatively steady rates over time. Even infants who score higher on the Uzgiris–Hunt scales at 12 months score higher at 18 months (Cione et al., 1993). Similarly, early test scores of mixed disabled populations – including children with cerebral palsy – predict later test scores for most young children, usually in the range of .60 to .80 when testing is performed when the child is 1 to 3 years old and then again a few years later (Bernheimer & Keogh, 1988; Maisto & German, 1986). Even at later ages, children with cerebral palsy (the most frequently studied group) display IQ scores that remain relatively stable throughout childhood (for a review see Burack et al., 1988).

Cross-Domain Relations

Cross-domain relations differ radically among children with different types of motor impairment. Children with cerebral palsy are relatively even in their intellectual abilities. Such evenness may occur as early as infancy. In one study, Uzgiris-Hunt subscales were factor-analyzed, and only two distinct types of intelligence emerged, one related to vocal imitation, the other to all other domains (Cione et al., 1993). In contrast, nondisabled infants possess several relatively separate domains of intelligence.

For children with cerebral palsy, intellectual evenness also occurs at later ages. In comparing language development in three groups of 3-year-old children – those with cerebral palsy (who were also premature), those with similar brain injuries but without cerebral palsy, and those without disabilities – Feldman, Janosky, Scher, and Wareham (1994) found that the groups were equivalent on various measures of grammar and vocabulary. Children with cerebral palsy displayed similar levels of linguistic and cognitive functioning. Similar levels from one domain to another are also found when one examines subdomains from IQ and other cognitive tests (Cruickshank, 1976).

In contrast, cross-domain discrepancies are the rule in spina bifida. Most salient here is the heightened verbal versus performance IQs of some of these children. At first glance, they seem highly verbal, which goes along with an interactive style that has been called "disinhibited" and "overly friendly."

Over the years, these children's hyperverbal behavior has come to be called the "cocktail party syndrome" (Tew, 1979). Although difficult to define exactly, this syndrome describes children who are hyperverbal, engaging in incessant, clearly articulated language. Though their language at first seems highly developed, it is actually superficial and often contains clichés (e.g., "My sense of direction flew out the window"; Hurley, 1993). In addition, many of their statements are irrelevant; these children seem to have a need to speak about anything that comes into their heads, and do so.

Although the cocktail party syndrome often occurs in spina bifida, it is more frequently related to spina bifida's co-occurring condition, hydrocephalus – which is caused by a variety of conditions (Hurley, Dorman, Laatsch, Bell, & D'Avignon, 1990). Further, this constellation of behaviors occurs most often in children with hydrocephalus who are mentally retarded. Cocktail party syndrome may also be related to these children's difficulties in maintaining attention on a single task and in focusing solely on relevant information (Horn, Lorch, Lorch, & Culatta, 1985). Attention-deficit disorder may also be more common in cocktail party children with spina bifida–hydrocephalus (Barkley, 1990).

At present, we do not know why children with spina bifida and hydrocephalus – or hydrocephalus alone – exhibit the cocktail party syndrome. A frontal lobe dysfunction may partially explain these children's attention problems, poor planning and organizational skills, and memory deficits (Snow et al., 1994). It is even less clear why these children are hyperverbal. Indeed, children with Williams syndrome, a genetic disorder of mental retardation (see Tables 3.1 and 3.3), have also been described as engaging in "cocktail party speech" (Udwin & Yule, 1990). The connections – if any – between Williams syndrome and hydrocephalus remain unknown.

For now, we can say only that cross-domain organization differs based on the child's type of motor impairment. Children with cerebral palsy display even, across-the-board functioning from one domain to another. Children with spina bifida–hydrocephalus do not, instead often showing heightened, though not always appropriate, verbal abilities. As in mental retardation, future research will undoubtedly focus on the extent to which these discrepancies occur, how they develop, and which brain structures seem implicated.

Contextual Issues

Mother–Child Interactions

As in the other disabilities described in this book, the behavior of mothers of children with motor impairments is both similar to and different from that of mothers of nondisabled children. Both groups seem similar in their MLUs and in the structural aspects of language, but different in their interactive styles. One study compared the mothers of four groups of 8- to 36-month-old infants: those with mental retardation; mental retardation plus cerebral palsy; MA matches; and CA matches (Hanzlik & Stevenson, 1986). Mothers of both disabled groups provided more commands to their children. Mothers of children with cerebral palsy, in particular, also touched their children more often. Children with cerebral palsy were more compliant, spent less time playing independently, and touched their mothers more often than children in the other groups.

One important issue in these interactions appears to be the perceptions of the mother. In an early study, Kogan, Tyler, and Turner (1974) noted that, over a 3-year period of early intervention, mothers of children with cerebral palsy also displayed increasingly less positive affect toward their children, in both therapy and play settings. Kogan et al. (1974) attributed this change to the mothers' decreasing optimism about their children's motor advances as the children got older; indeed, positive affect decreased least among mothers whose children began to walk independently over the 3-year period. At later ages, mothers of children with cerebral palsy show more concern that their children will achieve motor as opposed to communicative milestones, unlike mothers of children with Down syndrome, who are concerned about both (Hodapp, Dykens, Evans, & Merighi, 1992).

Because children with cerebral palsy seem more compliant and less independent than nondisabled children, several studies have begun examining mastery, defined as the child's need and pleasure in solving difficult tasks. Blasco, Hrncir, and Blasco (1990), for example, note that maternal involvement in interactions seems to foster development in infants with cerebral palsy. Ultimately, children with more involved mothers show more mastery and higher-level play. Even at later ages, motivation seems particularly important for children with motor impairments. In a study of two groups of 6- to 12-year-olds, Landry, Robinson, Copeland, and Garner (1993) found that children with spina bifida (but with normal IQs) showed lower-level play with toys and had parents who perceived their cognitive competencies to be lower than they actually were. Despite their low-level play, the children who were most physically impaired felt themselves equal in physical abilities to nondisabled agemates, whereas their parents were more accurate in their assessments of their children's physical disabilities. Motivation, mastery, and parental perceptions and behaviors, then, play an important role in the development of children with motor impairments.

Familial Reactions

Although families of children with motor impairments are thought to experience more stress than families of nondisabled agemates, this does not always appear to be the case. In a study that carefully matched parents of 5- to 15-year-old spina bifida children to families of children without disabilities, no differences were apparent in familial, parental, marital, or other measures (Spaulding & Morgan, 1986). The spina bifida group, however, was not retarded, and all families were headed by two parents who lived at home. Still, most of the children were highly impaired physically, and the research was carefully performed with standardized measures.

As with other disabilities, individual-differences work may ultimately prove more illuminating than work on group differences. Specifically, characteristics of the child and the family, as well as the quantity and quality of services available, influence the family's predisposition toward stress. McCormick, Charney, and Stemmler (1986) examined 201 children with spina bifida. Families reported that the most stressful aspect of raising these children was not the spina bifida per se, but concomitant functional disabilities such as the children's inability to take part in physical activities, or to walk, go to the toilet, bathe, dress, or play independently. The more associated disabilities the child had, the greater was the stress that the family experienced. Family demographics was also a determinant of stress level: Single-parent families, families in which the parents were not married, and relatively poor families, as well as those headed by a mother with a low level of education, experienced greater stress levels.

Finally, the need for specialized services also creates stress. Like children with severe and profound mental retardation (see Chapter 4), children with spina bifida often require special services and devices. Particularly stressful to parents was having to pay for braces, catheters, physical therapy, orthopedic or special shoes, crutches, and wheelchairs.

Some things help families to raise a child with motor impairments, particularly the mother's social support system and a positive outlook or style of coping. In a study examining families of children with several kinds of motor impairments, Wallander et al. (1989) found that the mother's social environment significantly predicted both her mental health and her social functioning. Other studies have focused more narrowly on families of children with spina bifida. Large social support networks, a significant proportion of family members within that network, and satisfaction with the perceived support were found to lead to better psychological adjustment for the mother (Barakat & Linney, 1992). High-quality marital support and a family environment that is not controlling may also be beneficial to the mother's emotional health (Kronenberger & Thompson, 1992).

According to Lazarus and Folkman's (1984) model of stress, appraisal, and coping, mothers of children with illness or disabilities can act in one of two ways. They can gather information, rely on religion, think positively, use social supports, and make realistic plans for the child's future. Conversely, they can deny the child's disability, withdraw from others, hope for a miracle cure, or blame others. Mothers of children with spina bifida rate themselves as having more psychological problems if they adopt this second, avoidant pattern of adjustment (Barakat & Linney, 1995).

Conclusion

Though motor impairments have been the subject of fewer developmental studies than other disabilities, some important work has begun. Such work is hampered by potential differences in development among children with different types of motor impairments and by the difficulties of examining these children. Nonetheless, both the organismic and contextual features of this work are of interest and fit well within the developmental perspective described in this book.

That children with motor impairments develop along sequences similar to those predicted by Piaget and others has been amply demonstrated during these children's early years. And, while fewer studies have been performed on sequential development during later childhood, these studies show developmental sequences that are identical to those traversed by nondisabled children.

Cross-domain relations depend on the type of motor impairment. Whereas children with cerebral palsy exhibit even or flat developmental profiles from one domain to another, children with spina bifida–hydrocephaly demonstrate better – and at times unusual – abilities in language. These children show the "cocktail party syndrome" and exhibit wide discrepancies across linguistic domains. How such discrepancies develop over time, what brain structures are involved, and what precisely are these children's strengths and weaknesses all constitute provocative questions for future research.

Several studies have shown that mothers of children with motor impairments differ stylistically from mothers of nondisabled children. Family work is increasingly taking a stress-coping perspective toward families of children with motor impairments. Like studies of other disabilities, these studies examine the relations between stress and support and the individual characteristics of the children and their parents.

Though important developmental work has begun on children with motor impairments, many critical gaps are also apparent. Few studies exist of the sequences or cross-domain relations of children who are older, except for those focused solely on children with spina bifida–hydrocephalus. Similarly, little work has been done on mother–child interactions (particularly after the toddler years), and family work is sporadic, with no studies yet examining siblings and many other aspects of family functioning.

We are left, then, with a population about which a great deal remains to be known. With increasing attention to these issues – and with greater attention to the child's type of motor impairment – future work promises to be more specific, precise, and informative. Such work should provide greater insights for both theory and intervention.

Part III

Implications and Applications

8

General Lessons

One could summarize the studies in Part II in a variety of ways. For example, one could judge the sheer quantity of developmental work on each of the disorders. Simply by comparing the lengths of the various chapters, one might conclude that much developmental work has been done on mental retardation, a fair amount on deafness and some aspects of blindness, less on motor impairments. Assessments of the quality of work in each field, though more subjective, would probably be similar.

In this chapter we evaluate these studies in a different way – by gleaning three lessons that are common to all four disability conditions discussed in this book. These general, multidisability lessons will, it is hoped, benefit the reader interested in only one of the four disability groups as much as the "multidisability" researcher or practitioner. In addition, these three lessons should lead toward a more elaborate developmental approach to childhood disabilities that transcends any individual condition.

Lesson 1: Similarities and Differences Mark Comparisons between the Development of Children with and without Disabilities

To some, this first lesson might seem obvious. The skeptical reader is excused for saying, "*Of course* children with and without disabilities show similarities and differences in their development."

Children with retardation develop more slowly than nondisabled children. Children with sensory or motor impairments do not have fully developed hearing, sight, or motor skills. Yet certain similarities (e.g., in the sequence of development) also exist.

Although it seems obvious, historically this issue is much more complex. Particularly in mental retardation, various researchers have been quick to note differences in development between children with and without retardation and to conclude that the developmental approach to mental retardation is unsupported, outmoded, or simply wrong (for a review see Hodapp & Zigler, 1996). But when developmental approaches are considered in a larger, more theoretical sense, we find that examining children with disabilities through the lens of normal development has many advantages. This does not mean, of course, that all developments of children with disabilities will be identical to those of nondisabled children; indeed, advocates of developmental approaches are particularly interested in differences that distinguish the two groups. Moreover, such differences tell us about normal developmental processes, a subject to which we return later in this chapter.

On the basis of a broader developmental perspective, we can make the following general statements about all four disabilities.

Sequences of Development are Similar

Since Piaget, development has generally been considered an orderly, sequential process. The development of children with mental retardation, deafness, blindness, and motor impairments generally follows the same sequences as does that of nondisabled children.

Similar sequences exist even in cases where they might not be expected – for example, in language acquisition. Deaf children acquire early language in the same general sequence as hearing children, even though they are learning signs or "babble" with their hands (Newport & Ashbrook, 1977). Similarly, the mistakes deaf children make while learning to sign are analogous to those hearing children make while acquiring spoken language. Recall Petitto's (1987) findings that deaf children reverse the seemingly iconic signs YOU and I in American Sign Language, just as same-age hearing children reverse the words *you* and *I* in speech (Chapter 6).

The similarities in developmental sequences between disabled and nondisabled children are impressive.

Structures of Development are Often Different

Children with disabilities show pronounced differences in developmental level from one domain to the next. This is demonstrated by the profound strengths or weaknesses in the language of children with mental retardation (e.g., Curtiss, 1977; Yamada, 1990); the higher-than-expected linguistic abilities of children with Williams syndrome (Bellugi et al., 1994); the superior cognitive performance of nonlinguistic deaf children (cf., Paul & Quigley, 1994); the delays in spatial abilities, locomotion, and Stage VI object permanence versus the normal development of vocabulary in blind children (Bigelow, 1990; Rodgers & Puchalski, 1988); and the marked linguistic abilities of children with spina bifida–hydrocephalus (even given their linguistic peculiarities) versus the poorer development of nonlinguistic skills. Although other children exhibit differences in development from one domain to another, children with disabilities often show cross-domain strengths and weaknesses to an exaggerated degree.

Though these differences become apparent in comparisons between disabled and nondisabled children and between children with different types of disabilities, the most interesting differences occur within a single disability group. Children with Williams syndrome have linguistic strengths that are not shared by children with Down syndrome or (presumably) children with other types of retardation (Bellugi et al., 1994). Boys with fragile X syndrome display relative weaknesses in sequential processing that are not observed in children with Down syndrome (Hodapp, Leckman, Dykens, Sparrow, Zelinsky, & Ort, 1992; see Table 3.3). So too do children with different types of motor impairments differ greatly in their cognitive-linguistic profiles. Children with cerebral palsy exhibit few distinguishing strengths and weaknesses, whereas children with spina bifida–hydrocephalus have heightened language abilities and relatively weak skills in visuospatial and abstract reasoning (Hurley et al., 1990).

Maternal Input Levels Are Similar, Styles Differ

In many respects, interactions between mothers and their children with disabilities are similar to those between mothers and nondisabled children. Mothers of children with Down syndrome (and with mixed etiologies of retardation) speak in short sentences, repeat key words, use exaggerated pronunciation and a high-pitched voice, and generally engage in the same "motherese" employed by mothers of nondisabled children at the same levels of language (Rondal, 1977). Similarly, deaf mothers hold a sign longer for their deaf infants than for deaf adults (Masataka, 1992), repeat a single sign as many as 12 times (Launer, 1982), and use a high proportion of one-sign sentences in communicating with their deaf infants (Harris et al., 1989). Mothers of children who are blind or motor-impaired also use motherese (Anderson et al., 1984; Moore & McConachie, 1994), although this has been documented by fewer studies. In all disabilities, mothers perform adaptations similar to those used by mothers speaking with their nondisabled children.

Yet there are differences in the interactions of these mothers. Mothers of children with disabilities seem much more didactic and intrusive than are mothers of nondisabled children. Mothers of children with retardation provide more commands and direct the interactions than do mothers of nonretarded children; these mothers often clash with – or speak at the same time as – their children (Vietze et al., 1978). Mothers of children who are deaf more often than mothers of hearing children touch and visually monitor their children; they also maintain a positive emotional tone (Erting et al., 1990; Maestas y Moores, 1980). Mothers of children who are blind give more commands than do mothers of sighted children (Kekelis & Anderson, 1984). Mothers of children with cerebral palsy give more commands and touch their children more often than do mothers of nondisabled children (Hanzlik & Stevenson, 1986).

The reasons for such stylistic differences are not clear. Mothers of children with disabilities may be acting out of their desire to teach their children. Indeed, Mahoney (1988) has developed an intervention to help these mothers become less didactic, to instead let the child lead and direct the interaction. Underlying this "mother-centered" view is the idea that the mothers' responses may be partly due to their own emotional goals, needs, and expectations (Hodapp, 1988).

But their responses are also based on the child's personal characteristics. Young children with Down syndrome are more lethargic and "floppy" than nonretarded MA-matched children (Cicchetti & Sroufe, 1976). Similarly, children who are deaf may require mothers who engage in more physical and visual contact and who provide a more emotional, upbeat interactive style. Because babies who are blind are often more passive than sighted infants (Rowland, 1983), much of the input provided by their mothers – for example, labels for common objects – may help them understand their surroundings. In the same way, children with cerebral palsy are often less active and more compliant than nondisabled children (Hanzlik & Stevenson, 1986). It thus remains unclear whether any aspects of maternal behavior should be considered correct or incorrect given the needs of the child, the mother, or both.

Interactive Principles Are Similar, Implementations Differ

Most mothers try to communicate with their child, engage in playful interactions, and foster their child's development, regardless of whether the child is disabled, even regardless of the child's particular disability.

Mothers differ, however, in the way they achieve these goals. Mothers of children with retardation, blindness, or motor impairments all shorten their sentences, and repeat and exaggerate words. Mothers of deaf children acquiring sign language shorten the length of their signed sentences and repeat these manual signs. They also exaggerate the size of signs and make the signs in places – for example, over objects – where the child can more easily observe them.

Sometimes, these mothers change the shape of the sign slightly to help the infant comprehend it; recall, for example, that the MOTHER sign that some mothers use for their young children differs from the sign used with adults (Erting, 1990). Mothers of children who are blind modulate their voices and touch their children to keep them engaged in interaction (Als et al., 1980a, 1980b); these mothers often foster interaction with simple, playful, and repeated routines and games (Urwin, 1978).

In these various ways, mothers help their children develop. Studies of children with Down syndrome (Harris et al., 1996), children who are deaf (Spencer et al., 1992), and children who are blind (Dote-Kwan, 1995) suggest that the child benefits when the mother follows the child's focus of attention, commenting on objects and events about which the child is already interested. Such joint participation, which, as we have seen, is achieved in slightly different ways in different disability conditions, is essential to good communication.

Lesson 2: Within-Disability Differences Are Important

Like other works on children with disabilities, this book is divided by disability type. We are accustomed to thinking this way, to considering as similar all children with a particular disability. However, like children without disabilities, no two children with the same disability are alike. Within-disability differences have surfaced in each of the four disabilities discussed in this book. We discuss each in turn.

Mental Retardation

In mental retardation, the issue revolves around the difference between "level-of-impairment" and "etiology-based" research (Hodapp & Dykens, 1994). To summarize from Chapter 3, many researchers – including most psychologists and special educators – divide groups by the child's degree of intellectual impairment. In contrast, etiology-based researchers, who are often more biomedically oriented, examine separately children with Down syndrome, fragile X syndrome, Williams syndrome, and Prader–Willi syndrome.

As in all within-disability debates, the issue concerns the best way to categorize children with mental retardation. Developmentally oriented workers are increasingly realizing that what matters most is the type of retardation – its exact cause or etiology. Children with Williams syndrome appear to have higher levels of language relative to overall intelligence, regardless of their level of intelligence (Bellugi et al., 1994). Children with fragile X syndrome show sequential processing deficits relative to their levels of simultaneous processing and achievement (Hodapp, Leckman, Dykens, Sparrow, Zelinsky, & Ort, 1992). In the same way, children with different types of retardation are at risk for different types of maladaptive behavior: overeating and obsessive-compulsive behavior in Prader–Willi syndrome, anxiety in Williams syndrome, and gaze avoidance and social problems in fragile X syndrome (Dykens & Hodapp, 1997).

But not every aspect of behavior in every syndrome is unique. For example, sequential processing deficits exist in children with both Prader–Willi syndrome and with fragile X syndrome (Dykens et al., 1992; Hodapp, Leckman, Dykins, Sparrow, Zelinsly, & Ort, 1992). Nonetheless, although subtle qualitative differences may occur from one syndrome to another (Dykens, 1995), particular strengths and weaknesses, trajectories, and maladaptive behaviors may be similar in two or more syndromes (called "partial specificity"; Hodapp, 1997a).

Deafness

This book focuses on deaf children who are acquiring American Sign Language rather than on children with milder hearing impairments who are acquiring speech or some other manual system. Here, several within-disability characteristics are important. Etiology exerts an indirect influence on children's development. For example, children whose deafness was caused by rubella have more developmental difficulties than do children who are deaf from other causes (Freeman et al. 1975), but such difficulties seem due as much to other problems associated with rubella – visual, mental, and emotional – as to rubella per se. While one could say that etiology affects the development of deaf children, its influence appears to be due to disabilities often associated with a specific cause of deafness.

Another important within-disability characteristic is the amount of language – be it sign or hearing – possessed by the child who is deaf. Deaf children with higher levels of language perform better on high-level cognitive tasks than do deaf children with lower language skills (cf., Greenberg & Kushe, 1989). Besides calling into question Furth's (1966) findings of cognition without language, these studies show the importance of language for cognition and other achievements.

The language of children who are deaf develops best when their parents are ASL signers who are deaf. These children develop language from their earliest years, in a natural way. Mothers who are deaf are more adept than hearing mothers at signing close to the object that both they and their deaf infant are looking at. These mothers sometimes change the shape, size, and orientation of the sign. In addition, mothers who are deaf interact sequentially with their deaf child, making their signed comments only when the child is looking toward them. All of these modifications would seem to be performed more naturally by mothers who are themselves deaf.

Blindness

Although certain differences among children who are blind have been hypothesized to be related to different etiologies, these results seem secondary to other associated problems. To date, the two causes of blindness that may cause developmental changes are retinopathy of prematurity (ROP), which results from too much oxygen in prenatal intensive care incubators, and retinoblastoma, a progressive tumor of the eye. Although occasional reports suggest differences in the IQs of these children and those of the larger blind population, such etiologically based differences have generally not been supported (Warren, 1994). Any additional difficulties these children may experience seem due to associated conditions such as mental retardation (often caused by the prematurity of ROP children). As in deafness, the real issue here involves associated impairments, most commonly hearing problems or mental retardation, which may slow development.

Even a small amount of vision helps children to develop. Indeed, one of the difficulties in performing studies on young children who are blind or visually impaired is ascertaining how much vision the child has. In addition, some children's vision may improve as they develop. Recall Cass et al.'s (1994) study comparing children who were totally blind, those whose vision improved as they developed, and those who continued to have a small amount of useful vision throughout the study. Whereas none of the children who were partially sighted or whose sight improved over time exhibited regressions, almost a third of the children who were totally blind showed areas in which they regressed as they got older. Most frequently, such regressions involved sensorimotor abilities or the ability to produce or comprehend language.

Motor Impairments

Individual differences in children with motor impairments are due both to the motor difficulties themselves and to their causes. In children with cerebral palsy (Cione et al., 1993) and in those exposed to thalidomide in utero (Pringle & Fiddes, 1970), the degree of impairment is related to cognitive abilities. But this association may be more due to the amount and quality of the child's motor experiences than to either cerebral palsy or thalidomide per se. Though motor experiences may not constitute a necessary condition for early cognitive development, children with motor impairments seem to develop at a faster rate when they have both a stimulating environment and the physical capacity to interact with their environments.

Different etiologies lead to different profiles of intellectual abilities. Most striking here are the marked discrepancies between the linguistic and nonlinguistic abilities of children with spina bifida–hydrocephalus. These children, with their "cocktail party speech," may not always have an in-depth understanding of their language, but they still show a marked linguistic strength.

Contextual Issues

In considering individual differences so far, we have focused on the children themselves. But another, more contextual sense of individual differences involves parents and families. As one might expect, children affect their families and vice versa.

Here, we adopt the Double ABCX model, which operates differently in different disorders. Examining the A term, we note that certain aspects of the child's personality affect parental and familial stress. The parents and families of individuals with Down syndrome – both children and adults – generally experience less stress and receive more support than do the parents and families of children with other types of retardation (see Table 4.1). It is not entirely clear why this is so, but these children, as a group, may possess a more engaging personality and enjoy relative freedom from many forms of psychopathology (Dykens, 1996). Conversely, other children may possess characteristics that lead to more parental and familial stress; for example, the overeating, obsessive behaviors, and stubbornness of children with Prader–Willi syndrome increase familial stress (Hodapp et al., 1997), and heavy caretaking demands cause stress in parents of young children with mental retardation (Beckman, 1983).

Examining the C factor, or the family's perceptions of the child, we note that in both mental retardation and deafness, familial stress may be heightened by the delay or uncertainty of diagnosis. Mothers of children for whom the cause of mental retardation is unknown experience more stress than do those of children with known etiologies (Goldberg, Marcovitch, MacGregor, & Lojkasek, 1986). Parents of infants who are deaf must endure a 1- to 2-year wait from the time they suspect something is wrong until they finally receive definitive diagnosis (Freeman et al., 1975).

In addition, most studies of parental and familial stress examine deaf children of hearing parents. To these parents, raising a child who is deaf constitutes a crisis. But parents within Deaf culture might not even consider the birth of a child who is deaf unusual (Padden & Humphries, 1988). Such is the power of parental and familial perceptions, as well as the cultural and subcultural contexts in which these perceptions occur.

In all of these ways, within-disability differences are important. It is clear that children, their parents, and families are not all the same. Even children with the same disability differ – a consideration that is often overlooked.

Lesson 3: Children with Disabilities Are Guides to Understanding Typical Development

So far, we have examined sequences, structures, rates, and regressions in children with disabilities, as well as mother–child interactions and family dynamics. We now turn the focus around, to examine what these findings tell us about typical developmental processes.

This is historically referred to as using "natural experiments." In a natural experiment, an existing event or condition sheds light on larger processes of interest to the researcher. Such events and conditions are unusual, or at least different from those observed in the researcher's everyday work. They are examined to discover what general lessons might be learned about functioning in general (Hodapp & Burack, 1990).

Such experiments occur in a variety of fields. Consider a famous, possibly apocryphal, example. Many years ago, the architect Frank Lloyd Wright designed and built a supposedly earthquake-proof hotel in Japan. A few years later, Japan suffered a devastating earthquake, with much destruction and loss of life. Naturally curious as to what had happened to "his" hotel, Wright was heartened to receive, by telegraph, the news: "Your building still stands." As a result of the information architects have gathered over the years, builders now know which structural characteristics help keep buildings standing when the earth shakes. Box 8.1 lists other well-known natural experiments.

Developmental psychologists have long used natural experiments to tell us about typical developmental processes. For example, they have examined Native American tribes who tightly swaddle their young infants to determine how the lack of early motor practice influences the infant's crawling and walking (Dennis, 1973). R. A. Spitz's (1945) famous study of infants institutionalized from birth shows the effects of maternal deprivation on children's later lives.

When considering natural experiments, developmentalists integrate data from three sources. The first consists of findings or the development of children in Western, industrialized societies, often White, middle-class children. Though limited to a few groups in a few societies, such studies represent an important first step. Especially concerning cognitive, linguistic, or otherwise organismic developments, such studies provide detailed clues as to the operation of typical developmental processes.

The second source consists of cross-cultural studies. Although the experiences of children vary tremendously from one culture to another, if certain commonalities in development persist among those cultures, one begins to suspect that such developments are universal. In a sense, comparing children from diverse cultures provides an "environmental" type of natural experiment.

The third source of data consists of findings on children with disabilities. In most such studies, the children have generally been Western and middle class. The question becomes how robust a particular development is in the face of the child's problems. Given mental retardation, deafness, blindness, or motor impairments, will a specific skill develop along the same sequence? Can we see various strengths and weaknesses? Do particular environments – especially those that have been shown to help typically developing children in both Western and non-Western cultures – also help these children? In short, in what ways is development the same and in what ways is it different in children with various disabilities? Most important, what do similarities *and* differences signify for our understanding of typical developmental processes?

Box 8.1. *Some famous natural experiments*

Elimination of Scurvy

For centuries, sailors at sea suffered from scurvy, a debilitating disease featuring bleeding around the teeth, gum, and bones and into the joints. First by accident and then by means of an early "experiment," British sailors discovered that eating limes prevented them from getting scurvy. We now know that vitamin C prevents scurvy; parenthetically, this is also why the British have historically – and derogatorily – been called "Limeys" (Carpenter, 1986; Cuppage, 1994).

The Voyage of the Beagle *and Darwin's Theory of Evolution*

As naturalist aboard the *Beagle* on its voyage around the world, Charles Darwin observed various natural phenomena. By observing volcanoes and finding bones of sea creatures high in the Andean mountains, Darwin realized that the earth's surface changes over time. From close observation of finches on the Galápagos Islands, he realized that species change from generation to generation due to local environmental variations. These observations led Darwin to his theory of natural selection (Barlow, 1958; Weiner, 1994).

Persistence of Beliefs in the Face of Contradictory Evidence

Various cults have prophesied that the world will end on a certain date. Researchers studied one such cult that held an elaborate belief system. When the world did not end on the specified day, cult members did not discount their prior beliefs; instead, they maintained them, now claiming that the world had been saved by the cult's warning (Festinger, Riecken, & Schachter, 1956).

Genetics of Huntington's Disease

Huntington's disease is a lethal hereditary disorder that first strikes during young adulthood. Folk singer Woody Guthrie was among its best-known victims. Capitalizing on the high prevalence of the disorder in three Venezuelan villages, Nancy Wexler, a psychologist who had the disease in her own family, helped discover the disorder's genetic causes. Using the genetic test she helped develop, Wexler discovered that she herself will not die an early death from Huntington's disease (Young et al., 1986; Wexler et al., 1987).

These studies, among the most exciting in the disabilities field, lead to the tentative conclusions outlined in the following sections.

Certain Developmental Sequences Are "Hard-Wired"

On the basis of data from research on children with disabilities as well as cross-cultural research, it has been concluded that all children develop early cognitive or language skills in the same sequences. This idea that early development is channeled in one and only one direction has been referred to as "canalization" (Scarr-Salapatek, 1975; see also McCall, 1982). Canalization may be based on the evolutionary necessity of acquiring such early skills. In order for human infants to survive, it may be essential for early development to follow a single path.

Sequential development occurs in children with retardation, deafness, blindness, and motor impairments. Though it applies mainly to the earliest developments (Hodapp, 1990), sequentiality is important. These examples demonstrate the power of canalization, the "hard-wired" nature of development during the earliest years.

Grammar is a Modular Domain

Over the past few decades, researchers have debated whether children develop at close to the same rates in all areas, or whether one or another domain develops separately from others – in a modular way.

The best examples of developmental modularity occur in children with disabilities. In mental retardation, Genie, Françoise, and Laura showed that individual children can have grammatical abilities that are markedly higher or lower than their skill levels in other areas (see Table 3.4). In Williams syndrome, an entire group of children have relatively intact grammatical abilities (Bellugi et al., 1994). In short, grammar may be modular, in that it develops separately from the child's other abilities.

Just as children with disabilities corroborate Fodor's (1983) logical argument that grammar is a separate, encapsulated system, these children may also show which sets of skills constitute a single domain of development. In a recent study, older French children with Williams syndrome had difficulty acquiring French grammatical gender agreement (Karmiloff-Smith, Grant, Berthoud, Bouthors, & Stevens, 1994). Since not all areas of grammar are equally intact in children with Williams syndrome, grammar itself may be composed of several, reasonably independent skills. We may have underestimated just how modular the human mind is.

A Sensitive Period Exists for Grammatical Development

From the mid-1960s, Eric Lenneberg (1967) hypothesized the existence of a critical age for language development, which ended at or around puberty. If the child had not acquired any language by this time, he or she would never do so. Adults learning a second language after puberty were hypothesized never to become as fluent as they were in their native tongue.

Although this hypothesis has been discussed for more than 30 years, children with disabilities provide new tests of the critical-age hypothesis. From observations of Genie (Curtiss, 1977) and from Newport's (1990) examinations of deaf adults who learned language at different ages during childhood, we can conclude that a critical age – or at least a sensitive period – for language acquisition does exist. Genie, for example, was unable to acquire language (i.e., grammar) after the pubertal years. But evidence from adults who are deaf illustrates that the critical age might have a more gradual onset than was originally supposed. Specifically, subjects who learned ASL during their earliest years performed better on certain language tasks (mainly, subtle morphological markers) than did those who first acquired sign at age 4 to 6. These adults, in turn, performed better still than those who acquired sign after age 12.

In addition, the critical age applies only to certain aspects of language. Genie developed the meanings of words and sentences (i.e., semantics) and used language correctly (pragmatics); only in grammar did she show little or no progress in the years after she was introduced to language (Curtiss, 1977; Rymer, 1993). In addition, neuropsychological tests showed that Genie had developed her language in the right (as opposed to the left) hemisphere; in cases in which young right-handed children have been exposed to language during the early years, language is almost never localized in the right hemisphere.

The ending of this sensitive period thus seems to herald a gradual "hardening" of the language centers in the brain; by puberty, these centers may no longer be as open for grammatical input. Although some grammatical development may occur after puberty, it is much slower and harder to achieve than grammatical development during the prepubertal years.

Maternal Modifications Promote Early Development

Children with disabilities illustrate how development proceeds even with the loss of certain abilities or modalities. As such, these children constitute what might be considered an organismic natural experiment, one that demonstrates the strong tendency for the organism to develop even in the face of an organic problem. But these children may also highlight the influence of environmental factors. For example, if children with different disabilities benefit from specific environmental inputs, we might speculate that these inputs are helpful, maybe even necessary, for development in general. Though not as direct a natural experiment for environmental as for organismic effects, we still learn something from the environments of children with disabilities.

The main conclusion is that specific maternal behaviors may help children to develop. Studies in mental retardation (Harris et al., 1996), deafness (Spencer et al., 1992), and blindness (Urwin, 1978) all point to the importance of the mother's and the child's joint attention to a single object or event, and of the mother's commenting on that object rather than calling the child's attention to a different object. Young children may be unable to concentrate on two things at once, to both comprehend the mother's sentence and change their focus of attention.

Such findings would seem to argue for the necessity of maternal input for children's early development. But among researchers who examine input language to nondisabled children, no such consensus exists. Whereas earlier researchers pointed out that specific maternal inputs exist in all cultures and societies (Ferguson, 1978), more recent workers question their necessity (Schieffelin & Ochs, 1986). These researchers note the Western bias of such views, and argue that different cultures socialize children differently.

Still, some input – from parents, siblings, relatives, or others – may help children to develop in every culture. Input may come in different ways: In Western countries, the mother or other caregiver speaks directly to the child; in other cultures, caretaking siblings may communicate with the child through games, rhymes, or sayings (Ochs, 1986). While the specifics may differ, it seems likely that all children – disabled or nondisabled, in industrialized or nonindustrialized cultures – benefit from certain interactions with others in their environment. What remains unknown is how widely these interactions vary, how and when they occur, and how children of certain ages (or developmental levels) benefit.

In reviewing natural experiments, then, we see that children with disabilities are at the center of many developmental debates. The modularity issue, for example, continues to be informed by observations of children with Williams syndrome, as well as by individual cases such as those of Genie, Laura, and Françoise. In addition, from the hand babbling of Petitto and Marentette's (1991) deaf infants we are discovering that language is not synonymous with speech, but that language may be amodal, expressed either orally or manually. From Newport's (1990) studies of adult deaf signers and from Curtiss's (1977) studies of Genie, we are discovering the timing and operation of the sensitive period for language. In adult–child interactions, we are learning that adult input may be helpful – though maybe not necessary – for children's later cognitive and linguistic development.

A Multidisability Developmental Approach

This chapter's general lessons point to the single conclusion that developmental issues are similar across these four disabilities. Sequences of development are identical across the four groups; pronounced strengths and weaknesses occur in each; and similar or at least analogous interactions promote development in children with each disability. In addition, individual differences play out similarly, though not identically, across the four conditions, and each can shed light on certain aspects of typical development.

Such similarities attest to the importance of more unified developmental approaches to children with disabilities. Granted, differences exist from one disability to another. Etiology, for example, seems more significant in mental retardation, cultural considerations more significant in deafness. Multiple impairments seem more important in blindness and motor impairments, less critical (or less often discussed) in deafness and mental retardation.

A larger, more comprehensive approach to these four disabilities is also in line with the larger field of developmental psychopathology. Over the past 20 years, some developmental workers have attempted to fuse typical developmental studies with fields associated with children with psychopathology. In many ways foreshadowed by developmental work on children with disabilities throughout this century (see Chapter 2), the field of developmental psychopathology uses the findings, approaches, and theories used in examining typically developing children to help us understand children with emotional and behavioral problems (Achenbach, 1974; Cicchetti, 1984, 1990). Featuring a relatively new, thriving journal (*Development and Psychopathology*) and interested researchers from several disciplines, developmental psychopathology takes an explicitly developmental approach to conceptualizing and intervening with children with psychopathology.

Many different disciplines and levels of analysis will be involved in developmental work with children with disabilities. In this book, we have drawn on findings from Western and cross-cultural developmental psychology, from genetics (etiologies of mental retardation), and from interactional and family studies. In short, a full-fledged developmental approach will require work in all these areas to flesh out both organismic and contextual developmental issues for children with disabilities.

Although this chapter presents the theoretical side of developmental approaches to children with disabilities, these approaches are not just intellectual enterprises. Indeed, the studies on the four disabilities also have practical implications. It is to these more practical considerations – guidelines for intervention and therapy with children and work with families – to which we now turn.

9

Toward Better Interventions

In discussing children with mental retardation, deafness, blindness, and motor impairments, the focus in this book has been on developmental theory and basic research findings. Sequences, cross-domain relations, rates, and regressions have been described, as have contextual issues – usually relating to families. The history of developmental approaches, as well as themes and new theoretical issues (e.g., natural experiments), have also been discussed.

Though the details of development are important for theory, they also suggest how one can intervene with children with disabilities. Sequences and cross-domain relations – or even family reactions and perceptions – serve as a baseline for intervention efforts. The more we know about the basic development of children with disabilities, the more we can help these children. The more we know about family perceptions and reactions, the more we can help these families to cope.

Few would disagree with this. But we can now go much further, to describe the interventions most likely to be successful for children with various types of disabilities and their families. We may even be in a position to describe effective interventions for children with different forms of a single disability. In mental retardation, for example, different interventions have been proposed for children with different genetic etiologies (Gibson, 1991; Hodapp & Dykens, 1991). Indeed, as we learn more about the most important aspects of the child and environment in each of the four disabilities, we will be able to design increasingly fine-grained, sophisticated programs of intervention.

As in prior discussions, this chapter focuses on both organismic and contextual issues. Here, however, the two terms will be given slightly different meanings. All interventions involve both the child and the environment; all are in some sense both organismic and contextual. In this chapter, then, interventions that focus primarily on the child and the child's functioning will be considered organismic. The two organismic interventions are educational interventions designed to foster children's cognitive-linguistic development and psychotherapeutic interventions to manage maladaptive behavior and psychopathology. The main contextual issues to be examined concern the supports necessary for families of children with disabilities.

Noncategorical Approaches

Before describing intervention issues that arise from developmental findings, we need to concern ourselves with noncategorical approaches. Such approaches consider together children with various forms of disabilities (Rowitz, 1988). Though used in many fields, noncategorical approaches are most often applied in special education. In both intervention and research, special education often groups children with various disabilities or groups various causes of single disabilities like mental retardation.

Although noncategorical approaches may ultimately prove less helpful than more specifically targeted interventions, its proponents' concerns are important. Advocates of noncategorical programming worry about labeling itself. They feel that once a child is labeled as having a disability, that child suffers. Classmates, teachers, and maybe even parents treat these children differently than other children. In addition, many labels – especially mental retardation and learning disabilities – have been applied disproportionately to poor and minority children as opposed to middle-class, White children, suggesting a biased diagnostic-labeling process. Finally, these professionals worry about the "self-fulfilling prophecy," the tendency of children to conform to the expectations of others. If teachers or parents expect little from a child with a disability, the child may perform poorly (for a review see Schwenn, Rotatori, & Fox, 1991).

In response, others note that professionals need labels to communicate with one another. In addition, children with a single diagnostic label often behave similarly, allowing for both research and intervention that might meet the needs of a certain category of child. Further, most federal and state laws demand that children be diagnosed: without a diagnostic label, the child is unable to qualify for a variety of special services. Overall, many professionals – even if they do not especially like the idea of labeling – consider labels and differential diagnoses to be necessary for intervention and research purposes.

This controversy has taken a recent twist. Forness and Kavale (1994) have expressed dismay about the proliferation of diagnostic categories in special education. Using as examples attention-deficit disorder, traumatic brain injury, fetal alcohol syndrome, prenatal substance abuse, and fragile X syndrome, they question the need for such fine-grained diagnoses in special education. They point to the administrative and practical problems arising when many disabilities receive separate labels and, frequently, distinct administrative categories. As time goes by, children in many of these categories may be placed in individual, specialized classrooms.

Besides discussing the administrative problems inherent in designing special programs for children with distinct diagnostic labels, Forness and Kavale (1994) note the behavioral similarities of children across their five sample diagnoses. Given the large degree of behavioral overlap, they argue that separate labels are unnecessary for education and that separate programs will ultimately not aid such children. They conclude that one must avoid the "Balkanization" of special education services, the proliferation of special education categories and labels that may not benefit the child, their schools, or even research.

Although such concerns are important, this chapter takes a different tack. Rather than special education policy or administration, the focus here is on more effective interventions for children within a single diagnostic category. Thus, children with different types of mental retardation, or motor impairments, or some other disability are considered to benefit from different approaches to special education, not from different categories per se. The goal is not to make the administration of special education programs more difficult by the proliferation of countless separate programs; indeed, many of these techniques can be used in programs ranging from special, segregated classes to fully inclusive classrooms.

Approaches focusing on children with different types of disabilities may be gaining favor among parents and special educators. We have been amazed, for example, at how supportive parents and teachers have been of our research on the behavioral development of children with various genetic disorders of mental retardation. In the past few years alone, more than 350 special educators and group home staff members attended a conference entitled "Genetics in the Classroom"; a mental retardation research conference (the Gatlinburg conference) was entitled "Genetics and Disabilities"; a newly founded quarterly publication, *genetworks* (Finucane, 1995), has met with widespread teacher and parent interest; and parent and teacher booklets have been published to aid in the intervention of children with several genetic disorders of mental retardation. Instead of decrying specialization, most teachers and parents welcome more information about children with specific disabilities. They hope that more programs of intervention can be tailored to the needs of children with many different disabilities as well as children having a common disability with different etiologies.

The point is that specificity may be beneficial. As shown in later sections, the child's personal characteristics might suggest particular interventions in several disabilities. But the goal is not to Balkanize special education, therapy, or family work.

Organismic Issues

Education

As already noted, the special education field has increasingly followed a noncategorical approach to intervention, grouping together children with different disabilities. But children with the four disabilities discussed in this book may require specific types and modes of intervention. For example, children who are deaf require visual input, and children who are blind require oral or tactile input. Other, more general issues that arise in intervention work will be discussed in the subsections that follow.

Using Strengths to Overcome Weaknesses. Most children exhibit certain strengths and weaknesses. In general, effective special education services have capitalized on children's strengths as opposed to their weaknesses. To take only the most obvious example, most professionals would agree that children who are deaf can learn ASL more easily than they can learn to speak and lip-read. The concern has always been that these children acquire some system of language. Although language may not be a necessary condition for higher-level thought, deaf children who possess higher-level linguistic skills (sign or oral) generally do better on reading and other academic tasks than children with lesser skills (Greenberg & Kushe, 1989). Leaders in the Deaf community note that the deaf child who, failing at oral methods, cannot adequately speak and lip-read has neither culture nor language; this child is essentially caught between two worlds, inhabiting neither.

For children with other disabilities, too, interventions are tailored to the child's strengths and weaknesses. Children with spina bifida–hydrocephalus are often friendly, verbose, and excessively "linguistic." On close inspection these children are often found to incorrectly assign words to objects, to show poor abstract thinking, to have visuoperceptual problems, and to exhibit a general inability to attend to the relevant dimensions of objects. As a result, testing and intervention are difficult (Hurley, 1993). In considering how to teach such children abstract concepts, Culatta (1993) notes the importance of presenting many, varied examples, exaggerating the defining characteristics of a particular concept, and providing real-world examples. For example, to test a child's understanding of a word like *first,* the teacher might lay out an array of objects and ask the child to "give me the block last and the pen first." In this way, the child is forced to learn the meaning of the word, rather than relying on word order or other, subtle cues. Children with cerebral palsy may not need as many "context-free" assessments as these children.

Similarly, there has been much discussion of how best to educate children with various types of mental retardation. Table 9.1 offers some tips for the education of children with fragile X syndrome,

Table 9.1. *Educational interventions for children with different types of mental retardation*

Salient characteristics	Suggested educational intervention
Fragile X syndrome	
Gaze avoidance	Minimize visual and auditory distractors
Perseveration	Emphasize individual vs. team tasks
Attentional problems	Deemphasize short-term memory
Depression (girls)	Reduce flow of people through school or work setting
Shyness	Emphasize contextual learning and sight-word reading
Social anxieties	Deemphasize child's making eye contact when speaking
Hyperactivity	
Low self-esteem (girls)	
Williams syndrome	
Hyperactivity	Deemphasize perceptual-motor tasks
Attentional problems	Emphasize team tasks
Overfamilarity	Provide schedule of upcoming events
Hyperacusis	Emphasize social skills and people-oriented tasks
Visuospatial deficits	Use language skills to teach concepts
Language strengths	Provide warning before predictable noises (hourly bells)
Engaging personality	
Difficulty modulating emotions	
Anxiety about upcoming events	
Prader–Willi syndrome	
Food seeking	Restrict food access and promote exercise
Temper tantrums	Provide extra support during transitions
Food preoccupations	Deemphasize short-term memory
Skin picking	Provide consistent behavioral limits at school and home
Stubbornness	Use contextual teaching strategies
Depression	
Nonfood obsessions-compulsions	

Information from Dykens and Hodapp (1997: Tables 1, 2, and 3); Levine (1994); and Spiridgliozzi et al. (1995a, 1995b).

Prader–Willi syndrome, and Williams syndrome. For example, in both fragile X syndrome and Prader–Willi syndrome, children perform more poorly on sequential than on simultaneous processing. In addition, both groups of children show reasonably good memories for facts, vocabulary, and general information (Dykens et al., Leckman, 1987; Dykens et al., 1992). As a result, M. L. Braden (1989) has proposed the use of the LOGOS reading method for children (especially boys) with fragile X syndrome. LOGOS matches words with symbols; the hexagonal, red stop sign is used to teach the word *stop,* and common signs for gas stations, road directions, and restaurants are used to teach the respective words. Because of their relative strengths in simultaneous processing, boys with fragile X syndrome should be better able to read using this "whole word" reading method than by sounding out letters in phonetically based systems. This is a good example of numerous approaches that make use of the child's strengths.

The hyperacusis – or extremely sensitive hearing – of children with Williams syndrome necessitates a small, quiet classroom, while these children's heightened linguistic and social skills may require the use of linguistic teaching methods. Given these children's very poor visuospatial skills, language might even be used to teach shapes, directions, or geography (see Levine, 1994). In contrast, such language-centered methods of instruction would seem counterproductive for children with most other types of mental retardation, particularly Down syndrome (Fowler, 1990).

Many of these educational recommendations seem obvious. It seems obvious, for example, that one should not allow a child with Prader–Willi syndrome free access to food (Dykens & Cassidy, 1996; Levine & Wharton, 1993); similarly, one should not try to make eye contact with boys with fragile X syndrome (Spiridgliozzi et al., 1995a, 1995b). Still, anecdotes abound of the failure of school personnel to consider the etiology of the child's retardation. For example, even after prolonged discussion about the role of food in Prader–Willi syndrome, the administrators of one school allowed a child with that syndrome to become a lunchroom monitor. Predictably, this girl gained even more weight. Following their common sense, school personnel often consider eye contact to be a communication goal for children with fragile X syndrome; for these children, however, eye contact increases tension and anxiety, and may even lead to more tantrums or self-injurious behavior.

Etiology-based interventions sometimes seem counterintuitive. It may seem strange to witness a conversation between a teacher who is looking directly at a boy with fragile X syndrome, while the boy is looking away and only occasionally glancing at the teacher, usually when the teacher looks away (Cohen, Vietze, Sudhalter, Jenkins, & Brown, 1991). It may even seem inhumane to limit the access of a child with Prader–Willi syndrome to food. And yet such practices may be beneficial. Several professionals working with individuals with Prader–Willi syndrome have recommended that schools, group homes, and other service systems be allowed to restrict access to food and, in many cases, access to money to buy it (Dykens et al., 1997). These professionals note that complications from obesity continue to be the primary cause of death among children and adults with this disorder (Hanchett et al., in press). What may seem a violation of the client's rights to self-determination and choice is, in the case of Prader–Willi syndrome, a protection against the life-threatening behaviors that characterize this disorder.

Combining General Principles and Disability-Specific Modifications to Achieve Fine-Grained Interventions. Developmental approaches do not assume that all development is the same in children with different disability conditions. Children with retardation develop more slowly than children with other disabilities; those with sensorimotor conditions use modalities to acquire information and experiment with their worlds that differ from the modalities used by other children with disabilities.

But some aspects of development – most notably, sequences in many areas – are the same across children with different disabilities as well as children without disabilities. Strengths and weaknesses in development can be found from one disability to another and even within the same disability.

This interplay between developmental similarities and differences shows itself clearly in the practice of early intervention. All young children, regardless of their disability, benefit from sensitive interactions with surrounding adults. For instance, all children benefit from language that is tailored to their needs. But the term "tailored to their needs" differs widely from one disability to the next. In the cases of mental retardation and motor impairments, such tailoring involves using language that is appropriate for the child's language age, that is delivered slowly, and in which key words are repeated. In the case of deafness, deaf mothers of infants who are deaf slow down their signed input and shorten and repeat signed utterances. They also physically enlarge their signs and even change the orientation of the sign so that the child can more easily observe the mother's handshape (Erting et al., 1990).

Concerning the focus of conversation, in all four disabilities it is best to follow the child's lead, to focus on the child's object of attention. In each case, however, mothers use different strategies to achieve this goal. In mental retardation, the mother follows the child's lead by simultaneously commenting on whatever has captured the child's attention. In deafness, the mother holds off on her signed comments and waits until the child has looked at the object or observed the event and then looked back at her. In blindness, the mother requests and describes the child's actions, relies on well-known routines, and comments about events that are occurring in the environment.

Across these four disabilities, then, though the goals of intervention are similar, the behaviors that parents and interventionists adopt to achieve them vary. Behaving in unique ways to achieve the same goal makes intervention both a science and an art: a science because these techniques are based on research, an art because they require careful, often counterintuitive behaviors on the part of the adult interactor.

Management of Maladaptive Behaviors

Since maladaptive behaviors often constitute an important associated handicap for many children with disabilities, therapeutic issues deserve our attention. But the very assessment of psychopathology is extremely difficult in these children. No valid scales exist for measuring maladaptive behavior and psychopathology in children who are deaf or blind. Children with mental retardation often cannot describe their feelings or thoughts. In addition, children with many of these disorders often have other, associated problems, experiences, and living situations. Is a young deaf child with an emotional or behavioral disorder troubled because that child is deaf, because the child has difficulty communicating with his or her parents or peers, or because of some other, associated central nervous system problem? Similar questions arise in relation to each disability.

Across all these conditions, two general findings emerge. First, there are higher rates of childhood psychopathology among these children than among nondisabled children. Second, certain features of either the children themselves or their environments predispose some children to psychopathology.

Mental Retardation. Researchers in the mental retardation field have probably paid the most attention to psychiatric problems (Bregman, 1991). In contrast to 30 years ago, when persons with retardation were thought to rarely suffer from emotional disorders, an entire subspecialty has now arisen to examine persons who are dually diagnosed with both retardation and emotional-behavioral problems (e.g., Matson & Frame, 1986). A general consensus exists that persons with mental retardation show psychopathology more often than do nonretarded populations.

Even this statement, however, must remain tentative due to the many problems of measuring psychopathology in mentally retarded populations. Most prominently, the communication of persons with mental retardation is often less advanced than that of nondisabled people. As a result, it becomes difficult to determine their mood, thoughts, and other information needed to make psychiatric diagnoses. In addition, many forms of psychopathology, including depression, involve feelings of despair, hopelessness, and low self-esteem – these are higher-level concepts that persons with mental retardation may not possess. Many mental health professionals may also hold a bias against diagnosing psychopathology in such persons, preferring instead to attribute their emotional-behavioral problems to mental retardation (Reiss, Levitan, & Szyskzo, 1982).

Despite these difficulties, the prevalence of psychiatric disorders is higher in populations with retardation than in those without. Depending on how a given study was performed, from 10–20% to 70–80% of persons with retardation have been considered to have psychiatric impairments (Borthwick-Duffy, 1994). In general, the lower figures (10–20%) come from reviews of the medical records of a large number of persons with retardation; the higher figures reflect persons already referred for psychiatric evaluations.

Several correlates of psychopathology have been noted. Although the prevalence of psychopathology is similar in males and females, the types of pathology may differ by gender. In a study of young adults with retardation during the postschool period, Koller, Richardson, Katz, and McLaren (1983) found that antisocial behavior was more prevalent in boys, whereas emotional disturbance was more common in girls. Similarly, the child's degree of disability may affect the amount and type of psychopathology. In a study of persons served by the California Department of Developmental Services, Borthwick-Duffy and Eyman (1990) found that 16% of those with mild mental retardation had an additional psychiatric diagnosis, whereas only 5.7% of persons with severe and profound mental retardation received such a diagnosis. In addition, children and adults with mild retardation may be more prone to depression than those with more severe retardation, while those with more severe mental retardation may be more likely to show severe stereotypical behaviors, various psychotic disorders (e.g., autism, schizophrenia), and hyperactivity-conduct disorders (Borthwick-Duffy, 1994).

Various types of mental retardation also seem prone to different types of psychopathology. Both males and females with fragile X syndrome exhibit shyness, gaze avoidance, and hyperactivity-attentional problems (Dykens, Hodapp, & Leckman, 1994). In Prader–Willi syndrome, food preoccupations and various obsessive-compulsive disorders are prominent (Dykens, Leckman, & Cassidy, 1996), whereas in Williams syndrome, social disinhibition, overfamiliarity, and anxiety are common. As a result, children with different disorders may require different therapeutic interventions. A verbal therapy that may work well for a person with

Williams syndrome will be less effective for a boy or girl with frag-ile X syndrome. The preoccupations with food and the obsessive behaviors seen in Prader–Willi syndrome seem different from the problems found in any other mental retardation condition. In short, different types of mental retardation make children and adults prone to different types of emotional-behavioral problems – any specific therapy that is successfully applied to one type may not be effective for another (Dykens & Hodapp, 1997).

Deafness. From 15% to 60% of all deaf and hearing-impaired chil-dren exhibit some kind of emotional-behavioral disorder. Al-though, as this range of percentages shows, rates vary enormously from study to study, Hindley and Brown (1994) conclude that the prevalence of psychiatric disorders in children who are deaf or hearing-impaired is from 2.5 to 3 times that seen in populations of hearing children. The degree of hearing impairment does not appear to be associated with the type or prevalence of psy-chopathology, and conduct and anxiety disorders seem most com-mon (for a review see Hindley, 1997).

Why such disorders arise is a difficult question. Schlesinger and Meadow (1972) have suggested that many children are frustrated by their inability to communicate with others. In addition, some studies (Fundudis et al., 1979) find a higher prevalence of disorders among children attending residential schools for the deaf; others do not (Hindley, Hill, McGuigan, & Kitson, 1994). Finally, children whose deafness is due to congenital rubella show greater impulsiv-ity and more attention difficulties, and the rates of autism – or of autistic-like symptoms – among these children may similarly be ele-vated (Chess, Korn & Fernandez, 1971; Desmond et al., 1978).

Although emotional problems are very common in children who are deaf, few systematic attempts at therapy have been undertaken. While four institutes in the United States (in New York, Chicago, Washington, D.C., and San Francisco) have treated deaf adults for more than 30 years, no U.S. psychiatric hospital currently has an inpatient unit for the treatment of deaf children (Moores, 1996). The psychiatric problems of children who are deaf have not, how-ever, gone totally unaddressed. Schlesinger (1978) has adapted

Erikson's early stages to promote healthy psychosocial development in these children, and more recently Greenberg and Kushe (1993) have instituted a school curriculum called PATHS, Promoting Alternative Thinking Strategies (Kushe & Greenberg, 1993). The PATHS program facilitates the deaf child's development of self-control, emotional understanding, and social problem solving. Consisting of 130 lessons, this curriculum is being used in North America and in several European countries.

Blindness. The prevalence of psychopathology is also extremely high among children who are blind. In the sole study of this issue, Jan et al. (1977) found that children who were blind and partially sighted showed high percentages of moderate or severe psychiatric impairments. Twenty-nine percent of these children were reported by their mothers to be suffering from emotional and behavioral problems. The problems ran the gamut of diagnostic categories; although mental retardation and developmental disorders accounted for a large portion of them (33.7% of the sample), there were also emotional-behavioral problems, including adjustment reaction (10.5%), personality disorder (8.1%), behavior disorder (7.0%), and organic brain syndrome (5.8%).

Several factors are associated with psychopathology in children who are blind or visually impaired. Whereas 30% of children with no additional abilities exhibit emotional-behavioral problems, 62.5% of multiply disabled blind children have emotional and behavioral problems (Jan et al., 1977). Many more of these children had also been given psychotropic medication, most commonly tranquilizers and anticonvulsants.

In addition to multiple disabilities, another factor concerns the etiology of blindness. Children with retinopathy of prematurity seem particularly prone to severe emotional problems. Most researchers agree that these children show more autistic-like symptoms (and, at times, full-blown autism) than children with other types of blindness (for reviews, see Hindley & Brown, 1994; Warren, 1994). It remains unclear why this is the case; prematurity, central nervous system damage, and sensory or emotional deprivation have been suggested over the years.

Motor Impairments. As in blind children, psychopathology in children with motor impairments stems more from associated problems than from the motor impairments per se. One such problem is the growing realization on the part of motor-impaired children that their disabilities are not transient. From about 10 to 14 years of age, children with cerebral palsy realize that they will be impaired throughout their lives (Minde, 1977). Adolescents with spina bifida become increasingly sensitive about their decreased feeling and lack of control of bladder and bowel movements (Hayden, Davenport, & Campbell, 1979).

Another problem concerns etiology. A large percentage of children with spina bifida are thought to have hyperactivity and attentional disorders (Wills, 1993). Such disorders may also occur to some degree in children with cerebral palsy (Alexander & Bauer, 1988). These may be related to impaired executive functioning (usually due to structural or functional problems in the prefrontal cortex). Indeed, children with spina bifida–hydrocephalus may behave like children with what have been called "nonverbal learning disabilities." Educational, therapeutic, and occupational guidelines have been proposed by Watson (1991) and others. Table 9.2 summarizes the major findings for each of the four disability conditions.

Contextual Issues

Children's educational and psychiatric problems do not occur in isolation. Parents, siblings, and families as a whole influence and are influenced by the child with disabilities. Many families of children with disabilities need help and support over the childhood years.

Before describing such support, however, it is necessary to point out that parents of children with disabilities are, at heart, parents raising children. Like all parents, parents of children with disabilities must provide for their child's physical and emotional well-being. Though often forgotten, this simple fact is important, because all children need to be cared for and given love, stimulation, and guidance throughout childhood.

Table 9.2. *Therapy issues in deafness, blindness, motor impairments, and mental retardation*

Deafness
High percentage of conduct and anxiety disorders
Frustration over inability to communicate with others
Importance of developing self-control and emotional understanding
PATHS program to promote healthy psychosocial development

Blindness
High percentage of associated psychopathology (mental retardation, adjustment reactions, personality and behavior disorders)
Extremely high prevalence of pathology in children with multiple handicaps
Predisposition to autism or autistic-like behaviors caused by retinopathy of prematurity

Motor impairments
Realization (from age 10 to 14) that motor disabilities are permanent
Adolescent sensitivity to bladder-control problems
High prevalence of hyperactivity-attentional problems in spina bifida–hydrocephalus

Mental retardation
More pathology in mild than in severe or profound mental retardation
Difficult measurement problems and possible diagnostic overshadowing
Ties to different genetic etiologies (see Table 9.1)

But providing even such basic requirements as food, protection, and shelter becomes more difficult when the child has a disability. Recall Birenbaum and Cohen's (1993) finding of the increased costs of parenting a child with severe and multiple impairments. The costs of shunts, specialized gear, medical care, and other supportive services are often borne by the parents themselves. Recognizing this situation, many states provide cash subsidies to families of children with disabilities; as of 1988, 20 states offered families such cash assistance (Agosta, 1989).

Support for Families of Children with Any Disability

Many needs seem common to families of all children with disabilities, and many of these needs revolve around attaining services for the children and themselves. In the United States, Part H of Public Law 99-457 – the Education of the Handicapped Amendments of 1986 – calls for an Individualized Family Service Plan (IFSP) as a component of the country's early intervention services. This plan involves a "statement of family strengths and needs relating to enhancing the development of the family's handicapped infant or toddler" (Healy, Keesee, & Smith, 1989; see also Krauss & Hauser-Cram, 1992). The family system is thereby acknowledged as important – even critical – for the provision of services during the preschool years. In Norway, Sweden, and Denmark, family-based training is provided for families of children with many low-incidence conditions. In Norway, the entire family (including the child with disabilities) is brought to a school outside of Oslo for a two-week period. There, the family receives information about the child's disability, intervention techniques, and local, regional, and national services.

Different programs and agencies approach early intervention services differently, and with different goals. In some programs, interventions focus on the child (Bricker & Veltman, 1990), while in others, they focus on the caregiver, usually the mother (Seitz & Provence, 1990). In others, the mother–child interaction is of concern (Bromwich, 1990; Mahoney, 1988), while in still others, family issues are given priority (Simeonsson & Bailey, 1990). Even within programs with the same focus, goals can vary widely. For example, some programs that focus on the mother emphasize developmental guidance, others treat the mother as a therapist, and still others promote the mother's becoming a good teacher to her child (Seitz & Provence, 1990). It thus remains unclear who should be the focus of early intervention, how such intervention should be performed, and with what goals (Meisels & Shonkoff, 1990).

Given these differences in professional practices, parents often feel bewildered by the child's needs and how to meet them. Consider the plight of a typical family upon the birth of a baby with a disability. Like most people, the members of this family have probably had little experience with developmental disabilities. Friends, relatives, and even the family physician know little about what services are needed or are available, how these services will be paid for, and how one finds out about them. Further, in the United States, the types of services – and who provides them – differ for children of different ages.

Table 9.3 provides an overview of the services necessary for children and their families at three age periods. Obviously, these services will depend on the nature of the child's disability, the family's needs, and the child's age. But at every period, a full range of services is available. The major problem concerns how families obtain services that are appropriate to the child and the family.

Obviously, a key ingredient of successful family coping is information – information about the child's disability, available services, and the many agencies serving children with disabilities and their families. First, information about the child's disability can best be obtained through national organizations, local and regional hospitals (often in pediatric, genetics, and genetics counseling services), and books, pamphlets, and other materials. Many of these information services have gone on-line, in Internet and World Wide Web listings and discussion groups.

Second, in the United States, Britain, and most Western countries, large but little-known systems of services exist, and these systems can also be fragmented and difficult to negotiate. In the United States, medical services are performed in hospitals and are sometimes paid for by state or federal subsidies.

Third, intervention services are under the aegis of a state agency (a different lead agency in each state) during the infancy and toddler years, then under the aegis of the local community's school system when the child reaches age 3 (until age 21). During the school years, camps and recreational or other activities are often run by private agencies based either locally or nationally but with local chapters (e.g., Special Olympics). In the postschool years, residential and work services are coordinated and paid for by each state's department of developmental disabilities (sometimes titled differently), though the programs are often contracted out to private group home or supervised apartment providers and private-sector employers and agencies.

Even with this information, families may still require help in advocating for their child. Consider, for example, the seemingly straightforward issue of obtaining special education services for a

Table 9.3. *Service needs and resources for families of children at different ages*

	Needs	Resources
Ages 0–3 years		
Child	Evaluation: physical, motor, cognitive, linguistic, social-emotional Early intervention services	Multidisciplinary evaluation, which results in an Individualized Family Service Plan (IFSP), with child and family receiving either center- or home-based early intervention services for set amount of hours per week
Mother	Emotional support Caretaking behaviors	Support groups by disability, region, and etiology – see Appendix Part of early intervention evaluation, intervention, and IFSP
Family	Support Financial assistance Information	Support groups Depending on problem, state developmental disabilities or insurance payment for some services Hospitals, agencies, groups
Ages 3–21 years		
Child	Evaluation, Referral, and Individualized Educational Program (IEP)	School system: involves legal process of evaluation and placement (notification, hearings, appeals if necessary); information on "transition" to adult services as child nears age 21 (and school services end)
Family	Information Financial assistance Support	Local and national groups State departments in some states Including respite care, camps, art (Very Special Arts) or athletic activities (Special Olympics), scholarships for adolescents with some disabilities (deafness, blindness)

Table 9.3 *(cont.)*

	Needs	Resources
Above 21 years		
Offspring	Residential services Work	Both run by state developmental disability departments (parents and offspring have major say concerning whether residential or work placements are appropriate)
Family	Support Information Guardianship issues	Continuation of many of the services provided during the school years Particularly for individuals with severe disabilities, provisions for residential and work status after parents can no longer serve as offspring's legal guardians

school-age child with a disability. In the United States, these services are guaranteed through Public Law 94-142, the Education for All Handicapped Children Act of 1975 (later replaced by the IDEA, or the Individuals with Disabilities Act of 1990). PL 94-142 and IDEA institute what is essentially a legal process. This process provides notice that the child is being considered for special services; a formal, scheduled hearing at which the parent(s) and school personnel discuss the most appropriate school placement and specialized services; the right to present a defense if parents disagree with school personnel; a written statement given to the parents notifying them of the school's decision; and the parents' right to appeal this decision, first to the school itself, then to district and state educational authorities, and eventually to the courts (see Hallahan & Kauffman, 1994). The process results in an Individualized Educational Program (or plan), called an IEP, which assesses the child's academic performance, suggests annual goals, provides instructional objectives, describes services the child will receive, and includes starting dates of services and when and how the child's progress will be reevaluated (Smith, 1989). In short, obtaining services for one's child can sometimes be complicated, bureaucratic, and contentious.

Support for Families of Children with Specific Disabilities

An additional group of issues is related to the child's type of disability. Besides generic, nonspecialized services, families often require specialized services that cater to the child's disability or its etiology.

As noted in earlier chapters, family issues vary widely from one disability to another and, in some cases, even within a single disability (Hodapp, 1995). The many cultural issues facing families of deaf children, for example, are unique to them: Obviously, the situation in which the hearing sibling acts as a translator for two deaf, ASL parents is specific to these families. Families of children with other disabilities confront their own problems. The rarity of blindness makes it difficult for the parents of children who are blind to find other parents who have had similar experiences. And paying for braces, physical therapy, wheelchairs, and other devices, as well as attending to the practicalities of coordinating the procedures the child must undergo, are problems faced mainly by families of children with motor impairments. Etiologically based problems – which stem from the differences between spina bifida–hydrocephalus and cerebral palsy and among the different types of mental retardation – are confronted by families of children with motor impairments and mental retardation, respectively.

Unfortunately, services that are targeted to the child's specific disability often fall outside the usual, noncategorical service delivery systems. Especially in the case of children with low-incidence conditions like blindness or deafness, local public schools are often ill-prepared to provide specialized services or equipment, particularly in rural areas. Educational services must often be performed either by itinerant teachers (often used in blindness) or through larger, regional schools that serve several adjoining or neighboring towns.

However, more and more special services are being established for children with a variety of disabilities and their families. For example, special "clinics" are currently being set up in large, university-based teaching hospitals, often those with influential programs in pediatrics, genetics, or clinical genetics. Such clinics provide specialized medical care, psychiatric interventions, and information about special schools, group homes, or other services that might be needed by families with children with specific disabilities (e.g., motor impairments) or specific types of a single disability (e.g., Prader–Willi syndrome or fragile X syndrome). Some of these services can also be obtained through mental retardation research centers, UAPs (University Affiliated Programs), or UAFs (University Affiliated Facilities), most of which are partially or totally funded by the federal government. Although changes in federal and insurance funding may mean that fewer such clinics and centers will exist in the future, they are at present an important resource for parents of children with disabilities. Parents, teachers, or other interested individuals can usually determine the location of specialized service clinics, schools, camps, or group homes by contacting the national groups listed in the Appendix.

Conclusion

Of all the issues discussed so far, educational, therapeutic, and family interventions are the ones that most concern children with disabilities and their families. Many services exist in the United States, Britain, and most industrialized countries, although the number of services available and their quality vary depending on the disability. The question remains how good these services are, who delivers and pays for them, and how families learn about and obtain them for their child.

Intervention for children with developmental disabilities is hampered by two theoretically based practices. The first, already mentioned, is the movement toward noncategorical programming. Teachers, therapists, and other interventionists need to pay greater attention to the evidence, albeit preliminary, that interventions can be aided by becoming more specialized, targeted, and focused.

Especially within the field of special education, it is time to go beyond thinking that "one size fits all."

From the other direction, researchers need to intersect more with interventionists. It remains unproven, for example, that children with different disabilities (or with different types of a single disability) are aided by more specialized intervention practices. As of today, few studies have directly compared the efficacy of one versus another type of educational or therapeutic practice. More, and better, research is needed in order to intervene most effectively with children with disabilities and their families.

10
Evaluating Developmental Approaches

At the beginning of Developmental Psychopathology, Thomas Achenbach (1974) noted, "This book is about a field that hardly exists" (p. 3). This statement applies equally to developmental approaches to children with disabilities. Some aspects of development have been examined in several disabilities, but major gaps remain. Some developmental theories and research methods have been employed with children with disabilities, but both could be applied more effectively and more frequently to these populations.

This book therefore concludes by assessing the current state of affairs in developmental research on children with disabilities. We then examine what major issues remain to be addressed and how to address them. Although it is always risky to assess where we are now, where we need to be, and how we can get there, it is hoped that this exercise will highlight some of the future issues in developmental approaches to children with the four disability conditions discussed in this book.

Where We Are Now: Current Issues

Two issues stand out here. The first concerns developmental approaches themselves, the second the quantity and quality of developmentally oriented work. Although in many ways the two are connected, it is helpful to examine them separately.

Status of Formal Developmental Approaches

No formal developmental approaches exist in any disability other than mental retardation. Few professionals have written in a general way about development in children who are deaf, blind, or motor-impaired (although see V. Lewis, 1987). Granted, many researchers have examined specific aspects of development in children with each disorder – language development in children who are deaf or blind, sensorimotor development in children who are blind or motor-impaired. And a few researchers have applied the similar-sequence hypothesis and other developmental ideas to children with motor impairments and other disabilities (e.g., Lister et al., 1991). This book is the first attempt to examine in one place the development of children with several disability conditions using a formally applied developmental approach.

Why do we need formal developmental approaches to children with disabilities? To answer this question, we rely on the history of developmental approaches in mental retardation. By articulating his ideas about similar sequences and structures in mental retardation, Zigler has helped to foster research on the development of these children in a variety of domains (Hodapp, 1997a). It seems unlikely that our understanding of development in children with retardation would be nearly as extensive in the absence of such a formal developmental perspective.

In a similar way, such workers as Cicchetti, Achenbach, Rutter, and Sroufe have found it helpful to incorporate in their studies the emerging field of developmental psychopathology. Again, many researchers have examined the course, causes, and correlates of children's psychopathology, but until recently no formal field has combined a specifically developmental perspective with childhood psychopathology. With its growing influence, however, developmental psychopathology offers new research opportunities and new ways of thinking about old problems (Cicchetti, 1993). The thriving journal Development and Psychopathology (begun in 1989), several handbooks (Cicchetti & Cohen, 1995; Lewis & Miller, 1990), and special journal issues devoted to the subject all attest to the importance of clearly stating what developmental psychopathology is and how it differs from its component fields. It is hoped, as well, that interest might increase in response to this book's description of a developmental approach to children with disabilities.

Quantity and Quality of Existing Work

In line with mental retardation's explicit, formally described developmental approach, a great deal of sophisticated research exists in that field. Work on deafness – though not as abundant – is also of high quality, possibly because many of the leading researchers (Bellugi, Pettito, Newport) are developmental psycholinguists examining deaf children's acquisition of American Sign Language. Much less work has been carried out on blindness and motor impairments.

Notable as well is the coverage of developmental work in each disorder. In all disabilities, the child's earliest achievements have been extensively documented. Other developmental periods have been studied to differing degrees in each disorder. In mental retardation, even noncognitive areas have received attention, including the development of self-image (Silon & Harter, 1985) and of morality (Kahn, 1985; Mahaney & Stephens, 1974), as well as the emotional development of children with Down syndrome (e.g., Kasari, Mundy, Yirmiya, & Sigman, 1990). In deafness, researchers have intensively examined children's development of ASL; in blindness, their spatial abilities and language using visual metaphors (Warren, 1994); and in motor impairments, the language characteristics of children with spina bifida–hydrocephalus versus those of children with cerebral palsy.

Contextual studies are also similar across disorders in certain respects, even as they are disability-specific in others. In all four disabilities, interactions have been examined between young children and their mothers. The amount of family work, however, varies greatly from one disability to the next. Extensive family work has been performed in mental retardation and, to some extent, in motor impairments. In contrast, family research is just beginning in deafness and is almost nonexistent in blindness.

Table 10.1. *Developmental work in the four disabilities*

Type of study	Mental retardation	Deafness	Blindness	Motor impairments
Early cognitive	3	2	2	2
Later cognitive	2	2	1	1
Early language	3	3	2	1
Later language	2	3	1	1
Noncognitive	2	1	1	2
Mother–child interactions	3	3	2	2
Families	3	2	1	2

Key: 1 = little or no work; 2 = some work; 3 = much work on this aspect of development.

Table 10.1 conveys a sense of this checkerboard pattern of developmental work, though it does not quite fully capture the state of affairs. For example, no interactional work of any kind exists in almost any disorder once the child is beyond 5 years old, nor are there sibling (or peer) studies in any disability except mental retardation (apart from the studies of hearing sibling translators when both parents are deaf). Like the situation Achenbach described more than 20 years ago, developmental work on children with disabilities is a field waiting to happen.

Where We Need to Be: Future Issues

A first obvious concern is the need for more research on the development of children with disabilities. Currently, with the exception of the developmentalists in mental retardation and the language development researchers in deafness, few professionals examine the development of children with disabilities. More alarming, perhaps, is the scarcity of an infrastructure to support such research. Few graduate programs in developmental psychology focus (or have faculty involved in) disability research, and the number of developmental courses and research opportunities are similarly sparse in such fields as special education and early intervention.

Moreover, many disabilities researchers have recently expressed concern about how few established researchers are under the age of 35 or 40. Partly to address this problem in mental retardation, one organization of researchers – the American Academy on Mental Retardation (AMR) – has initiated the presentation of graduate student research at the annual meetings of the American Association on Mental Retardation, the field's main professional organization. Like researchers in many areas of disability, the AMR is concerned that behavioral research in disabilities will eventually wither away if current professionals cannot cultivate the next generation of researchers.

In part, the low prestige of disability studies in a variety of behavioral and social science fields discourages developmental and clinical psychologists from undertaking such studies. In addition, few university positions are advertised in "atypical development," apart from those dealing with emotional disturbance and psychopathology. Conversely, not enough workers in special education or early intervention are interested in the findings and theories arising from developmental psychology. In short, for research to continue on the development of children with disabilities, a more expanded, wider institutional support structure will be necessary.

Research with Better Theoretical Grounding

In addition to more research, we need research that incorporates modern developmental theory. Two issues arise in this regard: first, a general adherence to "old" developmental theories; second, single-minded attention to single disabilities.

As this book illustrates, developmental approaches are not limited to the ideas of similar sequences and structures (see Chapter 3). These ideas, though appropriate in the late 1960s, do not take into account the many advances of developmental psychology during the past 30 years. This book argues that developmental approaches to disability must remain up-to-date, reflecting recent changes within developmental psychology.

Moreover, researchers interested in development in a particular disabled population need to adopt a more "cross-disability" focus.

Granted, researchers focus mainly on a single disability group because this is necessary for high-quality research. At the same time, however, researchers would be aided by entertaining a general interest in developmental issues in other disabilities. As noted in Chapter 8, analogous issues and findings arise when one examines the development of children with diverse disabilities.

Research that Describes Developmental Mechanisms and Employs Multilevel Analyses

Future work will need to describe the mechanisms of development. The issue of "mechanisms" is indeed a difficult one, and developmental researchers have often been accused of being better at describing development than in determining why development occurs.

Future work will also require diverse levels of analysis. One can examine the development of behavior itself, describe connections, or the lack of connections, among and within developmental domains, and investigate environmental factors that support, delay, or alter development. To say, for example, that children need either spoken or signed linguistic input within a circumscribed sensitive period, one must designate a developmental mechanism – specific input at a certain time leads to a certain development (see Chapter 8). Other mechanisms occur on other levels. On the neurological level, for example, the development of certain brain structures will inevitably be implicated in corresponding behavioral developments as the child matures. Fischer (1987) found that certain changes in the brain during the first two years of life are associated with specific sensorimotor cognitive advances. Mechanisms at other levels might include neurochemical changes and the turning on and off of genes over time.

Related to the concept of mechanisms is the issue of how studies are performed. At present, most disability studies adopt a group-differences approach: Children with a particular disability (or their families) are compared with nondisabled children. But no two children are alike. Children with different types of mental retardation vary along a host of behaviors (see Table 3.3). Similarly, children who are blind due to retrolental fibroplasia and children whose deafness is caused by rubella show higher rates of psychopathology than do children whose blindness or deafness arises from other causes. In addition, certain aspects of children, parents, and families are related to familial stress. The stress that deaf-of-deaf families experience differs from that experienced by hearing families with children who are deaf; similarly, differences in type and level of stress exist in families of children with different types of mental retardation (e.g., Prader–Willi versus Down syndrome).

Future studies will need to take greater account of individual differences from one child or family to another. Melding group- and individual-differences approaches will be necessary. Group-differences studies will tell us whether, on average, children with disabilities or their families differ from children and families without disabilities. Individual-differences studies will tell us some of the mechanisms by which such group differences occur and, more important, which characteristics are helpful for child or family adaptation. Although joining group- and individual-differences approaches will not be a panacea, it will aid the search for the mechanisms of developmental change.

Research Tied to Practical Concerns

Future developmental work will need to forge closer connections with practical concerns. At present, much of the information concerning the development of children with mental retardation, deafness, blindness, and motor impairments remains unconnected to intervention practices. As Chapter 9 notes, this is due in part to the recent practice of noncategorical programming.

Moreover, the findings presented in this book reveal the potential connections to early intervention, schooling, and family work. If children with different types of mental retardation show specific, etiologically based strengths and weaknesses, then specific intervention strategies might be attempted. If, for children with different disabilities or for children having a common disability with different etiologies, rates of development change at particular times or in response to particular developmental tasks, intervention may need to become more intensive or to focus on particular areas.

In the same way, work with families will benefit as we learn more about familial reactions to children with different disabilities. Some interventions may prove generic to families of children with all disorders – for example, parents of all children with disabilities may initially "mourn" the loss of the idealized infant and may need therapy or supportive services. In contrast, other issues will be specific to one disability, or even to one cause of a disability. With growing information about different family types and parental coping styles, intervention programs can be more directly targeted to specific groups.

To date, few of these ideas have been communicated from researchers to practitioners. One looks in vain for institutional structures – journals, organizations, grants, and training programs – that allow for the application of research findings to the everyday practice of professionals. When and if such supports emerge, developmental findings should improve intervention practices on a variety of levels.

How to Get There from Here: Future Research Strategies

A classic story from Maine ends with the Mainer telling the city slicker: "Eeeyah, you can't get there from here." So too might be the fate of the recommendations outlined in the preceding section. While it may be nice to have more theoretically grounded research, or research that examines mechanisms or has practical implications, getting from "here" to "there" may prove problematic.

Although many things will help advance future disability studies, probably the most important will be a cross-disciplinary perspective. Developmentalists will need to consult with geneticists, pediatricians, neurologists, communication specialists, occupational and physical therapists, social workers, psychiatrists, clinical psychologists, early interventionists, and special educators. Each professional offers expertise in a domain of interest (e.g., developmental psycholinguistics), a program of intervention (e.g., early intervention, special education, clinical psychology), a method of testing (e.g., auditory, visual) or a population (e.g., spina bifida, Prader–Willi syndrome).

Such cross-disciplinary collaborations will undoubtedly give rise to new problems. Professionals from diverse disciplines have different training and different ideas as to which aspects of a particular disability are worth studying. Different professionals also speak in different technical languages. To give one example, geneticists routinely use terms like cytogenetics and molecular genetics; imprinting; full versus partial mutation; deletion, disomy, and amplification; and trisomy, translocation, and mosaicism. Few nongeneticists will be able to slash their way through this jungle of jargon without the help of a friendly geneticist.

In addition to a mastery of the terms and concepts that prevail in different fields, successful cross-disciplinary efforts require an appreciation of the scope of each discipline. To a physician, the terms development and behavior may well be limited to the child's weight and height, IQ tests, general delays in language, and the presence or absence of gross psychopathology. To a developmentalist, these terms also include aspects of cognition, language, social development, mother–child interactions, and family dynamics. Developmentalists even realize that, within each speciality area, further degrees of specialization exist.

Language development is an example of a discipline that has witnessed increasing specialization. This single field alone involves many subfields. Language development researchers generally divide themselves into those interested in early and those interested in later language development, with the break point at approximately 3 years of age. Early-language researchers study in minute detail such topics as joint attention, pointing, pre-speech gestures, maternal spoken and gestural input, babbling, vocalization and articulation, relations of sensorimotor developments to early language production or comprehension, early word meanings, classification of objects, and individual styles of children's learning. Those interested in older children examine various aspects of grammar, linguistic routines (phrases such as good morning, excuse me, trick or treat), word mapping (the way that the child understands the exact referent of any word), conversational rules, code switching (i.e., speaking differently to one's boss than to one's

1-year-old), and, later, reading and writing. Each of these subdisciplines – one might even say sub-subdisciplines – has its own research traditions, procedures, instruments, and developmental theories and subtheories.

Given such complexity within disciplines and subdisciplines, can interdisciplinary collaborations succeed? Some preliminary efforts have been made to answer this question. In a federally sponsored conference in Tennessee (September 1995), various teams of researchers presented their thoughts on interdisciplinary collaboration. All spoke of the risks associated with such endeavors, and the tensions inherent in defining the scope of one professional's turf versus that of another's. At the same time, these teams expressed optimism about the ultimate benefits of such cross-disciplinary collaboration. The cross-disciplinary studies described in this book include Bellugi et al.'s (1994) work on the language of children with Williams syndrome (crossing language development and neurology) and Dykens et al.'s (1996) studies on the obsessive and compulsive behaviors of children with Prader–Willi syndrome (crossing child clinical psychology, child psychiatry, and pediatric genetics).

Concluding Thoughts

It is an article of faith in this book that it is worthwhile elucidating developmental approaches to children with disabilities. Focusing on mental retardation, deafness, blindness, and motor impairments, we have discussed both the organismic and contextual aspects of developmental approaches, as well as how such aspects have played themselves out in each disability.

Since the days of Werner, Piaget, and Vygotsky, children with disabilities have always been interesting to developmentalists. More recently, Zigler's developmental approach to mental retardation has formalized some of these ideas, and recent modifications and expansions have added to the vitality of the approach. In addition, recent studies have examined aspects of organismic and contextual development in children with other disability conditions. Future studies should pay greater attention to individual differences as well as to group differences, to cross-disciplinary collaboration, and to the many heretofore neglected aspects of development. Developmental approaches to children with disabilities, then, have a colorful history, a vivid present, and a bright future.

Appendix:
Resource Organizations
and Publications

Resource Organizations

General Disability

Council for Exceptional Children (CEC)
1920 Association Drive
Reston, Virginia 22091-1589
(703)620-3660

American Association of University Affiliated Programs for
  Persons with
Developmental Disabilities
8630 Fenton Street, Suite 410
Silver Spring, MD 20910
(301)588-8252

CAPP National Parent Resource Center
Federation for Children with Special Needs
95 Berkeley Street, Suite 104
Boston, MA 02116
(617)482-2915

Clearinghouse on Disability Information
Office of Special Education and Rehabilitative Services
330 "C" Street SW,
Switzer Building, Room 3132
Washington, DC 20202
(202)205-8241

National Information Center for Children & Youth with
  Disabilities
P.O. Box 1492
Washington, DC 20013
(800)695-0285

National Organization for Rare Disorders (NORD)
100 Route 37
P.O. Box 8923
New Fairfield, CT 06812
(203)746-6518; (800)999-6673

Alliance of Genetic Support Groups
35 Wisconsin Circle, Suite 440
Chevy Chase, MD 29815
(301)652-5553; (800)336-GENE

National Parent Network on Disabilities
1600 Prince Street, Suite 115
Alexandria, VA 22314
(703)684-6763

Sibling Information Network
1775 Ellington Road
South Windsor, CT 06074
(203)648-1205

National Center for Clinical Infant Programs (NCCIP)
P.O. Box 96529
Washington, DC 20090-6529

Resources for Children with Special Needs, Inc.
200 Park Avenue South, Suite 816
New York, NY 10003
(212)677-4650

Disability Rights Education and Defense Fund
2212 Sixth Street
Berkeley, CA 94710
(800)466-4232

I. Mental Retardation

General

Parent and Professional Organizations

Association of Retarded Citizens of the U.S. ("The ARC")
500 E. Border Street,
Arlington, TX 76010
(817)261-6003

American Association on Mental Retardation (AAMR)
1719 Kalorama Road NW
Washington, DC 20009-2683
(800)424-3688; (202)387-1968

TASH: The Association for Persons with Severe
  Handicaps
29 West Susquehanna Avenue, Suite 210
Baltimore, MD
(410)828-8274

Specific Syndrome or Condition

Association for Children with Down Syndrome
2616 Martin Avenue
Bellmore, NY 11710
(516)221-4700

National Down Syndrome Society
666 Broadway
New York, NY 10012
(800)221-4602

National Down Syndrome Congress
1800 Dempster Street
Park Ridge, IL 60068
(800)232-6372

National Fragile X Syndrome Foundation
1441 York Street, Suite 215
Denver, CO 80206
(800)688-8765; (303)333-6155

Prader–Willi Syndrome Association
5700 Midnicht Pass Road, Suite C
Sarasota, FL 34242
(800)926-4797

Prader–Willi Syndrome International Information Forum
40 Holly Lane
Roslyn Heights, NY 11577
(800)358-0682; (516)621-2445

International Prader–Willi Syndrome Organisation (IPWSO)
Jean Phillips-Martinsson
Farthings
44 Warwick Park
Turnbridge Wells
Kent TN2 5EF
United Kingdom

The Williams Syndrome Association
P.O. Box 297
Clawson, MI 48017-0297
(810)541-3630

II. Blindness

American Council of the Blind
1155 Fifteenth Street NW, Suite 720
Washington, DC 20005
(202)467-5081

American Foundation for the Blind
15 West 16th Street
New York, NY 10011
(212)620-2000

National Federation of the Blind
1800 Johnson Street
Baltimore, MD
(301)659-9314

American Association of the Deaf-Blind
814 Thayer Avenue, Suite 302
Silver Spring, MD 20910
(301)588-6545

National Information Clearinghouse on Children Who are
  Deaf-Blind
345 North Monmouth Avenue
Monmouth, OR 97361
(800)438-9376

National Family Association for the Deaf-Blind
111 Middle Neck Road
Sands Point, NY 11050
(516)944-8900

American Printing House for the Blind, Inc.
1839 Frankfort Avenue
Louisville, KY 40206
(502)895-2405

Carroll Center for the Blind
770 Centre Street
Newton, MA
(617)969-6200

National Library Service for the Blind and Physically
  Handicapped
The Library of Congress
Washington, DC 20542
(202)727-2142

Recording for the Blind
20 Roszel Road
Princeton, NJ 08540
(800)221-4792

III. Deafness

National Association for the Deaf
814 Thayer Avenue
Silver Spring, MD 20910
(301)587-1788

National Foundation for Children's Hearing Education and
  Research
928 McLean Avenue
Yonkers, NY 10704
(914)237-2676.

Self-Help for Hard of Hearing People
7800 Wisconsin Avenue
Bethesda, MD 20814
(301)657-2248

Gallaudet University
800 Florida Avenue NE
Washington, DC 20002
(202)651-5000

Convention of American Instructors of the Deaf
  (CAID – membership office)
P.O. Box 377
Bedford, TX 76095-0377
(817)354-8414

Alexander Graham Bell Association for the Deaf
3417 Volta Place NW
Washington, DC 20007
(314)739-5944

IV. Motor Impairments

National Easter Seal Society
230 West Monroe
Chicago, IL 60606
(800)221-6827; (312)726-6200

United Cerebral Palsy Associations, Inc.
7 Penn Plaza, Suite 804
New York, NY 10001
(800)USA-IUCP

March of Dimes Defects Foundation
1275 Mamaronek Avenue
White Plains, NY 10605
(914)428-7100

Spina Bifida Association of America
4590 MacArthur Boulevard NW, no. 250
Washington, DC 20007-4226
(800)621-3141

International and Foreign Resources

International

International Association for the Scientific Study of Mental
    Retardation
Terry Dolan, President
c/o Waisman Center
University of Wisconsin
1500 Highland Avenue
Madison, WI 53705-2280

International Association of Parents of the Deaf (IAPD)
814 Thayer Avenue
Silver Spring, MD 20910

Rehabilitation Institute
25 East 21st Street
New York, NY 10010

International Cerebral Palsy Society (ICPS)
12 Park Crescent
London W1N 4EQ
United Kingdom

International League of Societies for Persons with Mental
  Handicap
Avenue Louise 248
Box 17
B-1050 Brussels, Belgium

Britain

SENSE, The National Deaf-Blind and Rubella Association
311 Gray's Inn Road
London WC1X 8PT

SENSE-in-Scotland
168 Dumbarton Road
Glasgow G11 6XE

Health Education Authority
78 New Oxford Street
London WC1A 1AH

Scottish Council on Disability
Princess House
5 Shandwick Place
Edinburgh EH2 4RG
Tel. 031 229 8632

Royal Society for Mentally Handicapped Children and Adults
  (MENCAP)
The Lord Rix CBE
123 Golden Lane
London EC1Y 0RT
Tel. 0171-454 0454

The Spastics Society
16 Fitzroy Square
London W1P 5HQ
Tel. 01 387 9571

Disabled Living Centres Council
c/o TRIADS

76 Clarendon Park Road
Leicester LE2 3AD
Tel. 700747/8

The Family Fund (helps families of children under 16 with severe
   disabilities)
c/o Joseph Rowntree Trust
Beverly House
Shipton Road
York YO3 6RB

The Disabled Living Foundation
346 Kensington High Street
London W14 8NS

Canada

Canadian Association for Community Living
4700 Keele Street
Kinsman Building
York University
North York, ON M3J 1P3
(416)661-9611

Canadian Rehabilitation Council for the Disabled
45 Sheppard Avenue East, Suite 801
Willowdale, ON M2N 5W9
(416)250-7490

Spina Bifida Association of Canada
220-388 Donald Street
Winnipeg, MB R3B 2J4
(800)565-9488; (204)957-1784

Canadian Hearing Society
271 Spadina Road
Toronto, ON M5R 2V3
(416)964-9595

Canadian Hard of Hearing Association
2435 Holly Lane, Suite 205
Ottawa, ON K1V 7P2
(800)263-8068; (613)526-1584

Canadian National Institute for the Blind
1929 Bayview Avenue
Toronto, ON M4G 3E8
(416)486-2500

Canadian Down Syndrome Society
12837 76th Avenue, Suite 206
Surrey, BC V3W 2V3
(604)599-6009

Australia

Australian Council for Rehabilitation of the Disabled (ACROD)
P.O. Box 60
Curtin, ACT 2605

National Council on Intellectual Disabilities
Executive Officer: Mr. Roger Barson
GOP Box 647
Canberra, ACT 2601

New Zealand

Directory of Special Education and Guidance Services in New
    Zealand
Department of Education
Wellington

The Down's Association
P.O. Box 4142
Auckland

Parent-to-Parent
P.O. Box 4232
Hamilton East

Publications

Directories

American Federation for the Blind (1994). *AFB directory of services for blind and visually impaired persons in the United States and Canada* (2 vols.). New York: American Federation for the Blind.

Blindness and visual impairments: National information and advisory organizations. Washington, DC: National Library Service for the Blind and Physically Handicapped.

Dybwad, R. (1989). *International directory of mental retardation resources* (3rd ed.). Washington, DC: U.S. Dept of Health and Human Services (President's Committee on Mental Retardation).

Nadash, P. (1993). *Directory of local disability information providers.* London: Policy Studies Institute (NDIP Project Team, 100 Park Village E., London NW1 3SR; services throughout the United Kingdom).

National Institutes on Deafness and Other Communication Disorders (NIDCD) (1994). *Resources for deafness and other communication disorders: 1994 directory.* Washington, DC: The Clearinghouse.

National Institutes on Disability and Rehabilitation Research (1994). *Directory of national information services on disability, 1994–1995* (2 vols). NIDRR: Washington, DC.

Magazines and Journals

Exceptional Parent
P.O. Box 3000
Dept. EP
Denville, NJ 07834
(lists parent and advocacy groups and information resources in every January issue)

American Annals of the Deaf (every April issue contains a guide to educational programs for deaf students; university and college programs for personnel in deafness; programs for deaf–blind children and adults; and rehabilitative programs)

KDES PAS-6
800 Florida Avenue, NE
Washington, DC 20002-3693

Exceptional Children
1920 Association Drive
Reston, VA 22091-1589

Down Syndrome Today
P.O. Box 212
Holtsville, NY 11742

Down Syndrome Quarterly
Samuel J. Thios, Editor
Denison University
Granville, OH 43023

Down's Syndrome: Research and Practice
The Sarah Duffen Centre
Belmont Street
Southsea, Hants P05 1NA
United Kingdom

*Prader–Willi Perspectives: A Quarterly Journal of Prader–Willi
    Syndrome Information for Parents and Professionals*
Visible Ink Incorporated
40 Holly Lane
Roslyn Heights, NY 11577
(800)358-0682; (516)621-2445

*genetwork: Bridging the Gap between Genetic Diagnosis and
    Special Education*
Genetic Services at Elwyn
Elwyn, Inc.
111 Elwyn Road
Elwyn, PA 19063

References

Achenbach, T. (1974). Developmental psychopathology. New York: Ronald Press.

Adelson, E., & Fraiberg, S. (1974). Gross motor development of infants blind from birth. Child Development, 45, 114–116.

Agosta, J. (1989). Using cash assistance to support family efforts. In G. H. S. Singer & L. K. Irvin (Eds.), Support for caregiving families: Enabling positive adaptation to disability (pp. 189–204). Baltimore: Brookes.

Alexander, M. A., & Bauer, R. E. (1988). Cerebral palsy. In V. B. Van Hasselt, P. S. Strain, & M. Hersov (Eds.), Handbook of developmental and physical disabilities (pp. 215–226). New York: Pergamon.

Als, H., Tronick, E., & Brazelton, T. B. (1980a). Affective reciprocity and the development of autonomy. Journal of the American Academy of Child Psychiatry, 19, 22–40.

(1980b). Stages of early behavioral organization: The study of a sighted infant and of a blind infant in interaction with their mothers. In T. M. Field, S. Goldberg, D. Stern, & A. Sostek (Eds.), High-risk infants and children (pp. 181–204). New York: Academic Press.

Anderson, E. S., Dunlea, A., & Kekelis, L. (1984). Blind children's language: Resolving some differences. Journal of Child Language, 11, 645–664.

(1993). The impact of input: Language acquisition in the visually impaired. First Language, 13, 23–49.

Arnos, K. S., & Downs, K. (1994). A cultural and historical perspective on genetics and deafness. In C. J. Erting, R. C. Johnson, D. L. Smith, & B. D. Snider (Eds.), The Deaf way (pp. 295–310). Washington, DC: Gallaudet University Press.

Bangs, D. (1994). What is a Deaf performing arts experience? In C. J. Erting, R. C. Johnson, D. L. Smith, & B. D. Snider (Eds.), The Deaf way (pp. 751–761). Washington, DC: Gallaudet University Press.

Barakat, L. P., & Linney, J. A. (1992). Children with physical handicaps and their mothers: The interrelation of social support, maternal adjustment, and child adjustment. Journal of Pediatric Psychology, 17, 725–739.

(1995). Optimism, appraisals, and coping in the adjustment of mothers and their children with spina bifida. Journal of Child and Family Studies, 4, 303–320.

Barkley, R. A. (1990). Attention-deficit hyperactivity disorder: A handbook for diagnosis and treatment. New York: Guilford Press.

Barlow, N. (Ed.). (1958). The autobiography of Charles Darwin, 1809–1882. New York: Norton.

Baumeister, A. (1984). Some methodological and conceptual issues in the study of cognitive processes with retarded children. In P. Brooks, R. Sperber, & C. McCauley (Eds.), Learning and cognition in the mentally retarded (pp. 1–38). Hillsdale, NJ: Erlbaum.

(1987). Mental retardation: Some concepts and dilemmas. American Psychologist, 42, 796–800.

Baumeister, A., & MacLean, W. (1979). Brain damage and mental retardation. In N. R. Ellis (Ed.), Handbook of mental deficiency: Psychological theory and research (2d ed., pp. 197–230), Hillsdale, NJ: Erlbaum.

Bayley, N. (1955). On the growth of intelligence. American Psychologist, 10, 805–818.

Bayley, N. (1969). Bayley Scales of Infant Development: Birth to two years. New York: Psychological Corporation.

Beckman, P. (1983). Influence of selected child characteristics on stress in families of handicapped children. American Journal of Mental Deficiency, 88, 150–156.

Bell, R. Q. (1968). A reinterpretation of direction of effects in studies of socialization. Psychological Review, 75, 81–95.

Bell, R. Q., & Harper, L. V. (1977). Child effects on adults. Hillsdale, NJ: Erlbaum.

Bellugi, U., Marks, S., Bihrle, A., & Sabo, H. (1988). Dissociation between language and cognitive functions in Williams syndrome. In D. Bishop & K. Mogford (Eds.), Language development in exceptional circumstances (pp. 177–189). London: Churchill Livingstone.

Bellugi, U., Wang, P., & Jernigan, T. (1994). Williams syndrome: An unusual neuropsychological profile. In S. H. Broman & J. Grafman (Eds.), Atypical cognitive deficits in developmental disorders (pp. 23–56). Hillsdale, NJ: Erlbaum

Benedek, T. (1959). Parenthood as a developmental phase. Journal of the American Psychoanalytic Association, 7, 389–417.

Bernheimer, L., & Keogh, B. L. (1988). Stability of cognitive performance of children with developmental delays. American Journal on Mental Retardation, 92, 539–542.

Best, B., & Roberts, G. (1976). Early cognitive development in hearing impaired children. American Annals of the Deaf, 121, 560–564.

Bigelow, A. E. (1987). Early words of blind children. Journal of Child Language, 14, 47–56.

(1990). Relationship between the development of language and thought in young blind children. Journal of Visual Impairment and Blindness, 84, 414–419.

(1995). The effect of blindness on the early development of the self. In P. Rochat (Ed.), The self in infancy: Theory and research (pp. 327–347). Amsterdam: Elsevier Science.

Birenbaum, A., & Cohen, H. J. (1993). On the importance of helping families: Policy implications from a national study. Mental Retardation, 31, 67–74.

Blacher, J. (1984). Sequential stages of parental adjustment following the birth of a child with handicaps: Fact or artifact? Mental Retardation, 22, 55–68.

Blasco, P. M., Hrncir, E. J., & Blasco, P. A. (1990). The contribution of maternal involvement to mastery performance in infants with cerebral palsy. Journal of Early Intervention, 14, 161–174.

Bloom, L. (1970). Language development: Form and function in emerging grammars. Cambridge, MA: MIT Press.

Bobath, B., & Bobath, K. (1975). Motor development in the different types of cerebral palsy. London: William Heinemann Medical Books.

Bond, G. G. (1987). An assessment of cognitive abilities in hearing and hearing impaired preschool children. Journal of Speech and Hearing Disorders, 52, 319–323.

Bonvillian, J. D., Orlansky, M. D., & Novack, L. L. (1983). Developmental milestones: Sign language acquisition and motor development. Child Development, 54, 1435–1445.

Borthwick-Duffy, S. A. (1994). Epidemiology and prevalence of psychopathology in people with mental retardation. Journal of Consulting and Clinical Psychology, 62, 17–27.

Borthwick-Duffy, S. A., & Eyman, R. K. (1990). Who are the dually diagnosed? American Journal on Mental Retardation, 94, 586–595.

Boughman, J., & Shaver, K. (1982). Genetic aspects of deafness. American Annals of the Deaf, 127, 393–400.

Braden, J. P. (1994). Deafness, deprivation, and IQ. New York: Plenum Press.

Braden, M. L. (1989). Logo reading system. (Available from author, at 219 E. Street Vrain, Colorado Springs, CO 80903.)

Bradley, C. L., & Miller, H. (1990). Congenital rubella. In J. Hogg, J. Sebba, & L. Lambe (Eds.), Profound retardation and multiple impairment: Vol. 3. Medical and physical care and management (pp. 93–113). London: Chapman & Hall.

Brazelton, T. B., Koslowski, B., & Main, M. (1974). The origins of reciprocity: The early mother–infant interaction. In M. Lewis & L. A. Rosenblum (Eds.), The effect of the infant on its caretaker (pp. 49–76). New York: Wiley.

Bregman, J. D. (1991). Current developments in the understanding of mental retardation: Part II. Psychopathology. Journal of the American Academy of Child and Adolescent Psychiatry, 30, 861–872.

Breslau, N., Weitzman, M., & Messenger, K. (1981). Psychologic functioning of siblings of disabled children. Pediatrics, 67, 344–353.

Bricker, D., & Veltman, M. (1990). Early intervention programs: Child-focused approaches. In S. J. Meisels & J. P. Shonkoff (Eds.), Handbook of early intervention (pp. 373–399). Cambridge University Press.

Broman, S., Nichols, P., Shaughnessy, P., & Kennedy, W. (1987). Retardation in young children: A developmental study of cognitive deficit. Hillsdale, NJ: Erlbaum.

Bromwich, R. (1990). The interactional approach to early intervention. Infant Mental Health Journal, 11, 66–79.

Bronfenbrenner, U. (1979). The ecology of human development. Cambridge, MA: Harvard University Press.

Bronfenbrenner, U., Kessel, F., Kessen, W., & White, S. (1986). Toward a critical social history of developmental psychology: A propadeutic discussion. American Psychologist, 41, 1218–1230.

Brown, A. L., & Ferrara, R. (1985). Diagnosing zones of proximal development. In J. V. Wertsch (Ed.), Culture, communication, and cognition: Vygotskian perspectives (pp. 273–305). Cambridge University Press.

Brown, R. (1973). A first language. Cambridge, MA: Harvard University Press.

Bruner, J. (1982). The organization of action and the nature of adult–infant transaction. In E. Z. Tronick (Ed.), Social interchange in infancy (pp. 23–35). Baltimore: University Park Press.

Bryant, B. K. (1985). The neighborhood walk: Sources of support in middle childhood. Monographs of the Society for Research in Child Development, 50 (Whole No. 3).

Buchino, M. A. (1993). Perceptions of the oldest hearing child of deaf parents: On interpreting, communication, and role reversals. American Annals of the Deaf, 138, 40–45.

Budoff, M. (1974). Learning potential and educability among the educable mentally retarded. Cambridge, MA: Research Institute for Educational Problems.

Buium, N., Rynders, J., & Turnure, J. (1974). Early maternal linguistic environment of normal and Down syndrome language learning children. American Journal of Mental Deficiency, 79, 52–58.

Burack, J. A. (1990). Differentiating mental retardation: The two-group approach and beyond. In R. M. Hodapp, J. A. Burack, & E. Zigler (Eds.), Issues in the developmental approach to mental retardation (pp. 27–48). Cambridge University Press.

Burack, J. A., Hodapp, R. M., & Zigler, E. (1988). Issues in the classification of mental retardation: Differentiating among organic etiologies. Journal of Child Psychology and Psychiatry, 29, 765–779.

Bybee, J. A., & Zigler, E. (1992). Is outerdirectedness employed in a harmful or beneficial manner by students with and without mental retardation? American Journal on Mental Retardation, 96, 512–521.

Byrne, E., & Cunningham, C. (1985). The effects of mentally handicapped children on families: A conceptual review. Journal of Child Psychology and Psychiatry, 26, 847–864.

Cahill, B. M., & Glidden, L. M. (1996). Influence of child diagnosis on family and parent functioning: Down syndrome versus other disabilities. American Journal on Mental Retardation, 101, 149–160.

Calderon, R., Greenberg, M. T., & Kushe, C. A. (1991). The influence of family coping on the cognitive and social skills of deaf children. In D. S. Martin (Ed.), Advances in cognition, education, and deafness (pp. 195–200). Washington, DC: Gallaudet University Press.

Capute, A. J., & Accardo, P. J. (1991). Cerebral palsy: The spectrum of motor dysfunction. In A. J. Capute & P. J. Accardo (Eds.), Developmental disabilities in infancy and childhood (pp. 335–348). Baltimore: Brookes.

Cardoso-Martins, C., & Mervis, C. (1984). Maternal speech to prelinguistic children with Down syndrome. American Journal of Mental Deficiency, 89, 451–458.

Carpenter, K. J. (1986). The history of scurvy and vitamin C. Cambridge University Press.

Carter, B., & McGoldrick, M. (Eds.). (1988). The changing family life cycle: A framework for family therapy (2d ed.). New York: Gardner Press.

Cass, H. D., Sonksen, P. M., & McConachie, H. R. (1994). Developmental setback in severe visual impairment. Archives of Disease in Childhood, 70, 192–196.

Chess, S., Korn, S. J., & Fernandez, P. B. (1971). Psychiatric disorders of children with congenital rubella. New York: Brunner/Mazel.

Chomsky, N. (1968). Language and mind. New York: Harcourt, Brace, & World.

Cicchetti, D. (1984). The emergence of developmental psychopathology. Child Development, 55, 1–7.

(1990). An historical perspective on the discipline of developmental psychopathology. In J. Rolf, A. Masten, D. Cicchetti, K. Neuchterlein, & S. Weintraub (Eds.), Risk and protective factors in the development of psychopathology (pp. 2–28). Cambridge University Press.

(1993). Developmental psychopathology: Reactions, reflections, projections. Developmental Review, 13, 471–502.

Cicchetti, D., & Beeghly, M. (Eds.). (1990). Children with Down syndrome: A developmental approach. Cambridge University Press.

Cicchetti, D., & Cohen, D. (Eds.). (1995). Manual of developmental psychopathology (2 vols.). New York: Wiley.

Cicchetti, D., & Mans-Wagener, L. (1987). Sequences, stages, and structures in the organization of cognitive development in infants with Down syndrome. In I. Uzgiris & J. M. Hunt (Eds.), Infant performance and experience: New findings with the Ordinal Scales (pp. 281–310). Urbana: University of Illinois Press.

Cicchetti, D., & Pogge-Hesse, P. (1982). Possible contributions of the study of organically retarded persons to developmental theory. In E. Zigler & D. Balla (Eds.), Mental retardation: The developmental-difference controversy (pp. 277–318). Hillsdale, NJ: Erlbaum.

Cicchetti, D., & Sroufe, L. A. (1976). The relationship between affective and cognitive development in Down syndrome infants. Child Development, 47, 920–929.

(1978). An organizational view of affect: Illustration from the study of Down syndrome infants. In M. Lewis & L. A. Rosenblum (Eds.), The development of affect (pp. 309–350). New York: Plenum.

Cione, G., Paolicelli, P. B., Sordi, C., & Vinter, A. (1993). Sensorimotor development in cerebral-palsied infants assessed with the Uzgiris–Hunt Scales. Developmental Medicine and Child Neurology, 35, 1055–1066.

Cohen, I. L., Vietze, P., Sudhalter, V., Jenkins, E. C., & Brown, W. T. (1991). Effects of age and communication level on eye contact in fragile X males and non–fragile X autistic males. American Journal of Medical Genetics, 38, 498–502.

Correa, V. I. (1987). Working with Hispanic parents of visually impaired children: Cultural implications. Journal of Visual Impairments and Blindness, 81, 260–264.

Crawley, S., & Spiker, D. (1983). Mother–child interactions involving two-year-olds with Down syndrome: A look at individual differences. Child Development, 54, 1312–1323.

Crnic, K., Friedrich, W., & Greenberg, M. (1983). Adaptation of families with mentally handicapped children: A model of stress, coping, and family ecology. American Journal of Mental Deficiency, 88, 125–138.

Cross, T. G. (1978). Mother's speech and its association with rate of language acquisition in young children. In N. Waterson & C. Snow (Eds.), The development of communication (pp. 199–218). London: Wiley.

Cruickshank, W. M. (Ed.). (1976). Cerebral palsy: A developmental disability. Syracuse, NY: Syracuse University Press.

Culatta, B. (1993). Developing abstract concepts. In F. L. Rowley-Kelly & D. H. Riegel (Eds.), Teaching children with spina bifida (pp. 125–143). Baltimore: Brookes.

Cummings, S. (1976). The impact of the child's deficiency on the father: A study of fathers of mentally retarded and chronically ill children. American Journal of Orthopsychiatry, 46, 246–255.

Cummings, S., Bayley, H., & Rie, H. (1966). Effects of the child's deficiency on the mother: A study of mentally retarded, chronically ill, and neurotic children. American Journal of Orthopsychiatry, 36, 595–608.

Cuppage, F. E. (1994). James Cook and the conquest of scurvy. Westport, CT: Greenwood Press.

Curtiss, S. (1977). Genie: A psycholinguistic study of a modern day "wild child." New York: Academic Press.

Decarie, T. G. (1969). A study of the mental and emotional development of the thalidomide child. In B. M. Foss (Ed.), Determinants of infants' behaviour (Vol. 4). London: Methuen.

Dennis, W. (1973). Children of the creche. New York: Appleton-Century-Crofts.

Desmond, M. M., Fisher, E. S., Vorderman, A. L., Schaffer, H. G., Andrew, L. P., Zion, T. E., & Catlin, F. I. (1978). The longitudinal course of congenital rubella encephalitis in non-retarded children. Journal of Pediatrics, 93, 584–591.

Dolnick, E. (1993). Deafness as culture. Atlantic Monthly, 272(3), 37–53.

Dote-Kwan, J. (1995). Impact of mothers' interactions on the development of their young visually impaired children. Journal of Visual Impairment and Blindness, 89, 46–58.

Drotar, D., Baskiewicz, A., Irvin, N., Kennell, J., & Klaus, M. (1975). The adaptation of parents to the birth of an infant with congenital malformation: A hypothetical model. Pediatrics, 56, 710–717.

Dunst, C. J. (1980). Clinical and educational manual for use with the Uzgiris–Hunt Scales for infant psychological development. Baltimore: University Park Press.

(1988). Stage transitioning in the sensorimotor development of Down's syndrome infants. Journal of Mental Deficiency Research, 32, 405–410.

(1990). Sensorimotor development of infants with Down syndrome. In Cicchetti, D., & Beeghly, M (Eds.), Children with Down syndrome: A developmental approach (pp. 180–230). Cambridge University Press.

Dykens, E. M. (1995). Measuring behavioral phenotypes: Provocations from the "new genetics." American Journal on Mental Retardation, 99, 522–532.

(1996). DNA meets DSM: The growing importance of genetic syndromes in dual diagnosis. Mental Retardation, 34, 125–127.

Dykens, E. M., & Cassidy, S. B. (1996). Prader–Willi syndrome: Genetic, behavioral, and treatment issues. Child and Adolescent Psychiatry Clinics, 5, 913–927.

Dykens, E. M., Goff, B. J., Hodapp, R. M., Davis, L., Devanzo, P., Moss, F., Halliday, R. N., Shah, B., State, M., & King, B. (1997). Eating themselves to death: Have "personal rights" gone too far in Prader–Willi syndrome? Mental Retardation, 35, 312–314.

Dykens, E. M., & Hodapp, R. M. (1997). Treatment approaches in genetic mental retardation syndromes. Professional Psychology: Research and Practice, 28, 263–270.

Dykens, E. M., Hodapp, R. M., & Evans, D. W. (1994). Profiles and development of adaptive behavior in males with fragile X syndrome. Journal of Autism and Developmental Disorders, 23, 135–145.

Dykens, E. M., Hodapp, R. M., & Leckman, J. F. (1987). Strengths and weaknesses in the intellectual functioning of males with fragile X syndrome. American Journal of Mental Deficiency, 92, 234–236.

(1994). Behavior and development in fragile X syndrome. Newbury Park, CA: Sage.

Dykens, E. M., Hodapp, R. M., Ort, S., Finucane, B., Shapiro, L., & Leckman, J. F. (1989). The trajectory of cognitive development in males with fragile X syndrome. Journal of the American Academy of Child and Adolescent Psychiatry, 28, 422–426.

Dykens, E. M., Hodapp, R. M., Walsh, K., & Nash, L. (1992). Profiles, correlates, and trajectories of intelligence in individuals with Prader–Willi syndrome. Journal of the American Academy of Child and Adolescent Psychiatry, 31, 1125–1130.

Dykens, E. M., & Leckman, J. F. (1990). Developmental issues in fragile X syndrome. In R. M. Hodapp, J. A. Burack, & E. Zigler (Eds.), Issues in the developmental approach to mental retardation (pp. 226–245). Cambridge University Press.

Dykens, E. M., Leckman, J. F., & Cassidy, S. B. (1996). Obsessions and compulsions in Prader–Willi syndrome. Journal of Child Psychology and Psychiatry, 37, 995–1002.

Ellis, N. R. (1963). The stimulus trace and behavioral inadequacy. In N. R. Ellis (Ed.), Handbook of mental deficiency, psychological theory and research (pp. 134–158). New York: McGraw-Hill.

Ericson, M. (1969). MMPI profiles of parents of young retarded children. American Journal of Mental Deficiency, 73, 727–732.

Erikson, M., & Upshur, C. C. (1989). Caretaking burden and social support: Comparison of mothers of infants with and without disabilities. American Journal on Mental Retardation, 94, 250–258.

Erting, C. J., Johnston, R. C., Smith, D. L., & Snider, B. D. (Eds.). (1994). The Deaf way. Washington, D.C.: Gallaudet University Press.

Erting, C. J., Prezioso, C., & O'Grady Hynes, M. (1990). The interactional context of deaf mother–infant communication. In V. Volterra

& C. J. Erting (Eds.), From gesture to language in hearing and deaf children (pp. 97–106). Berlin: Springer.

Farber, B. (1959). The effects of the severely retarded child on the family system. Monographs of the Society for Research in Child Development, 24 (Serial No. 2).

———. (1970). Notes on sociological knowledge about families with mentally retarded children. In M. Schreiber (Ed.), Social work and mental retardation (pp. 118–124). New York: John Day.

Feldman, H. M., Janosky, J. E., Scher, M. S., & Wareham, N. L. (1994). Language abilities following prematurity, periventricular brain injury, and cerebral palsy. Journal of Communication Disorders, 27, 71–90.

Ferguson, C. (1978). Talking to children: A search for universals. In J. Greenberg (Ed.), Universals of human language: Vol. 1. Method and theory (pp. 203–224). Stanford, CA: Stanford University Press.

Festinger, L., Riecken, H. W., & Schachter, S. (1956). When prophesy fails: A social and psychological study of a modern group that predicted the destruction of the world. New York: Harper & Row.

Feurstein, R., Rand, Y., Hoffman, M., Hoffman, M., & Miller, R. (1979). Cognitive modifiability in retarded adolescents: Effects of instrumental enrichment. American Journal of Mental Deficiency, 83, 539–550.

Fine, R. A. (1972). The great drug deception: The shocking story of MER/29 and the folks who gave you thalidomide. New York: Stein & Day.

Finucane, B. (Ed.). (1995). genetwork: Bridging the gap between genetic diagnosis and special education (Vol. 1, editions 1–3). Elwyn, PA: Elwyn, Inc.

Fischer, K. (1987). Relations between brain and cognitive development. Child Development, 58, 623–632.

Flynt, S. W., & Wood, T. A. (1989). Stress and coping of mothers of children with moderate mental retardation. American Journal on Mental Retardation, 94, 278–283.

Fodor, J. (1983). Modularity of mind: An essay on faculty psychology. Cambridge, MA: MIT Press.

Folkman, S., Schaefer, C., & Lazarus, R. S. (1979). Cognitive processes as mediators of stress and coping. In V. Hamilton & D. S. Warburton (Eds.), Human stress and cognition (pp. 265–298). New York: Wiley.

Forness, S. R., & Kavale, K. A. (1994). The Balkanization of special education: Proliferation of categories for "new" behavioral disorders. Education and Treatment of Children, 17, 215–227.

Fowler, A. (1988). Determinants of rate of language growth in children with Down syndrome. In L. Nadel (Ed.), The psychobiology of Down syndrome (pp. 217–245). Cambridge, MA: Bradford / MIT Press.

(1990). The development of language structure in children with Down syndrome: Evidence for a specific syntactic delay. In D. Cicchetti & M. Beeghly (Eds.), Children with Down syndrome: A developmental approach (pp. 302–328). Cambridge University Press.

Fowler, A., Gelman, R., & Gleitman, L. (1994). The course of language learning in children with Down syndrome. In H. Tager-Flusberg (Ed.), Constraints on language acquisition: Studies of atypical children (pp. 91–140). Hillsdale, NJ: Erlbaum.

Fraiberg, S. (1977). Insights from the blind. New York: Basic Books.

Fraiberg, S., & Freedman, D. A. (1964). Studies in the ego development of the congenitally blind child. Psychoanalytic Study of the Child, 19, 113–169.

Fraiberg, S., Siegel, B., & Gibson, R. (1966). The role of sound in the search behavior of a blind infant. Psychoanalytic Study of the Child, 21, 327–357.

Franklin, M. B. (1990). Reshaping psychology at Clark: The Werner era. Journal of the History of the Behavioral Sciences, 26, 176–189.

Freeman, R. D., Malkin, S. F., & Hastings, J. O. (1975). Psychosocial problems of deaf children and their families: A comparative study. American Annals of the Deaf, 120, 391–405.

Freud, S. (1917/1957). Mourning and melancholia. Reprinted in J. Rickman (Ed.), A general selection from the works of Sigmund Freud (pp. 124–140). Garden City, NY: Doubleday.

Friedrich, W. L., & Friedrich, W. N. (1981). Psychosocial assets of parents of handicapped and nonhandicapped children. American Journal of Mental Deficiency, 85, 551–553.

Friedrich, W. N. (1979). Predictors of coping behavior of mothers of handicapped children. Journal of Consulting and Clinical Psychology, 47, 1140–1141.

Fundudis, T., Kolvin, I., & Garside, R. (1979). Speech retarded and deaf children: Their psychological development. London: Academic Press.

Furth, H. (1964). Research with the deaf: Implications for language and cognition. Psychological Bulletin, 62, 145–164.

(1966). Thinking without language. New York: Free Press.

Gallimore, R., Weisner, T., Kaufman, S., & Bernheimer, L. (1989). The social construction of ecocultural niches: Family accommodation of developmentally delayed children. American Journal on Mental Retardation, 94, 216–230.

Gannon, J. (1988). The week the world heard Gallaudet. Washington, DC: Gallaudet University Press.

Gardner, H. (1983). Frames of mind. New York: Basic Books.

(1985). The centrality of modules. Behavioral and Brain Sciences, 8, 12–14.

Gath, A. (1973). The mental health of siblings of congenitally abnormal children. Journal of Child Psychology and Psychiatry, 13, 211–218.

(1974). Sibling reactions to mental handicap: A comparison of brothers and sisters of mongol children. Journal of Child Psychology and Psychiatry, 15, 187–198.

(1977). The impact of an abnormal child upon the parents. British Journal of Psychiatry, 130, 405–410.

Gibson, D. (1966). Early developmental staging as a prophesy index in Down's syndrome. American Journal of Mental Deficiency, 70, 825–828.

(1978). Down syndrome: The psychology of mongolism. Cambridge University Press.

(1991). Down syndrome and cognitive enhancement: Not like the others. In K. Marfo (Ed.), Early intervention in transition: Current perspectives in programs for handicapped children (pp. 61–90). New York: Praeger.

Glick, J. (1992). Werner's relevance for contemporary developmental psychology. Developmental Psychology, 28, 558–565.

Glidden, L. M. (1993). What we do not know about families with children who have developmental disabilities: Questionnaire on Resources and Stress as a case study. American Journal on Mental Retardation, 97, 481–495.

Goldberg, S. (1977). Social competence in infancy: A model of parent–infant interaction. Merrill–Palmer Quarterly, 23, 263–277.

Goldberg, S., Marcovitch, S., MacGregor, D., & Lojkasek, M. (1986). Family responses to developmentally delayed preschoolers: Etiology and the father's role. American Journal on Mental Retardation, 90, 610–617.

Granich, L. (1940). A qualitative analysis of concepts in mentally deficient schoolboys. Archives of Psychology, 251, 1–47.

Greenberg, M. T., & Kushe, C. (1989). Cognitive, personal, and social development of deaf children and adolescents. In M. Wang, M. Reynolds, & H. Walberg (Eds.), The handbook of special education: Research and practice (Vol. 3, pp. 95–129). New York: Pergamon.

(1993). Promoting social and emotional growth in deaf children: The PATHS project. Seattle: University of Washington Press.

Gresham, F. M., MacMillan, D. L., & Siperstein, G. N. (1995). Critical analysis of the 1992 AAMR definition: Implications for school psychology. School Psychology Quarterly, 10, 1–19.

Grossman, F. K. (1972). Brothers and sisters of retarded children. Syracuse, NY: Syracuse University Press.

Hallahan, D. P., & Kauffman, J. M. (1994). Exceptional children: Introduction to special education (6th ed.). Boston: Allyn & Bacon.

Hanchett, J. M., Butler, M., Cassidy, S. B., Holm, V., Parker, K. R., Wharton, R., & Zipf, W. (in press). Age and causes of death in Prader–Willi syndrome patients. American Journal of Medical Genetics.

Hancock, K., Wilgosh, L., & McDonald, L. (1990). Parenting a visually impaired child: The mother's perspective. Journal of Visual Impairment and Blindness, 84, 411–413.

Hanzlik, J. R., & Stevenson, M. B. (1986). Interaction of mothers with their infants who are mentally retarded, retarded with cerebral palsy, or nonretarded. American Journal of Mental Deficiency, 90, 513–520.

Harris, M., Clibbens, J., Chasin, J., & Tibbits, R. (1989). The social context of early sign language development. First Language, 9, 81–97.

Harris, S., Kasari, C., & Sigman, M. (1996). Joint attention and language gains in children with Down syndrome. American Journal on Mental Retardation, 100, 608–619.

Hatton, D. D., Bailey, D. B., Burchinal, M. R., & Ferrell, K. A. (1997). Developmental growth curves of preschool children with vision impairments. Child Development, 68, 788–806.

Hayden, P. W., Davenport, S. L. H., & Campbell, M. M. (1979). Adolescents with myelodysplasia: Impact of physical disability on emotional maturation. Pediatrics, 1(64), 53–59.

Healy, A., Keesee, P. D., & Smith, B. S. (1989). Early services for children with special needs: Transactions for family support (2d ed.). Baltimore: Brookes.

Heller, T., Markwardt, R., Rowitz, L., & Farber, B. (1994). Adaptation of Hispanic families to a child with mental retardation. American Journal on Mental Retardation, 99, 289–300.

Henggeler, S. W., Watson, S. M., Whelan, J. P., & Malone, C. M. (1990). The adaptation of hearing parents of hearing-impaired youths. American Annals of the Deaf, 135, 211–216.

Higgins, L. C. (1973). Classification in congenitally blind children. New York: American Foundation for the Blind (Research Series No. 25).

Hindley, P. A. (1997). Psychiatric aspects of hearing impairments. Journal of Child Psychology and Psychiatry, 38, 101–117.

Hindley, P. A., & Brown, R. M. A. (1994). Psychiatric aspects of specific sensory impairments. In M. Rutter, E. Taylor, & L. Hersov (Eds.), Child and adolescent psychiatry: Modern approaches (3d ed., pp. 720–736). London: Blackwell Scientific.

Hindley, P. A., Hill, P. D., McGuigan, S., & Kitson, N. (1994). Psychiatric disorder in deaf and hearing impaired children and young people: A prevalence study. Journal of Child Psychology and Psychiatry, 35, 917–934.

Hirsch, B. (1979). Psychological dimensions of social supports: A multidimensional analysis. American Journal of Community Psychology, 7, 263–277.

Hodapp, R. M. (1988). The role of maternal emotions and perceptions in interactions with young handicapped children. In K. Marfo (Ed.), Early intervention in transition (pp. 41–60). New York: Praeger.

(1990). One road or many? Issues in the similar sequence hypothesis.

In R. M. Hodapp, J. A. Burack, & E. Zigler (Eds.), Issues in the developmental approach to mental retardation (pp. 49–70). Cambridge University Press.

(1994). Cultural–familial mental retardation. In R. Sternberg (Ed.), Encyclopedia of intelligence (pp. 711–717). New York: Macmillan.

(1995). Parenting children with Down syndrome and other types of mental retardation. In M. Bornstein (Ed.), Handbook of parenting (Vol. 1, pp. 233–253). Hillsdale, NJ: Erlbaum.

(1996). Down syndrome: Developmental, psychiatric, and management issues. Child and Adolescent Psychiatric Clinics of North America, 5, 881–894.

(1997a). Direct and indirect behavioral effects of different genetic disorders of mental retardation. American Journal on Mental Retardation, 102, 67–79.

(1997b). Developmental approaches to children with disabilities: New perspectives, populations, prospects. In S. S. Luthar, J. A. Burack, D. Cicchetti, & J. R. Weisz (Eds.), Developmental psychopathology: Perspectives on risk and disorder (pp. 189–207). Cambridge University Press.

Hodapp, R. M., & Burack, J. A. (1990). What mental retardation tells us about typical development: The examples of sequences, rates, and cross-domain relations. Developmental Psychopathology, 2, 213–225.

Hodapp, R. M., & Dykens, E. M. (1991). Toward an etiology-based strategy of early intervention for handicapped children. In K. Marfo (Ed.), Early intervention in transition: Current perspectives in programs for handicapped children (pp. 41–60). New York: Praeger.

(1994). Mental retardation's two cultures of behavioral research. American Journal on Mental Retardation, 98, 675–687.

Hodapp, R. M., Dykens, E. M., Evans, D. W., & Merighi, J. R. (1992). Maternal emotional reactions to young children with different types of handicaps. Journal of Developmental and Behavioral Pediatrics, 13, 118–123.

Hodapp, R. M., Dykens, E. M., Hagerman, R., Schreiner, R., Lachiewicz, A., & Leckman, J. F. (1990). Developmental implications of changing trajectories of IQ in males with fragile X syndrome. Journal of the American Academy of Child and Adolescent Psychiatry, 29, 214–219.

Hodapp, R. M., Dykens, E. M., & Masino, L. L. (1997). Families of children with Prader–Willi syndrome: Stress-support and relations to child characteristics. Journal of Autism and Developmental Disorders, 27, 11–24.

Hodapp, R. M., & Krasner, D. V. (1995). Families of children with disabilities: Findings from a national sample of eighth-grade students. Exceptionality, 5, 71–81.

Hodapp, R. M., Leckman, J. F., Dykens, E. M., Sparrow, S., Zelinsky, D., & Ort, S. (1992). K-ABC profiles in children with fragile X syndrome, Down syndrome, and nonspecific mental retardation. American Journal on Mental Retardation, 97, 39–46.

Hodapp, R. M., & Mueller, E. (1982). Early social development. In B. Wolman (Ed.), Handbook of developmental psychology (pp. 284–300). Englewood Cliffs, NJ: Prentice-Hall.

Hodapp, R. M., Young, K. T., & Zigler, E. (in press). American family policy and its relation to families of children with disabilities. In L. Rowitz (Ed.), The new partnership: The family and the service system. San Diego, CA: Singular.

Hodapp, R. M., & Zigler, E. (1990). Applying the developmental perspective to individuals with Down syndrome. In D. Cicchetti & M. Beeghly (Eds.), Children with Down syndrome: A developmental perspective (pp. 1–28). Cambridge University Press.

(1995). Past, present, and future issues in the developmental approach to mental retardation and developmental disabilities. In D. Cicchetti & D. J. Cohen (Eds.), Manual of developmental psychopathology (pp. 299–331). New York: Wiley.

(1996). New issues in the developmental approach to mental retardation. In W. E. MacLean (Ed.), Handbook of mental deficiency, psychological theory, and research (3d ed., pp. 115–136). Hillsdale, NJ: Erlbaum.

Holmes, T. H., & Rahe, R. H. (1967). The social readjustment rating scale. Journal of Psychosomatic Research, 11, 213–218.

Holroyd, J., & MacArthur, D. (1976). Mental retardation and stress on parents: A contrast between Down syndrome and childhood autism. American Journal of Mental Deficiency, 80, 431–436.

Horn, D. G., Lorch, E. D., Lorch, R. F., & Culatta, B. (1985). Distractibility and vocabulary deficits in children with spina bifida and hydrocephalus. Developmental Medicine and Child Neurology, 27, 713–720.

Hornby, G. (1995). Fathers' views of the effects on their families of children with Down syndrome. Journal of Child and Family Studies, 4, 103–117.

Humphries, T. (1993). Deaf culture and cultures. In K. M. Christensen & G. L. Delgado (Eds.), Multi-cultural issues in deafness (pp. 3–15). London: Longman.

Hurley, A. D. (1993). Conducting psychological assessments. In F. L. Rowley-Kelly & D. H. Reigel (Eds.), Teaching children with spina bifida (pp. 107–123). Baltimore: Brookes.

Hurley, A. D., Dorman, C., Laatsch, L. K., Bell, S., & D'Avignon, J. (1990). Cognitive functioning in patients with spina bifida, hydrocephalus, and the cocktail party syndrome. Developmental Neuropsychology, 6, 151–172.

Hyche, J., Bakeman, R., & Adamson, L. (1992). Understanding communicative cues of infants with Down syndrome: Effects of mothers' experience and infants' age. Journal of Applied Developmental Psychology, 13, 1–16.

Inhelder, B. (1943/1968). The diagnosis of reasoning in the mentally retarded (Will Beth Stephens and others, Trans.). New York: John Day.

(1966). Cognitive development and its contribution to the diagnosis of some phenomena of mental deficiency. Merrill–Palmer Quarterly, 11, 299–311.

Insight Team of the Sunday Times of London (1979). Suffer the children: The story of thalidomide. New York: Viking Press.

Jamieson, J. R. (1993). Instructional discourse strategies: Differences between hearing and deaf mothers of deaf children. First Language, 14, 153–171.

(1994). Teaching as transaction: Vygotskian perspectives on deafness and mother–child interaction. Exceptional Children, 60, 434–449.

Jan, J. E., Freeman, R. D., & Scott, E. P. (1977). Visual impairment in children and adolescents. New York: Grune & Stratton.

Jones, O. (1980). Prelinguistic communication skills in Down's syndrome and normal infants. In T. Field, S. Goldberg, D. Stern, & A. Sostek (Eds.), High-risk infants and children: Adult and peer interaction (pp. 205–225). New York: Academic Press.

Journal of Visual Impairment and Blindness. (1995). Special issue on deaf-blindness 89 (3).

Kahn, J. V. (1985). Evidence of the similar-structure hypothesis controlling for organicity. American Journal of Mental Deficiency, 89, 372–378.

Kampfe, C. M. (1989). Parental reactions to a child's hearing impairment. American Annals of the Deaf, 134, 255–259.

Karmiloff-Smith, A., Grant, J., Berthoud, I., Bouthors, B., & Stevens, T. (1994, July). The complex picture of the linguistic profile of individuals with Williams syndrome. Paper presented at the Sixth International Professional Meeting of the Williams Syndrome Association, San Diego, CA.

Karmiloff-Smith, A., Grant, J., Berthoud, I., Davies, M., Howlin, P., & Udwin, O. (1996). Language and Williams syndrome: How intact is "intact"? Child Development, 68, 246–262.

Kasari, C., Larson, M. A., & Veltman, M. A. (1987). Differences in neuromotor development. In J. T. Neisworth & S. J. Bagnato (Eds.), The young exceptional child: Early development and education (pp. 319–349). New York: Macmillan.

Kasari, C., Mundy, P., Yirmiya, N., & Sigman, M. (1990). Affect and attention in children with Down syndrome. American Journal on Mental Retardation, 95, 55–67.

Kasari, C., & Sigman, M. (1997). Linking parental perceptions to interactions in young children with autism. Journal of Autism and Developmental Disorders, 27, 39–57.

Kaufman, A. S., & Kaufman, N. L. (1983). Kaufman Assessment Battery for Children. Circle Pines, MN: American Guidance Service.

Kaye, K. (1982). The mental and social life of babies. Chicago: University of Chicago Press.

Kazak, A. (1987). Families with disabled children: Stress and social networks in three samples. Journal of Abnormal Child Psychology, 15, 137–146.

Kazak, A., & Marvin, R. (1984). Differences, difficulties, and adaptation: Stress and social networks in families with a handicapped child. Family Relations, 33, 67–77.

Kekelis, L. S., & Anderson, E. S. (1984). Family communication styles and language development. Journal of Visual Impairment and Blindness, 78, 54–65.

Keller, H. (1954). The story of my life. Garden City, NY: Doubleday.

Kessen, W. (1962). Stage and structure in the study of children. In W. Kessen & C. Kuhlman (Eds.), Thought in the young child. Monographs of the Society for Research in Child Development, 27, 444–449.

    (1968). The construction and selection of environments: Discussion of Richard H. Walter's paper on social isolation and social interaction. In D. C. Glass (Ed.), Environmental influences. New York: Rockefeller University Press and Russell Sage Foundation.

    (1984). The end of the age of development. In R. Sternberg (Ed.), Mechanisms of cognitive development (pp. 1–17). New York: Freeman.

Klima, E., & Bellugi, U. (1979). The signs of language. Cambridge, MA: Harvard University Press.

Knox, J. E., & Kozulin, A. (1989). The Vygotskian tradition in Soviet psychological study of deaf children. In W. O. McCagg & L. Siegelbaum (Eds.), The disabled in the Soviet Union (pp. 63–84). Pittsburgh: University of Pittsburgh Press.

Koester, L. S. (1992). Intuitive parenting as a model for understanding parent–infant interactions when one partner is deaf. American Annals of the Deaf, 137, 362–369.

Kogan, K. T., Tyler, N., & Turner, P. (1974). The process of interpersonal adaptation between mothers and their cerebral palsied children. Developmental Medicine and Child Neurology, 16, 518–527.

Koller, H., Richardson, S. A., Katz, M., & McLaren, J. (1983). Behavior disturbance since childhood among a 5-year birth cohort of all mentally retarded young adults in a city. American Journal of Mental Deficiency, 87, 386–395.

Kopp, C. B., & Shaperman, J. (1973). Cognitive development in the absence of object manipulation during infancy. Developmental Psychology, 9, 430.

Kounin, J. (1941a). Experimental studies of rigidity: I. The measurement of rigidity in normal and feebleminded persons. Character and Personality, 9, 251–272.

(1941b). Experimental studies of rigidity: II. The explanatory power of the concept of rigidity as applied to retarded persons. Character and Personality, 9, 273–282.

Krauss, M. (1993). Child-related and parenting stress: Similarities and differences between mothers and fathers of children with disabilities. American Journal on Mental Retardation, 97, 393–404.

Krauss, M. W., & Hauser-Cram, P. (1992). Policy and program development for infants and toddlers with disabilities. In L. Rowitz (Ed.), Mental retardation in the year 2000 (pp. 184–196). New York: Springer.

Krauss, M. W., & Seltzer, M. M. (1998). Life course perspectives in mental retardation research: The case of family caregiving. In J. A. Burack, R. M. Hodapp, & E. Zigler (Eds.), Handbook on mental retardation and development (pp. 504–520). Cambridge University Press.

Kronenberger, W. G., & Thompson, R. J. (1992). Psychological adaptation of mothers of children with spina bifida: Association with dimensions of social relationships. Journal of Pediatric Psychology, 17, 1–14.

Kuhn, T. S. (1970). The structure of scientific revolutions (2d ed.). Chicago: University of Chicago Press.

Kushe, C., & Greenberg, M. T. (1993). The PATHS curriculum. Seattle: Developmental Research & Programs.

Kyle, J., & Ackerman, J. (1987). Signing for infants. Deaf mothers using BSL in the early stages of development. Unpublished manuscript, University of Bristol, Education Research Unit, Bristol, England.

Labouvie-Vief, G., & Chandler, M. J. (1978). Cognitive development and life-span developmental theory: Idealistic versus contextual perspectives. In P. B. Baltes (Ed.), Life-span development and behavior (Vol. 1, pp. 181–210). New York: Academic Press.

Landau, B. (1983). Blind children's language is not "meaningless." In A. E. Mills (Ed.), Language acquisition in the blind child: Normal and deficient (pp. 62–76). London: Croom Helm.

Landau, B., & Gleitman, L. R. (1985). Language and experience: Evidence from the blind child. Cambridge, MA: Harvard University Press.

Landry, S. H., Robinson, S. S., Copeland, D., & Garner, P. W. (1993). Goal-directed behavior and perception of self-competence in children with spina bifida. Journal of Pediatric Psychology, 18, 389–396.

Lane, E. B., & Kinder, E. F. (1939). Relativism in the thinking of subnormal subjects as measured by certain of Piaget's tests. Journal of Genetic Psychology, 54, 107–118.

Lane, H. (1976). The wild boy of Aveyron. New York: Basic Books.

(1984). When the mind hears: A history of the deaf. New York: Random House.

(1995). The education of deaf children: Drowning in the mainstream and the sidestream. In J. M. Kauffman & D. P. Hallihan (Eds.), The illusion of full inclusion: A comprehensive critique of a current special education bandwagon (pp. 275–287). Austin, TX: Pro-Ed Press.

Launer, P. B. (1982). "A plane" is not "to fly": Acquiring the distinction between related nouns and verbs in American Sign Language (Doctoral dissertation, City University of New York). American Dissertations, 1982–1983, ADD83-02525, p. 254.

Lazarus, R. S., & Folkman, S. (1984). Stress, appraisal, and coping. New York: Springer.

Lederberg, A. R., & Mobley, C. E. (1990). The effect of hearing impairment on the quality of attachment and mother–toddler interaction. Child Development, 61, 1596–1604.

Lederberg, A. R., Willis, M. G., & Frankel, K. H. (1991, March). A longitudinal study of the effects of deafness on the early mother–child relationship. Paper presented at the biennial meetings of the Society for Research in Child Development.

Lenneberg, E. H. (1967). Biological foundations of language. New York: Wiley.

Lenneberg, E. H., Rebelsky, F. G., & Nichols, I. A. (1965). The vocalization of infants born to deaf and hearing parents. Vita Humana (Human Development), 8, 23–37.

Lenz, W. (1961). Kindiche Missbildungen nach Medikament-Einnahme wahrend der Graviditat. Deutche medizinische Wochenschrift, 86, 2555–2556.

Levine, K. (1994). Williams syndrome: Information for teachers. Clawson, MI: Williams Syndrome Association.

Levine, K., & Wharton, R. (1993). Children with Prader–Willi syndrome: Information for school staff. Roslyn Heights, NY: Visible Ink.

Lewin, K. (1936). A dynamic theory of personality. New York: McGraw-Hill.

Lewis, E. O. (1933). Types of mental deficiency and their social significance. Journal of Mental Science, 79, 298–304.

Lewis, M., & Miller, S. (Eds.). (1990). Handbook of developmental psychopathology. New York: Plenum.

Lewis, V. (1987). Development and handicap. London: Basil Blackwell.

Lister, C., Leach, C., & Udberg, L. (1991). The development of understanding of quantity in children with cerebral palsy: II. Early Child Development and Care, 74, 29–37.

Lobato, D. (1983). Siblings of handicapped children: A review. Journal of Autism and Developmental Disorders, 13, 347–364.

Lubs, H. A. (1969). A marker X chromosome. American Journal of Human Genetics, 21, 231–244.

Luria, A. R. (1963). Psychological studies of mental deficiency in the Soviet Union. In N. R. Ellis (Ed.), Handbook of mental deficiency (pp. 353–387). New York: McGraw-Hill.

(1979). The making of mind: A personal account of Soviet psychology. Cambridge, MA: Harvard University Press.

Luterman, D. (1987). Deafness in the family. Boston, MA: College-Hill.

MacMillan, D. L., Gresham, F. M., & Siperstein, G. N. (1993). Conceptual and psychometric concerns about the 1992 AAMR definition of mental retardation. American Journal on Mental Retardation, 98, 325–335.

Maestas y Moores, J. (1980). Early linguistic environment: Interactions of deaf parents with their infants. Sign Language Studies, 26, 1–13.

Mahaney, E., & Stephens, B. (1974). Two-year gains in moral judgment by retarded and nonretarded persons. American Journal of Mental Deficiency, 79, 134–141.

Mahoney, G. (1988). Enhancing the developmental competence of handicapped infants. In K. Marfo (Ed.), Parent–child interaction and developmental disabilities (pp. 203–219). New York: Praeger.

Mahoney, G., Fors, S., & Wood, S. (1990). Maternal directive behavior revisited. American Journal on Mental Retardation, 94, 398–406.

Maisto, A. A., & German, M. L. (1986). Reliability, predictive validity, and interrelationships of early assessment indices used with developmentally delayed infants and children. Journal of Child Clinical Psychology, 15, 327–332.

Marfo, K. (1990). Maternal directiveness in interactions with mentally handicapped children: An analytical commentary. Journal of Child Psychology and Psychiatry, 31, 531–549.

(1992). Correlates of maternal directiveness with children who are developmentally delayed. American Journal of Orthopsychiatry, 62, 219–233.

Marschark, M. (1993). Psychological development of deaf children. Oxford: Oxford University Press.

Marshall, N., Hegrenes, J., & Goldstein, S. (1973). Verbal interactions: Mothers and their retarded children versus mothers and their nonretarded children. American Journal of Mental Deficiency, 77, 415–419.

Masataka, N. (1992). Motherese in a signed language. Infant Behavior and Development, 15, 453–460.

Matson, J., & Frame, C. L. (1986). Psychopathology among mentally retarded children and adolescents. Newbury Park, CA: Sage.

Maurer, H., & Sherrod, K. (1987). Context of directives given to young children with Down syndrome and nonretarded children: Development over two years. American Journal of Mental Deficiency, 91, 579–590.

Maxfield, K. E., & Buckholz, S. (1957). A social maturity scale for blind preschool children: A guide for its use. New York: American Foundation for the Blind.

McBride, W. G. (1961). Thalidomide and congenital abnormalities. Lancet, 2, 1358.

(1977). Thalidomide embryopathy. Teratology, 16, 79–82.

McCall, R. B. (1982). Nature–nurture and the two realms of development: A proposed integration with respect to mental development. Child Development, 52, 1–12.

McCall, R. B., Eichorn, D., & Hogarty, P. (1977). Transitions in early mental development. Monographs of the Society for Research in Child Development, Whole No. 42.

McConachie, H. R., & Moore, V. (1994). Early expressive language of severely visually impaired children. Development Medicine and Child Neurology, 36, 230–240.

McCormick, M. C., Charney, E. B., & Stemmler, M. M. (1986). Assessing the impact of a child with spina bifida on the family. Developmental Medicine and Child Neurology, 28, 53–61.

McCune, L. (1991). Review of A. Dunlea, Vision and the emergence of meaning. Language and Speech, 34, 97–103.

McGinnis, A. R. (1981). Functional linguistic strategies in blind children. Visual Impairment and Blindness, 75, 210–214.

Meadow-Orlans, K. P. (1990). The impact of childhood hearing loss on the family. In D. Moores & K. P. Meadow-Orlans (Eds.), Educational and developmental aspects of deafness (pp. 321–338). Washington, DC: Gallaudet University Press.

Meisels, S. J., & Shonkoff, J. (Eds.). (1990). Handbook of early intervention. Cambridge University Press.

Miller, G. (1992). Cerebral palsies. In G. Miller & J. C. Ramer (Eds.), Static encephalopathies of infancy and childhood (pp. 11–26). New York: Raven Press.

Miller, J. G. (1984). Culture and the development of everyday social cognition. Journal of Personality and Social Psychology, 46, 961–978.

Mills, A. E. (1988). Visual handicap. In D. Bishop & K. Mogford (Eds.), Language development in exceptional circumstances (pp. 150–164). Edinburgh: Churchill Livingstone.

Minde, K. (1977). Coping styles of 34 adolescents with cerebral palsy. American Journal of Psychiatry, 135, 1344–1349.

Mink, I., Nihira, C., & Meyers, C. (1983). Taxonomy of family life styles: I. Homes with TMR children. American Journal of Mental Deficiency, 87, 484–497.

Minnes, P. (1988). Family stress associated with a developmentally handicapped child. International Review of Research on Mental Retardation, 15, 195–226.

Moore, V., & McConachie, H. (1994). Communication between blind and severely visually impaired children and their parents. British Journal of Developmental Psychology, 12, 491–502.

Moores, D. F. (1996). Educating the deaf: Psychology, principles, and practices (4th ed.). Boston: Houghton Mifflin.

Moores, D. F., & Sweet, C. (1990). Factors predictive of school achievement. In D. F. Moores & K. P. Meadow-Orlans (Eds.), Educational and developmental aspects of deafness (pp. 154–201). Washington, DC: Gallaudet University Press.

Morss, J. R. (1983). Cognitive development in the Down's syndrome infant: Slow or different? British Journal of Educational Psychology, 53, 40–47.

Moser, H. (1992). Prevention of mental retardation (genetics). In L. Rowitz (Ed.), Mental retardation in the year 2000 (pp. 140–148). New York: Springer.

Mulford, R. C. (1983). Referential development in blind children. In A. E. Mills (Ed.), Language acquisition in blind children: Normal and deficient (pp. 89–107). London: Croom Helm.

(1988). First words of the blind child. In M. D. Smith & J. L. Locke (Eds.), The emergent lexicon: The child's development of linguistic vocabulary (pp. 293–338). New York: Academic Press.

Mundy, P., & Kasari, C. (1990). The similar structure hypothesis and differential rate of development in mental retardation. In R. M. Hodapp, J. A. Burack, & E. Zigler (Eds.), Issues in the developmental approach to mental retardation (pp. 71–92). Cambridge University Press.

Neisser, A. (1990). The other side of silence: Sign language and the Deaf community in America. New York: Knopf.

Neisser, U. (1991). Two perceptually given aspects of the self and their development. Developmental Review, 11, 197–209.

Nelson, K. (1973). Structure and strategy in learning to talk. Monographs of the Society for Research in Child Development, 38 (1–2).

Nelson, K. B., & Ellenberg, J. H. (1986). Antecedents of cerebral palsy: Multivariate analysis of risk. New England Journal of Medicine, 315, 81–86.

Newport, E. L. (1990). Maturational constraints on language learning. Cognitive Science, 14, 11–28.

Newport, E. L., & Ashbrook, E. F. (1977). The emergence of semantic relations in American Sign Language. Papers and Reports in Child Language Development, 13, 16–21.

Newport, E. L., & Meier, R. P. (1985). The acquisition of American Sign Language. In D. Slobin (Ed.), The cross-linguistic study of language acquisition (pp. 881–938). Hillsdale, NJ: Erlbaum.

Nixon, H. L. (1988). Reassessing social support groups for parents of visually impaired children. Journal of Visual Impairment and Blindness, 82, 271–278.

Norris, M., Spaulding, P. J., & Brodie, F. H. (1957). Blindness in children. Chicago: University of Chicago Press.

Nover, S. M. (1993). Politics and language: American Sign Language and English in Deaf education. In C. Lucas (Ed.), Sociolinguistis in Deaf communities (pp. 109–163). Washington, DC: Gallaudet University Press.

Ochs, E. (1986). Introduction. In B. B. Schieffelin & E. Ochs (Eds.), Language socialization across cultures (pp. 1–13). Cambridge University Press.

Olshansky, S. (1962). Chronic sorrow: A response to having a mentally defective child. Social Casework, 43, 190–193.

(1966). Parent responses to a mentally defective child. Mental Retardation, 4, 21–23.

Opitz, J. M. (1996, March). Historiography of the causal analysis of mental retardation. Speech to the 29th Gatlinburg Conference on Research and Theory in Mental Retardation, Gatlinburg, TN.

Orlansky, M. D., & Trap, J. J. (1987). Working with Native American persons: Issues in facilitating communication and providing culturally relevant services. Journal of Visual Impairments and Blindness, 81, 151–155.

Padden, C. (1990). Folk explanation in language survival. In D. Middleton (Ed.), Collective remembering (pp. 190–202). Seabury, CA: Sage.

(1996). From the cultural to the bi-cultural: The modern Deaf community. In I. Parasnis (Ed.), Cultural and linguistic diversity and the Deaf experience (pp. 79–98). Cambridge University Press.

Padden, C., & Humphries, T. (1988). Deaf in America: Voices from a culture. Cambridge, MA: Harvard University Press.

Parasnis, I. (1983). Effects of parental deafness and early exposure to manual communication on the cognitive skills, English language skills, and field independence of young deaf adults. Journal of Speech and Hearing Research, 26, 588–594.

Parasnis, I. (Ed.). 1996. Cultural and language diversity and the Deaf experience. Cambridge University Press.

Paul, P. V., & Quigley, S. P. (1994). Language and deafness (2d ed.). San Diego, CA: Singular.

Pearson, K., & Jaederholm, G. A. (1914). On the continuity of mental defect. London: Delau.

Pepper, S. (1942). World hypotheses. Berkeley: University of California Press.

Perez-Pereira, M., & Castro, J. (1992). Pragmatic functions of blind and sighted children's language: A twin case study. First Language, 12, 17–37.

Perlmutter, D. M. (1991). The language of the deaf [review of O. Sachs, Seeing voices]. New York Review of Books, 38(6), 65–72.

Petitto, L. (1987). On the autonomy of language and gesture: Evidence from the acquisition of personal pronouns in American Sign Language. Cognition, 27, 1–52.

Petitto, L., & Marentette, P. F. (1991). Babbling in the manual mode: Evidence for the ontogeny of language. Science, 251, 1493–1496.

Piaget, J. (1928). Judgment and reasoning in the child. New York: Harcourt, Brace.

(1943/1968). Preface to the first edition. In B. Inhelder, The diagnosis of reasoning in the mentally retarded. New York: John Day.

(1952). Autobiography. In E. G. Boring et al. (Eds.), A history of psychology in autobiography (Vol. 4, pp. 237–256). Worcester, MA: Clark University Press.

(1954). The construction of reality in the child. New York: Ballantine.

Piaget, J., & Inhelder, B. (1947). Diagnosis of mental operations and theory of intelligence. American Journal of Mental Deficiency, 51, 401–406.

(1969). The psychology of the child. New York: Basic Books.

Piattelli-Palmarini, M. (1980). Language and learning: The debate between Jean Piaget and Noam Chomsky. Cambridge, MA: Harvard University Press.

Pitcairn, T. K., & Wishart, J. G. (1994). Reactions of young children with Down's syndrome to an impossible task. British Journal of Developmental Psychology, 12, 485–489.

Pizzuto, E. (1990). The early development of deixis in American Sign Language: What is the point? In V. Volterra & C. J. Erting (Eds.), From gesture to language in hearing and deaf children (pp. 142–152). Berlin: Springer.

Plomin, R., & Rende, R. (1991). Human behavioral genetics. Annual Review of Psychology, 42, 161–190.

Pober, B. R., & Dykens, E. M. (1996). Williams syndrome: An overview of medical, cognitive, and behavioral features. Child and Adolescent Psychiatric Clinics of North America, 5, 929–943.

Poizner, H., Klima, E. S., & Bellugi, U. (1987). What the hands reveal about the brain. Cambridge, MA: MIT Press.

Prendergast, S. G., & McCollum, J. A. (1996). Let's talk: The effect of maternal hearing status on interactions with toddlers who are deaf. American Annals of the Deaf, 141, 11–18.

Pringle, M. L. K., & Fiddes, D. O. (1970). The challenge of thalidomide. London: Longman.

Prior, M. R., Glazner, J., Sanson, A., & Debelle, G. (1988). Research note: Temperament and behavioral adjustment in hearing-impaired children. Journal of Child Psychology and Psychiatry, 29, 209–216.

Proctor, A. (1988). Noncry vocal development in normal and at-risk infants: A review of the first 12 months. In K. Marfo (Ed.), Parent–

child interaction and developmental disabilities (pp. 95–113). New York: Praeger.

Prothro, E. T. (1943). Egocentricity and abstraction in children and in adult aments. American Journal of Psychology, 56, 66–77.

Pueschel, S. R., Gallagher, P. L., Zartler, A. S., & Pezzullo, J. C. (1986). Cognitive and learning processes in children with Down syndrome. Research in Developmental Disabilities, 8, 21–37.

Reese, H. W., & Overton, W. F. (1970). Models of development and theories of development. In L. R. Goulet & P. Baltes (Eds.), Life-span developmental psychology (pp. 115–145). New York: Academic Press.

Reilly, J. S., Klima, E., & Bellugi, U. (1990). Once more with feeling: Affect and language in atypical populations. Development and Psychopathology, 2, 367–391.

Reiss, S., Levitan, G. W., & Szyskzo, J. (1982). Emotional disturbances and mental retardation: Diagnostic overshadowing. American Journal of Mental Deficiency, 86, 567–574.

Reynell, J. (1978). Developmental patterns of visually handicapped children. Child: Care, Health, and Development, 4, 291–303.

Reynell, J., & Zinkin, P. (1975). New procedures for the developmental assessment of young children with severe visual handicaps. Child: Care, Health, and Development, 1, 61–69.

Rieber, R. W., & Carton, A. S. (Eds.). (1993). The collected works of L. S. Vygotsky: Vol. 2. The fundamentals of defectology (J. Knox & C. B. Stephens, Trans.). New York: Plenum Press.

Rienzi, B. M. (1990). Influence and adaptability in families with deaf parents and hearing children. American Annals of the Deaf, 135, 402–408.

Robinson, C. C., & Rosenberg, S. (1987). A strategy for assessing infants with motor impairments. In I. Uzgiris & J. M. Hunt (Eds.), Infant performance and experience: New findings with the Ordinal Scales (pp. 311–339). Urbana: University of Illinois Press.

Rodgers, S. J., & Puchalski, C. (1988). Development of object permanence in visually-impaired infants. Journal of Visual Impairments and Blindness, 82, 137–142.

Rondal, J. (1977). Maternal speech in normal and Down syndrome children. In P. Mittler (Ed.), Research to practice in mental retardation: Vol. 3, Education and training (pp. 239–243). Baltimore: University Park Press.

(1995). Exceptional language development in Down syndrome. Cambridge University Press.

(1996). Oral language in Down syndrome. In J. Rondal, J. Perera, L. Nadel, & A. Comblain (Eds.), Down's syndrome: Psychological, psychobiological, and socio-educational perspectives (pp. 99–117). London: Whurr.

Rondal, J., Ghiotto, M., Bredart, S., & Bachelet, J.-F. (1988). Mean length of utterance of children with Down syndrome. American Journal on Mental Retardation, 93, 64–66.

Rosenberg, S. A., & Robinson, C. C. (1990). Assessment of the infant with multiple handicaps. In E. D. Gibbs & D. M. Teti (Eds.), Interdisciplinary assessment of infants (pp. 177–188). Baltimore: Brookes.

Rowitz, L. (1988). The homogenization of deviance. Mental Retardation, 26(1), 1–3.

Rowland, C. (1983). Patterns of interaction between three blind infants and their mothers. In A. E. Mills (Ed.), Language acquisition in the blind child (pp. 114–132). London: Croom Helm.

Rymer, R. (1993). Genie: An abused child's flight from silence. New York: HarperCollins.

Sameroff, A., & Chandler, M. (1975). Reproductive risk and the continuum of caretaker casualty. In F. D. Horowitz, M. Hetherington, S. Scarr-Salapatek, & G. Siegel (Eds.), Review of child development research (Vol. 4, pp. 187–244). Chicago: University of Chicago Press.

Sandler, A.-M. (1963). Aspects of passivity and ego development in the blind infant. Psychoanalytic Study of the Child, 18, 343–360.

Sattler, J. M. (1992). Assessment of children (3d ed.). San Diego, CA: Sattler.

Scarr-Salapatek, S. (1975). An evolutionary perspective on infant intelligence: Species patterns and individual variations. In M. Lewis (Ed.), Origins of intelligence (pp. 165–197). New York: Plenum.

Scheerenberger, R. C. (1983). A history of mental retardation. Baltimore: Brookes.

Schieffelin, B. B., & Ochs, E. (Eds.). (1986). Language socialization across cultures. Cambridge University Press.

Schildroth, A. (1988). Recent changes in the educational placement of deaf students. American Annals of the Deaf, 133, 61–67.

(1994). Congenital cytomegalovirus and deafness. American Journal of Audiology, 3, 27–38.

Schlesinger, H. (1978). The effects of deafness on child development. In L. Liben (Ed.), Deaf children: Developmental perspectives (pp. 157–172). New York: Academic Press.

Schlesinger, H., & Meadow, K. P. (1972). Sound and sign: Childhood deafness and mental health. Berkeley: University of California Press.

Schwenn, J. O., Rotatori, A. F., & Fox, R. A. (Eds.). (1991). Understanding students with high incidence exceptionalities: Categorical and non-categorical perspectives. Springfield, IL: Thomas.

Seitz, V., & Provence, S. (1990). Caregiver-focused models of early intervention. In S. J. Meisels & J. P. Shonkoff (Eds.), Handbook of early intervention (pp. 400–427). Cambridge University Press.

Seltzer, M. M., Greenberg, J. S., & Krauss, M. W. (1995). A comparison of coping strategies of aging mothers of adults with mental illness or mental retardation. Psychology and Aging, 10, 64–75.

Seltzer, M. M., & Krauss, M. W. (1989). Aging parents with mentally retarded children: Family risk factors and sources of support. American Journal on Mental Retardation, 94, 303–312.

Seltzer, M., Krauss, M., & Tsunematsu, N. (1993). Adults with Down syndrome and their aging mothers: Diagnostic group differences. American Journal on Mental Retardation, 97, 496–508.

Seltzer, M., & Ryff, C. (1994). Parenting across the lifespan: The normative and nonnormative cases. Life-Span Development and Behavior, 12, 1–40.

Silon, E., & Harter, S. (1985). Assessment of perceived competence, motivational orientation, and anxiety in segregated and mainstreamed educable mentally retarded children. Journal of Educational Psychology, 77, 217–230.

Simeonsson, R. J., & Bailey, D. B. (1990). Family dimensions in early intervention. In S. J. Meisels & J. P. Shonkoff (Eds.), Handbook of early intervention (pp. 428–444). Cambridge University Press.

Sloper, P., Knussen, C., Turner, S., & Cunningham, C. (1991). Factors related to stress and satisfaction with life in families of children with Down's syndrome. Journal of Child Psychology & Psychiatry, 32, 4, 655–676.

Smith, D. D. (1989). Teaching students with learning and behavior problems (2d ed.). Englewood Cliffs, NJ: Prentice-Hall.

Snow, J. H., Prince, M., Souheaver, G., Ashcraft, E., Stefans, V., & Edmonds, J. (1994). Neuropsychological patterns of adolescents and young adults with spina bifida. Archives of Clinical Neuropsychology, 9, 277–287.

Solnit, A., & Stark, M. (1961). Mourning and the birth of a defective child. Psychoanalytic Study of the Child, 16, 523–537.

Spaulding, B. R., & Morgan, S. B. (1986). Spina bifida children and their parents: A population prone to family dysfunction? Journal of Pediatric Psychology, 11, 359–374.

Spencer, P. E., Bodner-Johnson, B. A., & Gutfreund, M. K. (1992). Interacting with infants with a hearing loss: What can we learn from mothers who are deaf? Journal of Early Intervention, 16, 64–78.

Spencer, P. E., & Gutfreund, M. K. (1990). Directiveness of mother–infant interactions. In D. R. Moores & K. P. Meadow-Orlans (Eds.), Educational and developmental aspects of deafness (pp. 350–365). Washington, DC: Gallaudet University Press.

Spiridgliozzi, G., Lachiewicz, A., MacMurdo, C., Vizoso, A., O'Donnell, C., McConkie-Rosell, A., & Burgess, D. (1995a). Educating boys with fragile X syndrome: A guide for parents and professionals. Durham, NC: Duke University Medical Center, Child Development Unit.

(1995b). Fragile X syndrome: Strategies for the classroom. genetwork, 1(1), 7, 11.

Spitz, H. (1983). Critique of the developmental position in mental retardation research. Journal of Special Education, 17, 261–294.

Spitz, R. A. (1945). Hospitalism: An inquiry into the genesis of psychiatric conditions in early childhood. Psychoanalytic Study of the Child, 1, 53–74.

Stanley, F. J. (1994). The aetiology of cerebral palsy. Early Human Development, 36, 81–88.

Stokoe, W. (1960). Sign language structure: An outline of the visual communication systems of the American Deaf. Studies in Linguistics (Occasional Papers No. 8). Buffalo, NY: University of Buffalo, Department of Anthropology and Linguistics.

(1994). A sign language dictionary. In C. J. Erting, R. C. Johnson, D. L. Smith, & B. D. Snider (Eds.), The Deaf way (pp. 331–334). Washington, DC: Gallaudet Press.

Stoneman, Z. (1989). Comparison groups in research on families with mentally retarded members: A methodological and conceptual review. American Journal on Mental Retardation, 94, 195–215.

(1998). Research on siblings of children with mental retardation: Contributions of developmental theory and etiology. In J. A. Burack, R. M. Hodapp, & E. Zigler (Eds.), Handbook on mental retardation and development (pp. 669–692). Cambridge University Press.

Suelzle, M., & Keenan, V. (1981). Changes in family support networks over the life cycle of mentally retarded persons. American Journal of Mental Deficiency, 86, 267–274.

Supalla, S. (1994). Equality in educational opportunities: The Deaf version. In C. J. Erting, R. C. Johnson, D. L. Smith, & B. D. Snider (Eds.), The Deaf way (pp. 584–592). Washington, DC: Gallaudet Press.

Super, C. M., & Harkness, S. (1986). The developmental niche: A conceptualization at the interface of child and culture. International Journal of Behavioral Development, 9, 545–569.

Sutherland, G. V. (1977). Fragile sites on human chromosomes, demonstration of their dependence on the type of tissue culture medium. Science, 197, 265–266.

Swisher, M. V. (1992). The role of parents in developing visual turn-taking in their young deaf children. American Annals of the Deaf, 137, 92–100.

Tager-Flusberg, H., & Sullivan, K. (1998). Early language development in children with mental retardation. In J. A. Burack, R. M. Hodapp, & E. Zigler (Eds.), Handbook of mental retardation and development (pp. 208–239). Cambridge University Press.

Tannock, R. (1988). Mothers' directiveness in their interactions with children with and without Down syndrome. American Journal on Mental Retardation, 93, 154–165.

Taussig, H. B. (1962). A study of the German outbreak of phocomelia: The thalidomide syndrome. Journal of the American Medical Association, 180, 1106–1114.

Tew, B. (1979). The "cocktail party syndrome" in children with hydrocephalus and spina bifida. British Journal of Disorders of Communication, 14, 89–101.

Tew, B., & Laurence, K. M. (1973). Mothers, brothers, and sisters of patients with spina bifida. Developmental Medicine and Child Neurology, 15, 69–76.

Thomas, V., & Olson, D. H. (1993). Problem families and the circumplex model: Observational assessment using the Clinical Rating Scale (CRS). Journal of Marital and Family Therapy, 19, 159–175.

Turnbull, A. P., Patterson, J. M., Behr, S. K., Murphy, D. L., Marquis, J. G., & Blue-Banning, M. J. (Eds.), Cognitive coping, families, and disability. Baltimore: Brookes.

Udwin, O., & Yule, W. (1990). Expressive language of children with Williams syndrome. American Journal of Medical Genetics, 6 (Suppl.), 108–114.

Urwin, C. (1978). The development of communication between blind infants and their parents. In A. Lock (Ed.), Action, gesture, and symbol: The emergence of language (pp. 79–108). London: Academic Press.

(1983). Dialogue and cognitive functioning in the early language development of three blind children. In A. E. Mills (1983), Language acquisition in the blind child (pp. 142–161). London: Croom Helm.

Uzgiris, I., & Hunt, J. McV. (1975). Assessment in infancy: Ordinal Scales of Infant Psychological Development. Urbana: University of Illinois Press.

Vadasy, P. F., & Fewell, R. R. (1986). Mothers of deaf–blind children. In R. R. Fewell & P. F. Vadasy (Eds.), Families of handicapped children: Needs and supports across the life-span (pp. 121–148). Austin, TX: Pro-Ed Press.

van der Veer, R., & Valsiner, J. (1991). Understanding Vygotsky: A quest for synthesis. Oxford: Basil Blackwell.

Vernon, P. (1979). Intelligence: Heredity and environment. San Francisco: Freeman.

Vietze, P., Abernathy, S., Ashe, M., & Faulstich, G. (1978). Contingency interaction between mothers and their developmentally delayed infants. In G. P. Sackett (Ed.), Observing behavior (Vol. 1, pp. 115–132). Baltimore: University Park Press.

Vygotsky, L. S. (1927/1993). Defect and compensation. In R. W. Rieber & A. S. Carton (Eds.), The collected works of L. S. Vygotsky: Vol.

2. The fundamentals of defectology (pp. 52–64). New York: Plenum. (Original work published in 1927.)

(1934/1962). Thought and language (E. Hanfmann & G. Vaker, Trans.). Cambridge, MA: MIT Press.

(1978). Mind in society. Cambridge, MA: Harvard University Press.

Wallander, J. L., Varni, J. W., Babani, L., DeHaan, C. B., Wilcox, K. T., & Banis, H. T. (1989). The social environment and the adaptation of mothers of physically handicapped children. Journal of Pediatric Psychology, 14, 371–387.

Warren, D. H. (1984). Blindness and early childhood development (2d ed.). New York: American Foundation for the Blind.

(1994). Blindness and children: An individual differences approach. Cambridge University Press.

Watson, D. (1991). Occupational therapy guidelines for children and adolescents with spina bifida. Child: Care, Health, and Development, 17, 367–380.

Weiner, J. (1994). The beak of the finch: The story of evolution in our time. New York: Knopf.

Weisner, T. S., Beizer, L., & Stolze, L. (1991). Religion and families of children with developmental disabilities. American Journal on Mental Retardation, 95, 647–662.

Weiss, B., Weisz, J. R., & Bromfield, R. (1986). Performance of retarded and nonretarded persons on information-processing tasks: Further tests of the similar-structure hypothesis. Psychological Bulletin, 100, 157–175.

Weisz, J. R. (1990). Cultural-familial mental retardation: A developmental perspective on cognitive performance and "helpless" behavior. In R. M. Hodapp, J. A. Burack, & E. Zigler (Eds.), Issues in the developmental approach to mental retardation (pp. 137–168). Cambridge University Press.

Weisz, J. R., & Yeates, O. W. (1981). Cognitive development in retarded and nonretarded persons: Piagetian tests of the similar structure hypothesis. Psychological Bulletin, 90, 153–178.

Weisz, J. R., Yeates, O. W., & Zigler, E. (1982). Piagetian evidence and the developmental-difference controversy. In E. Zigler & D. Balla (Eds.), Mental retardation: The developmental-difference controversy (pp. 213–276). Hillsdale, NJ: Erlbaum.

Wells, G. (1986). Variation in child language. In P. Fletcher & M. Garman (Eds.), Language acquisition: Studies in first language development (pp. 109–139). Cambridge University Press.

Werner, H. (1926/1948). Comparative psychology of mental development (rev. ed.). New York: International Universities Press. (Original work published 1926.)

(1937). Process and achievement: A basic problem of education and developmental psychology. Harvard Educational Review, 7, 353–368.

(1938). Approaches to a functional analysis of mentally handicapped problem children. American Journal of Mental Deficiency, 43, 105–108.

(1941). Psychological processes investigating deficiencies in learning. American Journal of Mental Deficiency, 46, 233–235.

(1957). The concept of development from a comparative and organismic point of view. In D. Harris (Ed.), The concept of development (pp. 125–148). Minneapolis: University of Minnesota Press.

(1959/1978). Significance of general experimental psychology for the understanding of abnormal behavior and its correction or prevention. In S. S. Barton & M. B. Franklin (Eds.), Developmental processes: Heinz Werner's selected writings (pp. 327–345). New York: International Universities Press (first presented as a talk in 1959).

Werner, H., & Kaplan, B. (1963). Symbol formation. New York: Wiley.

Werner, H., & Strauss, A. (1939). Problems and methods of functional analysis in mentally deficient children. Journal of Abnormal and Social Psychology, 34, 37–62.

Wertsch, J. V. (1985). Vygotsky and the social formation of mind. Cambridge, MA: Harvard University Press.

Wexler, N. S., Young, A. B., Tanzi, R. E., Travers, H., Starosta-Rubinstein, S., Penney, J. B., Snodgrass, S. R., Shoulson, I., Gomez, F., Ramos-Arroyo, M. A., Penshaszadeh, G. K., Moreno, H., Gibbons, K., Faryniarz, A., Hobbs, W., Anderson, M. A., Bonilla, E., Conneally, P. M., & Gusella, J. F. (1987). Homozygotes for Huntington's disease. Nature, 326, 194–197.

Wikler, L. (1986). Periodic stresses in families of mentally retarded children: An exploratory study. American Journal of Mental Deficiency, 90, 703–706.

Wikler, L., Wasow, M., & Hatfield, E. (1981). Chronic sorrow revisited: Attitudes of parents and professionals about adjustment to mental retardation. American Journal of Orthopsychiatry, 51, 63–70.

Wilbur, R. B. (1979). American Sign Language and sign systems. Baltimore: University Park Press.

Wills, K. E. (1993). Neuropsychological functioning in children with spina bifida and/or hydrocephalus. Journal of Clinical Child Psychology, 22, 247–267.

Winefield, R. (1987). Never the twain shall meet: Bell, Gallaudet, and the communications debate. Washington, DC: Gallaudet University Press.

Wishart, J. G. (1993). The development of learning difficulties in children with Down's syndrome. Journal of Intellectual Disability Research, 37, 389–403.

(1995). Cognitive abilities in children with Down syndrome: Developmental instability and motivational deficits. In C. J. Epstein, T. Hassold, I. T. Lott, L. Nadel, & D. Patterson (Eds.), Etiology and pathogenesis of Down syndrome (pp. 57–91). New York: Wiley-Liss.

Wishart, J. G., & Duffy, L. (1988). Instability of performance on cognitive tests in infants and young children with Down's syndrome. British Journal of Educational Psychology, 60, 10–22.

Wishart, J. G., & Johnston, F. H. (1990). The effects of experience on an attribution of a stereotyped personality to children with Down's syndrome. Journal of Mental Deficiency Research, 34, 409–420.

Witkin, H. (1964). Heinz Werner: 1890–1964. Child Development, 30, 307–328.

Wohlheuter, M. J., & Sindberg, R. (1975). Longitudinal development of object permanence in mentally retarded children: An exploratory study. American Journal of Mental Deficiency, 79, 513–518.

Wood, D. (1991). Communication and cognition: How the communication styles of hearing adults may hinder – rather than help – deaf learners. American Annals of the Deaf, 136, 247–251.

Wood, D., Wood, H. A., Griffiths, A. J., & Howarth, C. I. (1986). Teaching and talking with deaf children. New York: Wiley.

Woodward, J., Allen, T., & Schildroth, A. (1988). Linguistic and cultural role models for hearing-impaired children in elementary school programs. In M. Strong (Ed.), Language learning and deafness (pp. 184–191). Cambridge University Press.

Woodward, M. (1959). The behavior of idiots interpreted by Piaget's theory of sensorimotor development. British Journal of Educational Psychology, 29, 60–71.

(1961). Concepts of number of the mentally subnormal studied by Piaget's method. Journal of Child Psychology and Psychiatry, 2, 249–259.

(1962). Concepts of space of the mentally subnormal studied by Piaget's method. British Journal of Social and Clinical Psychology, 1, 25–37.

(1963). The application of Piaget's theory of research in mental deficiency. In N. R. Ellis (Ed.), Handbook of mental deficiency, psychological theory, and research (pp. 297–324). New York: McGraw-Hill.

(1979). Piaget's theory and the study of mental retardation. In N. Ellis (Ed.), Handbook of mental deficiency, psychological theory, and research (2d ed., pp. 169–195). Hillsdale, NJ: Erlbaum.

Yamada, J. E. (1990). Laura: A case for the modularity of language. Cambridge, MA: MIT Press.

Young, A. B., Shoulson, I., Penney, J. B., Starosta-Rubinstein, S., Gomez, F., Travers, H., Ramos-Arroyo, M. A., Snodgrass, S. R., Bonilla, E., Moreno, H., & Wexler, N. S. (1986). Huntington's disease in

Venezuela: Neurologic features and functional decline. Neurology, 36, 244–249.

Zeaman, D., & House, B. (1963). The role of attention in retardate discriminant learning. In N. R. Ellis (Ed.), Handbook of mental deficiency, psychological theory and research (pp. 159–223). New York: McGraw-Hill.

Zigler, E. (1967). Familial mental retardation: A continuing dilemma. Science, 155, 292–298.

(1969). Developmental versus difference theories of retardation and the problem of motivation. American Journal of Mental Deficiency, 73, 536–556.

(1971). The retarded child as a whole person. In H. E. Adams & W. K. Boardman (Eds.), Advances in experimental clinical psychology (pp. 47–121). Oxford: Pergamon.

(1984). A developmental theory on mental retardation. In B. Blatt & R. Morris (Eds.), Perspectives in special education: Personal orientations (pp. 173–209). Santa Monica, CA: Scott, Foresman.

Zigler, E., & Burack, J. A. (1989). Personality development and the dually diagnosed person. Research in Developmental Disabilities, 10, 225–240.

Zigler, E., & Glick, M. (1986). A developmental approach to adult psychopathology. New York: Wiley.

Zigler, E., & Hodapp, R. M. (1986). Understanding mental retardation. Cambridge University Press.

Zuk, G. H. (1959). The religious factor and the role of guilt in parental acceptance of the retarded child. American Journal of Mental Deficiency, 64, 139–147.

Author Index

Subject Index